T0330239

Internal Controls Toolkit

Founded in 1807, John Wiley & Sons is the oldest independent publishing company in the United States. With offices in North America, Europe, Asia, and Australia, Wiley is globally committed to developing and marketing print and electronic products and services for our customers' professional and personal knowledge and understanding.

The Wiley Corporate F&A series provides information, tools, and insights to corporate professionals responsible for issues affecting the profitability of their company, from accounting and finance to internal controls and performance management.

Internal Controls Toolkit

Christine H. Doxey

WILEY

Published by John Wiley & Sons, Inc., Hoboken, New Jersey.
Published simultaneously in Canada.

For general information on our other products and services or for technical support, please contact our Customer Care Department within the United States at (800) 762–2974, outside the United States at (317) 572–3993, or fax (317) 572–4002.

Wiley publishes in a variety of print and electronic formats and by print-on-demand. Some material included with standard print versions of this book may not be included in e-books or in print-on-demand. If this book refers to media such as a CD or DVD that is not included in the version you purchased, you may download this material at http://booksupport .wiley.com. For more information about Wiley products, visit www.wiley.com.

Library of Congress Cataloging-in-Publication Data

Names: Doxey, Christine H., 1955- author.
Title: Internal controls toolkit / Christine H. Doxey.
Description: First Edition. | Wiley : Hoboken, New Jersey, [2019] | Series:
  Wiley corporate F&A series | Includes index. |
Identifiers: LCCN 2019011646 (print) | LCCN 2019021944 (ebook) | ISBN
  9781119554400 (Adobe PDF) | ISBN 9781119554417 (ePub) | ISBN 9781119554394
  (hardcover)
Subjects: LCSH: Managerial accounting. | Auditing, Internal. | Corporate
  governance.
Classification: LCC HF5657.4 (ebook) | LCC HF5657.4 .D69 2019 (print) | DDC
  658.15/11—dc23
LC record available at https://lccn.loc.gov/2019011646

Cover Design: Wiley
Cover Image: © Liyao Xie/Getty Images

Printed in the United States of America

V10010977_061019

Contents

Introduction to the Internal Controls Toolkit

 INTRODUCTION

Companies of all sizes are subject to a variety of risks. Among them are legal, regulatory, strategic, operational, financial, and reputational. Each functional organization is subject to one or more of these types of risk, each of which may impact the company's bottom line. Companies use a number of policies and tools, such as insurance, establishment of reserve funds, and investment policies, and standards of control to manage risk.

The concept of internal control is one of the trademarks of effective governance and good business operations. Without a strong system of internal control, organizations cannot ensure that the interests of company stakeholders are being protected. Strong internal controls support organizational goals and objectives, while helping safeguard against the risks of financial loss, operational waste, environmental irresponsibility, corporate fraud, and even reputational damage that can be irreparable. Internal control over financial reporting continues to be a major area of importance in the governance of an organization.

This toolkit provides a series of standards of internal control and the risks they mitigate for all enterprise-wide operations. The fraud risks for today's corporate environment are significant as indicated by the statistics provided in the following sections. The standards will set the foundation for good control and will help to mitigate the risk of fraud. According to the 2018 Report to the Nations prepared by the Association of Certified Fraud Examiners (ACFE), Anti-fraud controls work. The ACFE analyzed 18 anti-fraud controls were analyzed and every one correlated to lower fraud losses and faster fraud detection.

Internal Controls and Fraud Prevention

PwC's 2018 Global Economic Crime and Fraud survey states that:

- 49% of organizations globally said they've been a victim of fraud and economic crime—up from 36%.
- 64% of respondents said losses due directly to their most disruptive fraud could reach US$1 million.
- 52% of all frauds are perpetrated by people inside the organization.
- 31% of respondents who suffered fraud indicated they experienced cyber-crime.

Internal Controls and Fraud Prevention: Additional Statistics

Payment and Business Process Fraud Statistics			
Organization	**Report**	**Key Findings**	**Source of Information**
Association of Certified Fraud Examiners (ACFE)	2018 Report to the Nations	Occupational fraud is extremely costly. Twenty-two percent of occupational frauds caused at least $1 million in losses.	https://www.acfe.com/article.aspx?id=4295001895
		Fraud schemes can be very difficult to detect. The typical occupational fraud lasted 16 months before it was discovered.	
		Tips are the most effective way to detect fraud. Forty percent of cases were detected by a tip—far more than by any other method.	
		Anti-fraud controls work. Eighteen anti-fraud controls were analyzed, and every one correlated to lower fraud losses and faster fraud detection.	
		High-level perpetrators do the most damage. The median loss in frauds committed by owners/executives was $850,000. Among non-owners/executives the median loss was $100,000.	

Payment and Business Process Fraud Statistics

Organization	Report	Key Findings	Source of Information
		Criminal fraud referrals are declining. Over the past 10 years, the percentage of occupational frauds referred to law enforcement has declined by 16 percent.	
Association of Finance Professionals (AFP)	2018 AFP Payments Fraud and Control Survey Report	Seventy-seven percent of organizations experienced business email compromise (BEC).	https://commercial.jpmorganchase.com/pages/commercial-banking/services/2018-AFP-Survey
		Fifty-four percent of BEC scams targeted wires, followed by checks at 34%.	
		Seventy-seven percent of organizations implemented controls to prevent BEC scams.	
		Seventy-four percent of organizations experienced check fraud, a slight decrease from 2016.	
		Twenty-eight percent were subject to ACH debit fraud and 13% were subject to ACH credit fraud.	
		Sixty-seven percent of payments fraud was discovered by the organization's treasury staff.	
Kroll	Global Fraud & Risk Report 10th Annual Edition 2017–2018	84% of companies surveyed worldwide experienced a fraud incident in 2017.	https://www.kroll.com/en-us/global-fraud-and-risk-report-2018
		86% reported at least one cyber-incident, and 70% reported security incidents.	
		Confidential information is coming under increasing threat. Executives are feeling a heightened sense of vulnerability to fraud, cyber-, and security risks.	

Payment and Business Process Fraud Statistics			
Organization	**Report**	**Key Findings**	**Source of Information**
		Information theft, loss, or attack (29%), virus/worm attack (36%), physical theft or loss of intellectual property (41%).	
		Theft of physical assets or stock (27%), email-based phishing attack (33%), environmental risk (including damage caused by natural disasters such as hurricanes, tornadoes, floods, earthquakes, etc.) (28%).	
		Management conflict of interest (26%), data breach resulting in loss of customer or employee data, IP/trade secrets/R&D (27%), workplace violence (23%).	
Experion	The 2018 Global Fraud and Identity Report	With most consumers owning smartphone and mobile devices (91%), followed closely by laptop computers (83%), the digital marketplace is here now. Technology is supporting the large volume of online interactions between businesses and consumers. But the real currency of digital commerce is trust.	https://www.experian.com/assets/decision-analytics/reports/global-fraud-report-2018.pdf
		When it comes to online engagement, three-quarters (75%) of businesses are interested in more advanced security measures and authentication processes that have little or no impact on the customer. At the same time businesses understand that their customers take comfort in the security measures they already have in place for digital transactions.	
		In contrast, almost three-quarters of businesses (72%) cite fraud as a growing concern over the past 12 months and nearly two-thirds (63%) report the same or higher levels of fraudulent losses over that same period.	

Who Will Benefit from This Toolkit

The intended audience for this toolkit includes individuals whose responsibilities fall within the functions delineated later. Within companies, those roles may include the chief executive officer (CEO), chief financial officer (CFO), chief human resources officer, controller, internal controls management, internal audit management, treasurer, and anyone within the chain of command for procurement, AP, payment processing, payroll, sales, AR, collections, treasury, company operations, security, and IT.

This toolkit defines the standards of internal control for all aspects of a manufacturing enterprise that also provides customer and professional services. In addition to the breadth of coverage, this toolkit addresses the depth of processes within each category, and offers a wealth of information about the functions and available controls to manage risk associated with each of them. As such, it is a great reference for many roles within these wide-ranging corporate functions within companies of many sizes. It may serve as a training tool for corporate employees who wish to learn more about internal controls standards and risk management processes.

This toolkit also provides guidelines, best practices, and other tools to assist companies in their enterprise-wide focus on risk management through the standards of internal control.

About the Standards of Internal Control

How were the standards developed?

The standards are the product of over 30 years of experience in the finance, accounting, and internal controls field. The standards are a body of work that leverages experience at large technology, telecommunications, and manufacturing companies. They were developed when implementing internal control programs for approximately 100 business processes and sub-processes that include all aspects of financial operations, the fiscal closing process, logistics, and procurement.

How are the standards used?

Since the standards were compiled from internal controls best practices used to mitigate risk, they can be used to set the foundation for the requirements of the Sarbanes Oxley (SOX) Act 404. This is a perfect fit, since the standards follow the COSO internal control framework and philosophy and are easily customizable to meet the needs of an organization. When the concept was launched at large technology companies, the standards were used as part of a quarterly balance sheet review process to validate the effectiveness of internal control programs, to ensure that risk was mitigated, and to determine that remediation activities were completed. The standards of internal control can be leveraged to enhance an existing controls program or to validate your current SOX 404 work.

What is the basic premise of the standards?

The basic premise of the standards is that critical corporate controls should be the foundation for all internal control programs, regardless of the company's size or industry. The three critical controls are: (1) Segregation of Duties, (2) Delegation of Authority, and (3) System Access. The standards stress that these critical controls should be embedded for all business processes and sub-processes to properly mitigate risk.

When should the standard be updated?

The standards are updated when there is a significant change to the business process or system environment. As an example, standards are updated when a business process is automated, or a new ERP system is implemented, upgraded, or consolidated.

The standards should be immediately revised if a fraud has been perpetrated. A fraud indicates that the risk has not been properly evaluated or a critical control has not adequately implemented. Lastly, the standards should be reviewed if the cost of the control is not in line with the overall benefit to the organization.

What is a best practice for implementing and using the standards?

As noted, the standards of internal control can be easily customized to fit any company and can be linked to an entity's corporate policies as suggested in the diagram below. Standards can also be integrated with functional policies, procedures, work instructions, and systems of controls using a solid foundation of business ethics establishing the support for the overall program.

A quarterly review process is highly recommended with the inclusion of a series of self-assessment, assertions, and action item follow-ups to ensure that open issues are remediated in a timely manner. An example is the quarterly balance sheet review program previously mentioned. This review includes a review of the standards applicable for the business process, a look at pending remediation items and plans, and a review of account reconciliations. This approach not only supports the requirements for SOX programs but defines the specifics of a *continuous control monitoring* (CCM) process.

Key Point: The standards define a series of internal controls that address the risks associated with key business processes, sub-processes, and entity-level processes. The following example takes a look at the standard for the invoice processing sub-process within accounts payable.

 ## GENERAL STANDARDS OF INTERNAL CONTROL

The following general standards of internal control apply to all business processes. It should be noted that any of these general requirements may be superseded by a more stringent or specific control within an individual business process.

General Standards of Internal Control

1.1 Managers are responsible for integrating effective internal controls into all company operations. This responsibility includes identifying, assessing, and managing risks that affect the accomplishment of their business objectives. The resulting internal control activities must be monitored to verify they are effective and working as intended.

1.2 All employees must comply with the company code of conduct.

1.3 Statements of corporate policy must be adhered to by all operating units. Policies and procedures established within operating units must, at a minimum, meet and not be in conflict with the control requirements specified by corporate policy. Policies and procedures must be periodically reviewed and updated.

1.4 The company's financial statements must be prepared in conformity with accounting principles. In addition, no false or intentionally misleading entries shall be made in the company's accounting records.

1.5 Adequate segregation of duties and control responsibilities must be established and maintained in all functional areas of the company as one of the three critical corporate controls. In general, custodial, processing/operating, and accounting responsibilities should be separated to promote independent review and evaluation of company operations. Where adequate segregation cannot be achieved, other compensating controls must be established and documented.

1.6 All representations made in the annual letter of representation must be supported and the appropriate documentation must exist and be retained in accordance with the controller, financial representation, and controls assurance process and statements of corporate policy.

1.7 Costs and expenses of all operating units must be maintained under budgetary control. Comparisons of actual expenses to budgeted amounts must be performed on a regular basis, and all significant variances explained.

1.8 All operating units must develop a system of internal controls to ensure that the assets and records of the company are adequately protected from loss, destruction, theft, alteration, or unauthorized access.

1.9 Critical transactions in the company's business processes must be traceable, authorized, authenticated, have integrity, and be retained in accordance according to corporate policies.

General Standards of Internal Control

1.10 The business records of the company must be maintained and retained in accordance with corporate policies.

1.11 The corporate policy on proprietary, confidential, or trade secret information must be adhered to. As a result, employees and contractors must refrain from unauthorized disclosure of sensitive or confidential information. Adequate security must also be maintained in disposing of this information.

1.12 All computer systems and/or software applications that will impact the operation of a business process must have the adequacy of their internal controls verified through the user acceptance process prior to implementation.

1.13 Contracts that legally bind company or a subsidiary company to any obligation can only be executed by purchasing personnel (for agreements pertinent to their areas of responsibility) or individuals duly authorized under company's delegation of authority policy. Legal should review and approve all contracts and "right to audit" clauses should be included in the contracts.

1.14 The company's internal control standards apply to all third parties who are in the possession of company assets. Examples of such third parties include outsourcing partners, sub-contractors, or public warehouses. Operating units are required to take appropriate actions to ensure compliance.

1.15 All operating units must develop, maintain, and enforce written policies and procedures that include internal controls, processes, roles, and responsibilities.

 HOW THIS TOOLKIT IS ORGANIZED

This toolkit is organized by 16 business processes and sub-processes. Each business process section has an Introduction, Process Overview, Metrics, and Statement on the Application of Internal Controls.

The metrics included in this toolkit provide recommendations and definitions for measurements, indicators, and analytics for each of the 16 business processes included. Metrics can be used to analyze a process and determine if there are fluctuations in results that may indicate a fraud risk or anomaly.

Some business process sections include key definitions that will help understand the details of the business process and the necessary internal control standards. Each sub-process has an introduction and defines the applicable standards of internal control and identifies the risk if the standard is not implemented. A glossary and addendum are also provided as additional references.

The table below depicts the organizational structure of the material provided in "The Internal Controls Toolkit."

Introduction

1. Background

Financial Controls

2. Order to Cash (O2C)

3. Treasury

4. Procure to Pay (P2P)

5. Hire to Retire (H2R)

7. Record to Report (R2R)

Operational Controls

6. Supply Chain

8. Government Contracts

14. Customer Services

15. Professional Services

IT, Information Management and Telecommunication Controls

9. Records and Information Management

10. Computer and Telecommunication Systems Controls

Protection of Assets and Employees

11. Protection of Assets – Human, Physical, and Intellectual

12. Insurance Process

13. EH&S

16. Entity Level Controls

Glossary

Addendum and Additional Tools

"The Internal Controls Toolkit" Structure

CHAPTER ONE

Background on Internal Controls

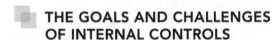 THE GOALS AND CHALLENGES OF INTERNAL CONTROLS

The success of an internal controls program is dependent upon ongoing management commitment as an operating requirement that is measured with the operating unit held accountable. As important as an internal control structure is to an organization, an effective system is not a guarantee that the organization will be successful. An effective internal control structure will keep the right people informed about the organization's progress (or lack of progress) in achieving its objectives, but it cannot turn a poor manager into a good one.

Even effective internal control can only help an entity achieve these objectives. It can provide management information about the entity's progress toward their achievement of business goals. However, internal control cannot change an inherently poor manager into a good one. In addition, shifts in government policy or programs, competitors' actions, or economic conditions can be beyond management's control. Internal control cannot ensure success, or even survival.

Internal control is not an absolute assurance to management and the board about the organization's achievement of its objectives. It can only provide reasonable assurance due to limitations inherent in all internal control systems.

For example, breakdowns in the internal control structure can occur due to a simple error or mistake, as well as faulty judgments that could be made at any level of management. In addition, controls can be circumvented by collusion or by management override and a fraudulent payment.

Finally, the design of the internal control system is a function of the resources available, meaning that a cost-benefit analysis must be in the design of the system. The cost of payment controls should never exceed the benefits of the internal system. And the value of a good internal control system should always adequately reduce and help to mitigate risk for the corporate payment process.

Risk-Based Internal Controls

Many companies have ineffective internal controls programs due to an overwhelming amount of controls that don't adequately consider risk. These organizations are only focused on testing the controls and not properly evaluating the effectiveness of the control when conducting a self-assessment or preparing for the annual SOX 404 internal controls assessment process.

A risk-based controls approach properly leverages resources and can reduce the cost of an overall internal controls program and, more importantly, this approach ensures that the control properly mitigates the risk. Risk-based controls focus on the key controls that will mitigate risk within the business process. Failing to take a true risk-based approach may result in identifying more controls than the operation needs. The operation may erroneously focus on perceived "key controls" that do not properly address the risk for a specific business process.

All companies, regardless of size, structure, nature, or industry, encounter risks at all levels within their organization. Risks affect each company's ability to survive, successfully compete within its industry, maintain financial strength and positive public image, and maintain the overall quality of its products, services, and people. Since there is no practical way to reduce risk to zero, management should determine how much risk should be prudently accepted, and strive to maintain risk within acceptable levels by considering the implementation of risk-based controls.

Risk is exposure to a potential loss as a consequence of uncertainty. There are global risks and risks in every phase and stage of a business process, with certain risks of greater importance during each stage. Understanding the types of risk faced within each process sets the foundation for the development of risk-based controls.

As an additional reference, here are ten tips for implementing risk-based controls:

1. The focus should be on the business process and any sub-processes rather than just the audit process.
2. The control should be focused on the end-to-end process and its dependencies rather than just on transactions. Although the control should address the accuracy of a transaction, a risk-based control addresses the total business process and not just a single transaction.
3. The expected outcome is to identify and mitigate risk as well as determine opportunities for process improvements within the operation.
4. There should be a focus on risk management rather than solely on current policies and procedures. Current policies and procedures may be outdated or incorrect.
5. The goal should be on continual risk assessment coverage through a continuous controls monitoring (CCM) process.
6. Risk-based internal controls facilitate change since they should be updated when there is a significant change to the business process or if the control is found to inadequately mitigate a potential risk.
7. This approach should set the foundation for implementing operational metrics and analytics.
8. Risk-based controls can identify risks and business process gaps across financial operations.
9. Risk-based controls can help prevent and detect fraud since they should represent the end-to-end business process.
10. Risk-based controls should always be developed by the business process owners, but approved by management with well-defined implementation and remediation plans.

Here are five questions to ask when developing a series of risk-based controls along with the five key metrics to consider when measuring results.

Five Questions to Ask
1. Does the control consider a failure that may rise to the level of a material weakness?
2. Can the control be relied upon to either prevent or detect (in a timely manner) a material misstatement of the filed financial statements?
3. Has the control been updated recently to reflect the current business process?

4. Has your organization considered remediation actions resulting from a fraudulent activity, findings from external and internal audits, and other control self-assessment processes?
5. Is the control a key component of your continuous controls monitoring (CCM) initiative?

Five Metrics to Consider
1. Number of incidents per period
2. Average value of incidences identified per period
3. Estimate of total value of incidences identified per period
4. Average hourly rate of person remediating incidents per period
5. Percentage of transactions tested per period

Application of Internal Controls

Internal controls should be applied within an operating unit of a corporation in an effective and efficient manner and provide reasonable assurance that the operating unit and corresponding business process will meet its objectives.

Internal control objectives are achieved through the competence and integrity of personnel, the independence of their assigned function, their understanding of prescribed procedures, and the effectiveness of monitoring accepted risk.

The effectiveness of an internal controls system is dependent upon the following factors:

■ Senior management commitment and communication
  ■ The tone set by senior management is the most important factor contributing to the ongoing success of the internal controls system. This is referred to as the "tone at the top" and is supported by a corporate's code of conduct.
■ Managers and employees understanding the internal control system along with their responsibilities as business process owners
  ■ Internal controls should be understood, supported, and promoted throughout the company. This is accomplished by formal training and communication programs for each corporate process.
■ Appropriate method of communication
  ■ Coordination and cooperation among employees is a key dependency. Impediments to necessary communication should be minimized.

■ Adequate time and resources
  ■ Business operations need sufficient time and resources to create, maintain, and review internal controls.

Key Point: A company needs internal controls to ensure business is conducted in accordance with applicable laws and regulations and management's directives and authorities. Effective internal controls will support the company in achieving the goals of minimizing exposure to loss of integrity in operations and financial records, including:

■ Loss of assets
■ Undetected errors
■ Compromise of proprietary data, etc.
■ Managing identified risks down to acceptable levels
■ Providing the company with disciplined process management
■ Facilitating achieving business objectives effectively and efficiently

Key Point: Some of the root causes for internal control problems are listed below.

■ The need for controls not recognized throughout the organization
■ Inadequate instruction/training
■ Insufficient capital or human resources provided to support the controls initiative
■ Improper priorities assigned
■ Attitudes of employees, supervisors, and managers
■ Human error
■ Management unaware or not informed of problems within business processes
■ Supervisors not monitoring ongoing process

The Three Critical Corporate Controls

The three most critical internal controls for any company can be established by corporate policies that should be "operationalized" into your company's business processes and monitored by the applicable internal control programs. The implementation of these controls set the foundation for good payment controls and risk mitigation. These controls are: (1) segregation of duties, (2) systems access, and (3) delegation of authority. Many companies have implemented these controls as "core controls" but need to keep them updated by following some of the best practices that are recommended below. The three critical controls will be referenced throughout the standards of internal control provided in this toolkit.

1. **The Segregation of Duties (SoD)** control is one of the most important controls that your company can have. Adequate segregation of duties reduces the likelihood that errors (intentional or unintentional) will remain undetected by providing for separate processing by different individuals at various stages of a transaction and for independent reviews of the work performed.

    The SoD control provides four primary benefits: (1) the risk of a deliberate fraud is mitigated as the collusion of two or more persons would be required in order to circumvent controls; (2) the risk of legitimate errors is mitigated as the likelihood of detection is increased; (3) the cost of corrective actions is mitigated as errors are generally detected earlier in their lifecycle; and (4) the organization's reputation for integrity and quality is enhanced through a system of checks and balances.

    Although SoD is a basic, key internal control, it is one of the most difficult to accomplish, often due to limited headcount, broadly defined responsibilities, and constantly changing responsibilities. Basically, the general duties to be segregated are: planning/initiation, authorization, custody of assets, and recording or reporting of transactions. Additionally, control tasks such as review, audit, and reconcile should not be performed by the same individual responsible for recording or reporting the transaction.

    Best Practice: Among the most common root causes of fraud are the lack of SoD controls, weak SoD controls, inappropriate compensating controls, or failure to update SoD controls when responsibilities change. As a best practice, many organizations review their SoD controls on a quarterly basis, and whenever staff turnover occurs, as part of their control self-assessment (CSA) process. As a result of this review, the applicable SoD controls are updated appropriately.

2. **System Access:** The principle of SoD in an information system environment is also critical as it ensures the separation of different functions such as transaction entry, online approval of the transactions, master file initiation, master file maintenance, system access rights, and the review of transactions.

In the context of application level controls, this means that one individual should only have access rights which permit them to enter, approve, or review transactions, but no combination of two for the same transaction. Therefore, assigning different security profiles to various individuals supports the principle of SoD. As an example, operational or process SoD within an AP department will determine the system access rights that should be granted for each associate based on roles and responsibilities.

Best Practice: System access rights are reviewed on a periodic basis (usually monthly or quarterly) to ensure that system access capabilities are appropriate for current staff members and reflect any changes in responsibilities or movements to other departments.

3. **Delegation of Authority (DoA):** The last critical control for your company is the DoA policy and control. The purpose of the DoA is to ensure the efficient operation of the company while maintaining fiscal integrity and adherence to policy. Accountability for the overall management of the property, assets, financial, and human resources of the company rests with the chief executive officer (CEO). In many cases the governance of the DoA is the responsibility of the controller. Individuals that have been assigned authority under the terms of the DoA must safeguard company resources by establishing and maintaining internal controls that deter and detect any potential misuse of resources.

Best Practice: Many companies assign levels of authority to the job grades or levels within the organization and apply workflow to streamline the approval process. If an individual is promoted or moves to another department, his or her level of authority is automatically updated in the employee master file.

The Background and History of Internal Controls

The idea of internal controls is nothing new. In fact, it dates back to ancient civilizations as early as the thirteenth century. It was not until the signing of the Security and Exchange Commission (SEC) Acts of 1933 and 1934, however, that a form of internal control was mandated in the United States. At this point, organizations were officially put on the path to corporate accountability by mitigating risk as a result of better, more effective internal controls. This chapter reviews various milestones, requirements, obstacles, and key events along the way.

Securities Act of 1933

When the stock market crashed in 1929 and billions of investor dollars disappeared, the public lost faith in the capital markets and the United States fell into the Great Depression. In search of solutions, Congress held hearings that resulted in passing the Securities Act of 1933, commonly called the "truth in securities" law. This law required that investors be provided important information about securities for public sale and prohibited fraudulent activity in the sale of securities, such as insider trading. It mandated that securities, with the exception of those exempt, be registered and that related financial information is disclosed.

Securities Exchange Act of 1934

With the passing of the Securities Exchange Act of 1934, Congress created the Securities and Exchange Commission (SEC) and gave it authority over all aspects of the securities industry. The Act granted the SEC disciplinary powers and the authority to mandate reporting, disclosures, and registration of regulated entities. The Securities Act of 1933 and the Securities Exchange Act of 1934 put into place a mechanism for monitoring the securities industry to ensure that companies taking investment dollars tell the truth, are transparent about the risks, and safeguard the interests of their stakeholders.

Trust Indenture Act of 1939

Designed to prevent fraud by providing full and fair disclosure of the character of securities sold in interstate and foreign commerce and through the mails, the Trust Indenture Act of 1939 applies to debt securities offered for public sale. It requires those who issue bonds and the bondholder to enter into a formal agreement in conformance with the standards laid out in the Act.

Investment Company Act of 1940

This law requires companies that offer securities to the public and engage primarily in investing and trading to disclose to the public their financial standing, structure and operations, and investment policies. Although the Act does not permit the SEC to directly supervise the actions of the companies, it is designed to minimize conflicts of interest in complex operations.

Investment Advisors Act of 1940

This act, which was amended in 1996, protects investors by requiring certain financial advisors to register with the SEC. Firms and individuals affected by the regulation are those who manage assets of at least $25 million or who advise registered investment company clients about securities.

Foreign Corrupt Practices Act (FCPA) of 1977

As a result of American corporations having made improper payment to government officials in a number of countries, Congress passed the Foreign Corrupt Practices Act of 1977 in an effort to eliminate such payments to foreign governments, politicians, and political parties, and to restore the reputation of American business. This law generally applies to U.S. corporations, partnerships, and other businesses and persons acting on their behalf, and prohibits any payment, offer of payment, or promise of giving anything of value to a foreign official in an attempt to obtain business.

In addition to its anti-bribery provisions, the law includes broad accounting and recordkeeping rules for companies required to file financial reports. The FCPA requires the companies to maintain toolkits, records, and accounts that accurately reflect the company's transactions and dispositions. Violations of the FCPA by a company and its employees can result in stiff penalties and imprisonment as evidenced by the recent well-publicized Wal-Mart case.

Comprehensive Crime Control Act—1984

This act expanded federal powers to seize assets in civil cases. The law included the Sentencing Reform Act provision, which created the U.S. Sentencing Commission, an independent agency in the judicial branch of government. The Sentencing Commission establishes sentencing policies and practices for federal courts, advises Congress and the executive branch in regard to effective and efficient crime policies, and serves as an information resource on federal crime and sentencing issues.

Federal Sentencing Guidelines for Organizations—1991

Following the savings-and-loan crisis of the 1980s, the U.S. Sentencing Commission responded to the public's frustration with the criminal justice system by releasing the Federal Sentencing Guidelines for organizations, which imposed harsh penalties on organizations whose employees or other agents have committed federal crimes. The guidelines—seven steps for mitigating the risk of such crimes—include implementing compliance standards and procedures, assigning compliance oversight responsibility to high-level personnel, avoiding delegation to individuals prone to commit crimes, providing information and training on standards, establishing systems for monitoring and reporting criminal conduct without fear of reprisal, enforcing standards and assigning responsibility for detecting offenses, and taking all reasonable steps to guard against offenses in the future.

Internal Control—Integrated Framework—1992 and 2013

Landmark guidance that has been embraced all around the world, Internal Control—Integrated Framework was developed by the Committee of Sponsoring Organizations of the Treadway Commission (COSO).

A commission led by James C. Treadway, Jr., then–Executive Vice President and General Counsel, Paine Webber Incorporated and a former Commissioner of the U.S. Securities and Exchange Commission, was set up. This commission was sponsored and funded by five U.S. private-sector organizations made up of the American Accounting Association (AAA), the American Institute of Certified Public Accountants (AICPA), Financial Executives International (FEI), The Institute of Internal Auditors (IIA), and the National Association of Accountants (now the Institute of Management Accountants [IMA]). These organizations are collectively called the Committee of Sponsoring Organizations of the Treadway Commission (COSO).

The Committee of Sponsoring Organizations was charged by the Treadway Commission to develop an integrated guidance on Internal Control. As a result of this, a framework for designing, implementing, and evaluating internal control for organizations was released.

The COSO Framework was designed to help businesses establish, assess, and enhance their internal control. The importance of *internal control in the operations and financial reporting* of an entity cannot be overemphasized as the existence or the absence of the process determines the quality of output produced in the financial statements. A present and functioning *internal control process* provides the users with a "reasonable assurance" that the amounts presented in the financial statements are accurate and can be relied upon for informed decision making.[1]

---

[1]Uwadiae, Oduware, "COSO—An Approach to Internal Framework," accessed October 1, 2018, https://www2.deloitte.com/ng/en/pages/audit/articles/financial-reporting/coso-an-approach-to-internal-control-framework.html.

The timeless concepts of the framework are: Internal controls is a process affected by people; it provides reasonable assurance; and it is geared to the achievement of objectives related to operations, compliance, and financial reporting.

The internal control framework consists of five interrelated components of an internal control system:

1. **Control Environment**, which sets the ethical tone of an organization and influences the control consciousness of its people
2. **Risk Assessment**, which identifies and analyzes the risks to achieving objectives, and determines how the risks should be managed
3. **Control Activities**, which are the policies and procedures that help ensure risks are addressed and management directives are carried out
4. **Information and Communication**, which include operational, financial, and compliance-related reports designed to help ensure information flows down, across, and up the organization; and effective communication with stakeholders
5. **Monitoring**, which assesses the quality of the internal control system's performance on an ongoing basis, through separate evaluations, or a combination of both; reports on findings; and helps ensure continuous improvement of the system, organizational efficiencies, and reduced costs

The five components of the COSO model are depicted in the chart below. The COSO model has driven many internal controls systems and Sarbanes-Oxley efforts in the corporate environment.

Component	Principle
Control Environment	1. Demonstrates commitment to integrity and ethical values
	2. Exercises oversight responsibility
	3. Establishes structure, authority, and responsibility
	4. Demonstrates commitment to competence
	5. Enforces accountability
Risk Assessment	6. Specifies relevant objectives
	7. Identifies and analyzes risk
	8. Assess fraud risk
	9. Identifies and analyzes significant change
Control Activities	10. Selects and develops control activities
	11. Selects and develops general controls over technology
	12. Deploys through policies and procedures

Component	Principle
Information and Communication	13. Uses relevant information
	14. Communicates internally
	15. Communicates externally
Monitoring Activities	16. Conducts ongoing and/or separate evaluations
	17. Evaluates and communicates deficiencies

COSO's Monitoring Guidance

COSO's Monitoring Guidance, which was updated in 2009, builds on two fundamental principles originally established in COSO's 2006 Guidance:

1. Ongoing and/or separate evaluations enable management to determine whether the other components of internal control continue to function over time.
2. Internal control deficiencies are identified and communicated in a timely manner to those parties responsible for taking corrective action and to management and the board as appropriate.

The updated monitoring guidance further suggests that these principles are best achieved through monitoring that is based on three broad elements:

1. Establishing a foundation for monitoring, including (a) a proper tone at the top; (b) an effective organizational structure that assigns monitoring roles to people with appropriate capabilities, objectivity and authority; and (c) a starting point or baseline of known effective internal control from which ongoing monitoring and separate evaluations can be implemented
2. Designing and executing monitoring procedures focused on persuasive information about the operation of key controls that address meaningful risks to organizational objectives
3. Assessing and reporting results, which includes evaluating the severity of any identified deficiencies and reporting the monitoring results to the appropriate personnel and the board for timely action and follow-up if needed

As recommended in COSO's Guidance for Monitoring Internal Control Systems (Published by the AICPA), organizations may select from a wide variety of monitoring procedures, including but not limited to the list below. The monitoring procedures selected along with the skills and the objectivity of the evaluators of internal controls will establish the roles and responsibilities.

- Periodic evaluation and testing of controls by internal audit
- Continuous monitoring programs built into information systems
- Analysis of, and appropriate follow-up on, operating reports or metrics that might identify anomalies indicative of a control failure
- Supervisory reviews of controls, such as reconciliation reviews as a normal part of processing
- Self-assessments by boards and management regarding the tone they set in the organization and the effectiveness of their oversight functions
- Audit committee inquiries of internal and external auditors
- Quality assurance reviews of the internal audit department

Continued advancements in technology and management techniques ensure that internal control and related monitoring processes will change over time. However, the fundamental concepts of monitoring, as outlined in COSO's Monitoring Guidance, are designed to stand the test of time. The guidance also covers other concepts that are important to effective and efficient monitoring, including:

- The characteristics associated with the objectivity of the evaluator
- The period of time and the circumstances by which an organization can rely on adequately designed indirect information—when used in combination with ongoing or periodic persuasive direct information—to conclude that internal control remains effective
- Determining the sufficiency and suitability of information used in monitoring to ensure that the results can adequately support conclusions about internal control
- Ways in which the organization can make monitoring more efficient without reducing its effectiveness

COBIT—1996

Control Objectives for Information and Related Technology (COBIT) was created in 1996 by the Information Systems Audit and Control Association (ISACA) and the IT Governance Institute. COBIT helps management derive the greatest benefit from information technology through appropriate IT governance and control. Its framework delineates processes and control objectives for planning/organization, acquisition/implementation, delivery/support, and monitoring/evaluation. This framework also focuses on criteria—effectiveness, efficiency, confidentiality, integrity, availability, compliance, and reliability—resources, and control objectives necessary for successful IT systems. In addition, COBIT provides management guidelines which comprise maturity models, critical success factors, key goal indicators, and key performance indicators.

SysTrust—1999

Jointly developed by the American Institute of Certified Public Accountants (AICPA) and the Canadian Institute of Chartered Accountants (CICA), SysTrust is a professional service designed to build confidence and garner trust in the systems that support an entity or activity. It allows for measuring reliability in regard to a system's availability, security, integrity, and maintainability. Certified Public Accountants (CPAs) use SysTrust to verify and provide assurance that system controls are operating effectively.

Corporate Frauds—2001–2002

The late 1990s and early 2000s painted a shameful picture of corporate America—a picture of unbridled greed and arrogance with a no-holds-barred approach to personal gains, an absence of corporate integrity and ethics, aggressive engagement in questionable or fraudulent business practices, highly compromised corporate governance, and—not surprising—the demise of public trust. Although the many corporate frauds perpetrated during this time would fill a toolkit on their own, only two will be covered here: Enron and WorldCom.

Prior to its bankruptcy in late 2001, Enron, the organization named "America's Most Innovative Company" by *Fortune* magazine every year from 1996 to 2001, was one of the world's leading electricity, natural gas, pulp and paper, and communications companies. It employed approximately 22,000 workers. In 2000, the same year Enron was on Fortune's "100 Best Companies to Work for in America" list, it claimed revenues of nearly $101 billion. Enron was widely recognized as an exemplary company with excellent long-term pensions, fine benefits, and extremely effective management.

In August 2001, however, financial analyst Daniel Scotto became concerned about the company's practices and warned his investors to sell Enron stocks and bonds. As later became widely known, many of Enron's recorded assets and profits were inflated, or even wholly fraudulent and nonexistent. The company hid debts and losses by setting up inappropriate "off-balance sheet" entities. Because these debts were not included in the firm's financial statements, Enron looked more profitable to investors than it actually was. To continue the illusion of billions in profits, even though the company was on the edge of collapse, those at the top of the company perpetrated more and more financial deception, which drove Enron's stock to higher levels. At this point, Chief Financial Officer Andrew Fastow and other executives who had manipulated the deals used insider information and traded millions of dollars of the stock, leaving the company in shambles and Enron stockholders with devastating losses.

Not unlike Enron, the story of WorldCom is one of deception and greed of those at the top who used fraudulent practices to mask declining profits. They classified operating expenses as capital expenditures, creating an illusion of financial growth and profitability to drive up the company's stock. In 2002, when Cynthia Cooper, an internal auditor, discovered the questionable accounting practices and uncovered a $3.8 billion fraud, she blew the whistle by reporting her findings to the WorldCom Audit Committee. The accounting fraud perpetrated by WorldCom executives led to the largest bankruptcy in history, and investors lost an estimated $180 billion.

U.S. Sarbanes-Oxley Act of 2002

The U.S. Sarbanes-Oxley Act of 2002 (SOX) was passed in an effort to hold corporate America responsible for its actions and to help rebuild the trust of the public following the various corporate financial reporting scandals of the late 1990s and early 2000s. It changed the requirements for internal control programs, corporate governance, and corporate accountability for publicly traded companies.

Named after its primary architects—Senator Paul Sarbanes (D-Maryland) and Representative Michael Oxley (R-Ohio)—SOX includes mandates for enhanced corporate governance and financial accountability. I had the pleasure of meeting Senator Sarbanes at an International Accounts Payable Professionals Annual Forum in 2007.

In a nutshell, the law addresses:

Summary of Sarbanes-Oxley Requirements

■ Management's certification of the accuracy of financial statements, management's responsibility for ensuring and reporting on the effectiveness of the company's internal controls, and the external auditors' attestation to management's assertion of internal controls

---
Summary of Sarbanes-Oxley Requirements

- New requirements for corporate boards and audit committees, including enhancing the audit committee's (ACs) oversight responsibility for the financial management of the organization, hiring and overseeing the external auditors, and ensuring that a financial expert is a part of the AC
- Disclosure of a code of conduct for financial officers, protection of whistleblowers, and accelerated reporting of insider trading
- Establishment of the independent Public Accounting Oversight Board (PCAOB) as the standard setting body for auditing
- Criminal penalties for management's issuance of fraudulent financial certifications
- Reinforcement of the external auditors' independence, ensuring they are not "involved" in the management or implementation of activities they audit; and required five-year rotation of the lead auditor

---

Key Point: Section 404 requires an annual report by management on the design and effectiveness of internal controls over financial reporting, and an attestation by the company's auditors as to the accuracy of management's assessment:

- Evaluate and test internal controls over financial reporting using COSO to opine on effectiveness (broad and deep).
- Assessment must be based on procedures sufficient to evaluate design and test operating effectiveness. Inquiry alone will not provide adequate basis for assessment.
- Significant support is required from operations and controller organizations as up to 70% of key controls can be outside of financial reporting.

Management's responsibilities include:

- Evaluate design and effectiveness of internal controls over financial reporting.
- Support evaluation with sufficient evidence, including documentation and test results.
- Written assessment of effectiveness of internal controls over financial reporting as of the end of the company's most recent fiscal year.
- Management must maintain evidential matter, including documentation, to provide reasonable support for its assessment and testing of both design and operating effectiveness.

Key Point: Definitions to describe a controls weakness are:

Significant deficiency: A control deficiency, or combination of control deficiencies, that adversely affects the company's ability to initiate, authorize, record, process, or report external financial data reliably in accordance with generally accepted accounting principles such that there is more than a remote likelihood that a misstatement of the company's annual or interim financial statements that is more than inconsequential will not be prevented or detected.

Material weakness: A significant deficiency, or combination of significant deficiencies, that results in more than a remote likelihood that a material misstatement of the annual or interim financial statements will not be prevented or detected. To ensure successful outcome, many organizations have listed the following items as best practices that can be followed by privately held companies:

Sarbanes-Oxley Best Practices

- Have strong steering and disclosure committees.
- Engage the external auditor early.
- Develop organization-wide communications for every annual event.
- Management buy-in is essential with key stakeholders.
- Balance documentation effort and use automation where possible.
- Ensure that company resources and process owners are engaged throughout the process.
- Identify and support champions for keeping information current.
- Develop livable, structured process for updating documentation to conflict organization or system changes.
- Ensure periodic reviews of the organization's internal controls programs.

 ## ENTERPRISE RISK MANAGEMENT (ERM) INTEGRATED FRAMEWORK—2004 AND 2013

COSO defines enterprise risk management (ERM) as a "process, effected by an entity's board of directors, management, and other personnel; applied in strategy setting and across the enterprise; designed to identify potential events that may affect the entity; and manage risk to be within its risk appetite, to provide reasonable assurance regarding the achievement of entity objectives."

In the Enterprise Risk Management Integrated Framework, COSO expands its highly acclaimed Internal Control Integrated Framework to more broadly explore and expand risk management from four perspectives: strategic, operational, financial, and compliance. Building upon the internal control framework, the components of the ERM framework include the internal environment, objective setting, event identification, risk assessment, risk response, control activities, information and communication, and monitoring.

Example: Enterprise Risk Management (ERM) and the Application to the Procure to Pay (P2P) Cycle

Enterprise risk management (ERM) in business includes the methods and processes used by organizations to manage risks and seize opportunities related to the achievement of their objectives. ERM provides a framework for risk management, which typically involves identifying particular events or circumstances relevant to the organization's objectives (risks and opportunities), assessing them in terms of likelihood and magnitude of impact, determining a response strategy, and monitoring process. By identifying and proactively addressing risks and opportunities, business enterprises protect and create value for their stakeholders, including owners, employees, customers, regulators, and society overall.[2]

ERM can also be described as a risk-based approach to managing an enterprise, integrating concepts of internal control, the Sarbanes-Oxley Act, data protection, and strategic planning. ERM is evolving to address the needs of various stakeholders, who want to understand the broad spectrum of risks facing complex organizations to ensure they are appropriately managed. Regulators and debt rating agencies have increased their scrutiny on the risk management processes of companies.

We have all been focused on implementing internal controls within our organizations in order to meet the requirements of the Sarbanes-Oxley Act (SOX), Section 404. Many companies have asked if their control processes are headed in the right direction, and started to wonder if they are "just going through the motions." Another question to consider: Do the controls adequately address the risk of an organization or entity that is not

---

[2]Wikipedia, "Enterprise Risk Management," accessed October 2, 2018, https://en.wikipedia.org/wiki/Enterprise_risk_management.

meeting its objectives or accomplishing a key strategy? Lastly, can the risk be managed?

The Committee of Sponsoring Organizations of the Treadway Commission (COSO) issued *Internal Control—Integrated Framework* to help businesses and other entities assess and enhance their internal control systems. That framework has since been incorporated into policies, rules, and regulations, which are used by thousands of enterprises to better control the process to achieve established objectives.

ERM is a process, affected by an entity's board of directors, management, and other personnel, that is applied during strategy setting across an enterprise in order to:

- Identify potential events that may affect the entity and manage risks to be within its "risk appetite," which can be defined as the risk tolerance that a firm is willing to allow.

   Some firms are very conservative and avoid risk by the focus on too many controls. As an example, a firm may have multiple levels of approvals for expenditure. This can become a signature-gathering process rather than a true approval process.
- Provide reasonable assurance regarding the achievement of entity objectives.

   ERM is a process that provides a reasonable level of assurance that the firm's total objectives will be achieved.

ERM is designed to raise a consistent "risk-and-control consciousness" throughout an enterprise and become a commonly accepted model for discussing and evaluating the risk management process.

ERM consists of eight interrelated components that are developed from the way management runs an enterprise and should be integrated with the management process. The components are:

1. **Internal Environment**—The internal environment encompasses the tone of an organization. It sets the basis for how risk is viewed and addressed, including risk management philosophy, risk appetite, integrity, ethical values, and the environment in which they operate.
2. **Objective Setting**—Objectives must exist before management can identify potential events affecting their achievement. ERM ensures that

management has a process established to set objectives and that the chosen objectives support and align with the entity's mission and are consistent with its risk appetite.

3. **Event Identification**—Internal and external events affecting achievement of an entity's objectives must be identified, distinguishing between risks and opportunities. Opportunities are channeled back to management's *strategy or objective-setting processes.*

4. **Risk Assessment**—Risks are analyzed, considering likelihood and impact, as a basis for determining how they should be managed.

5. **Risk Response**—Management selects risk responses—avoiding, accepting, reducing, or sharing risk—to develop a set of actions that align risks with the entity's risk tolerance.

6. **Control Activities**—Policies and procedures are established and implemented to help ensure the risk responses are carried out effectively.

7. **Information and Communication**—Relevant information is identified, captured, and communicated in a form and timeframe that enables people to carry out their responsibilities. Effective communication also occurs in a broader sense, flowing down, across, and up the entity.

8. **Monitoring**—The entirety of ERM is monitored and modifications made as necessary. Monitoring is accomplished through ongoing management activities, separate evaluations, or both. Management activities are defined as business planning, internal controls, communication, corporate governance, and corporate infrastructure.

An ERM Checklist

Starting at the enterprise level, control considerations include:

1. **Established and communicated enterprise-level objectives**, including how they are supported by strategic plans and complemented on a process/application level. A risk assessment process, including estimating the significance of risks, assessing the likelihood of their occurrence, and determining needed actions, should be established.
   ▪ Does cthose levels?
   ▪ Are acquisitions and divestitures of significant assets appropriately controlled (e.g. a completed due diligence procedure that has been reviewed by the appropriate level of management)?
   ▪ Are there adequate mechanisms for identifying business risks, including those resulting from:

- New markets or lines of business?
- New products and services?
- Privacy and data protection compliance requirements?
- Other changes in the business, economic, and regulatory environment?

2. **Adequate organization-level communication** to enable people to discharge their responsibilities effectively, allowing management to take timely and appropriate follow-up action on communications received from customers, vendors, regulators, and/or other external parties.
   - Is there a process for tracking communication?
   - Is ownership assigned to specific management personnel to help ensure the entity responds appropriately, timely, and accurately to communications?

Key Point: ERM involves companywide motivation. While ERM is not a regulatory requirement, it can establish a competitive advantage. The diagram below matches key Section 404 activities with the ERM model. As you can see, the ERM model supports and complements the requirements of SOX 404.

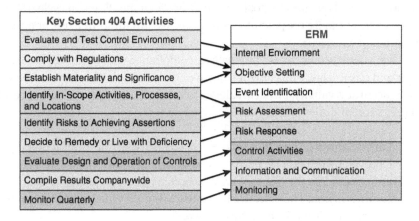

Internal Control over Financial Reporting—Guidance for Smaller Public Companies—2006

For years, smaller companies struggled to apply COSO's Internal Control — Integrated Framework. In this guidance, COSO provides a principles-based approach to internal control, uniquely designed for smaller companies. It actually has proved beneficial, however, to companies of all sizes. This guidance helps management to establish and maintain effective internal control over financial reporting and provides information on complying with new rules and regulations while containing costs.

Guidance on Monitoring Internal Control Systems—2009

Recognizing the absence of available resources on monitoring, COSO released this guidance to help organizations ensure they have an accurate understanding of the effectiveness of their internal controls so that they can take corrective action as warranted. This guidance advocates a proper tone at the top that supports monitoring, an effective organizational structure that assigns monitoring roles to people with appropriate capabilities, objectivity and authority, and a "baseline" at which the monitoring begins and from which accurate conclusions about improvement can be drawn. Other activities include the design and execution of monitoring procedures, assessing and reporting results, and following up as needed.

Definition and Objectives of Internal Controls

Internal controls are desired goals or conditions for a specific event cycle which, if achieved, minimize the potential that waste, loss, unauthorized use, or misappropriation will occur.

For a control objective to be effective, compliance with it must be measurable and observable. The control objectives include authorization, completeness, accuracy, validity, physical safeguards and security, error handling, and segregation of duties and are described below.

- **Authorization:** The objective is to ensure that all transactions are approved by responsible personnel in accordance with specific or general authority before the transaction is recorded.
- **Completeness:** The objective is to ensure that no valid transactions have been omitted from the accounting records.
- **Accuracy:** The objective is to ensure that all valid transactions are accurate, consistent with the originating transaction data, and information is recorded in a timely manner.
- **Validity:** The objective is to ensure that all recorded transactions fairly represent the economic events that actually occurred, are lawful in nature, and have been executed in accordance with management's general authorization.

- **Physical Safeguards and Security:** The objective is to ensure that access to physical assets and information systems is controlled and properly restricted to authorized personnel.
- **Error Handling:** The objective is to ensure that errors detected at any stage of processing receive prompt corrective action and are reported to the appropriate level of management.
- **Segregation of Duties:** The objective is to ensure that duties are assigned to individuals in a manner that ensures that no one individual can control both the recording function and the procedures relative to processing the transaction. As noted, segregation of duties is one of the three critical corporate controls.

Types of Internal Controls and Control Mechanisms

Major Types of Internal Control

There are three main types of internal controls: preventive, detective, and corrective as defined below.

1. **Detective:** Designed to detect errors or irregularities that may have occurred
2. **Corrective:** Designed to correct errors or irregularities that have been detected
3. **Preventive:** Designed to keep errors or irregularities from occurring within the business process

The table below applies the control type to standard risk objectives, and control measures or activities:

Risk Management Objective	Control Measure	Type of Control
Segregation/ Authorization	■ Physical and logical access control ■ Audit trails	■ Preventive ■ Detective
Accuracy	■ Automatic validation ■ Data verification ■ Application change control ■ Audit trails	■ Preventive ■ Detective or Corrective ■ Preventive ■ Detective
Completeness	■ Application change control ■ Record counts ■ Cross-totals ■ Audit trails	■ Preventive ■ Detective ■ Detective ■ Detective

Risk Management Objective	Control Measure	Type of Control
Confidentiality	■ Physical and logical access control ■ Audit trails	■ Preventive ■ Detective
Auditability	■ Only access production data through authorized programs ■ Audit trails	■ Preventive ■ Detective
Continuity/ Recovery	■ Backups and recovery plans	■ Corrective

Compensating Controls

Effective compensating controls can improve the design of a process that has inadequate segregations of duties and ultimately provide reasonable assurance to managers that the anticipated objective(s) of a process or a department will be achieved.

However, compensating controls are less desirable than the segregation of duties internal control because compensating controls generally occur after the transaction is complete. Also, it takes more resources to investigate and correct errors and to recover losses than it does to prevent an error.

Other Controls

Other organization and corporate defined controls are described in the following sections. These types of controls are embedded in the governance structure of a corporation and support the major types of controls that are integral to the payments process.

Organization Controls

Organizational controls should cover all aspects of the company's business processes without overlap, and be clearly assigned and communicated.

- Responsibility should be delegated down the level at which the necessary expertise and time exists.
- No single employee should have exclusive knowledge, authority, or control over any significant transaction or group of transactions.
- Agreeing realistic qualitative and quantitative targets strengthens responsibility.

■ The structure of accountability depends upon continuing levels of competence of employees in different positions and the development of competence so that responsibility and reporting relationships can be regrouped in more efficient ways.

Policy Controls

Policy controls are the general principles and guides for action that influence decisions. They indicate the limits to choices and the parameters or rules to be followed by the company and its employees. Major policies should be reviewed, approved, and communicated by senior management. Policies are derived by:

■ Considering the business environment and process objectives
■ Identifying the potential categories of risks that the environment poses toward achievement of the objectives

Procedure Controls

Procedure controls prescribe how actions are to be performed consistent with policies. Procedures should be developed by those who understand the day-to-day actions that will be subject to the procedures.

Supervisory Controls

Examples of supervisory controls are situations in which managers ensure that all employees understand their responsibilities and authorities, and the assurance that procedures are being followed within the operating unit.

Review Controls

Review controls include an ongoing self-assessment process as required by the Sarbanes-Oxley Act of 2002. A controls self-assessment (CSA) process is a series of questions that validate the effectiveness of the control environment. As a best practice, a self-assessment must be conducted every fiscal quarter for a specific business process or sub-process. In some situations, the manager of the operating unit may elect to conduct a self-assessment test more frequently if automated continuous monitoring tools are used. It is imperative that all weaknesses found in the testing process are remediated through a corrective action and follow-up process.

LEVERAGING THE STANDARDS OF INTERNAL CONTROL TO IMPLEMENT A CONTROLS SELF-ASSESSMENT (CSA) PROGRAM

The Institute of Internal Auditors (IIA) defines CSA as a process through which internal control effectiveness is examined with the objective of providing reasonable assurance that all business objectives are met. The employees performing CSA work are in the functional area being examined rather than upper-level managers that are above the system of internal controls.

These employees have a wealth of information about internal controls and fraud (if it exists). While internal (or independent) auditors can be involved with CSA initiatives, auditors do not "own" the process and do not make the assessments and evaluations.

Key Point: If there is an environment of internal control, controls are understood and embedded at the tactical level, and the process is validated by a CSA, cost of controls can be reduced drastically. More importantly, the risk of fraudulent behavior is significantly mitigated. The standards of internal control provided in this toolkit will help to determine the areas of risk and key controls to focus on in a CSA process.

The most common approaches to performing CSA activities are facilitated team meetings, CSA surveys, and management's focus on a specific internal control or area of their business.

■ A **facilitated team meeting** is the most popular form of CSA. The facilitated sessions consist of 6 to 15 employees who are subject on a day-to-day basis to the internal controls being evaluated. A trained facilitator guides the meeting, and another individual records the activity.

■ The **survey approach** uses questionnaires to elicit data about controls, risks, and processes. It differs from traditional internal control questionnaires used by auditors because the operational employees (not the auditors) use the survey results to self-evaluate the controls or processes. At some companies a survey approach may be used to evaluate "soft" controls. It may be used to evaluate the effectives of an ethics program that is considered an entity-level control. (Refer to Chapter 16.)

The steps below support the self-assessment approach in a CSA program. Self-testing on a regular basis validates the effectiveness and design of the control. This approach can be used when management would like to review the controls of a specific process. Lastly, this approach can also be used in a workshop setting.

1. **Understand the operating unit or business process.** A key component of a CSA program is ensuring that the control points and responsibilities of the operating unit are understood.
2. **Determine the scope of the CSA initiative.** Clearly define the CSA scope and the controls that will be assessed for a specific business process.
3. **Ensure there is management commitment.** This is crucial to the ongoing support and success of the program. It is demonstrated by full management understanding of the value-added benefits of a CSA program.
4. **Match the CSA program to the operating unit.** Develop a program that represents the operating unit or process or select from the recommendation standards of internal control
5. **Form a CSA team or work team.** Work teams or process teams, with the assistance of a facilitation team, identify obstacles to overcome or strengths to be leveraged and agree upon appropriate action steps to improve the group's effectiveness. As an example, a process-based CSA Team will focus on a process that may only entail one activity of a particular business unit or processes such as procure to pay and accounts payable. Suitable candidates for the CSA tem are:
   - Work teams that work together on a single business process that may cut across functional management boundaries
   - Work teams that are about to implement a new process or application system
   - Teams that tend to be staff-based in that most of those attending should be the individuals performing the work
   - Areas where basic day-to-day processes require improvement
6. **Plan and schedule the evaluation of internal controls.** Although an internal controls program should be flexible to address the changing business environment, a quarterly plan and schedule for the CSA program helps to work around peak periods of activity.
7. **Complete the evaluation of internal controls.**
8. **Develop deficiency findings and remediation activities.** A deficiency finding is a factual statement of a problem without judgment or conclusion and should be quantified where possible. Findings should address the root cause of the problem and identify "what is really broken."
9. **Develop a corrective action plan.** A corrective action plan is an internal controls team and/or management plan that addresses the status

of findings on an ongoing, scheduled basis. The CSA team is responsible for managing the implementation of the corrective action plan. The plan needs to include:

- Finding reference
- Corrective action
- Owner of the individual corrective action. An individual should own the corrective action plan to ensure accountability.
- Commitment date
- Status
- Actual date the correction occurred
- Revised or retesting recommended
- Review of recommended corrective action
- Attached supporting documentation as evidence of completion of the corrective action (e.g. process change, system access issues due to segregation of duties issues corrected)

10. **Follow-up and retest the finding.** Corrected findings need to be verified by following up and retesting the issue by the review of audit trails, process changes, and sampling transactions after the correction took place.

11. **Management reporting and review.** Ongoing management review of internal controls program results indicates the commitment and strengthens the accountability in each organization within the operating unit.

12. **Conduct ongoing training.** Internal controls training is key to the operating unit understanding of internal controls components and requirements and should be provided on an annual basis. Business process owners responsible for the payments process should have specific training programs for new hires if there has been a process change or a new system or solution has been implemented.

13. **Update standards of internal control (key controls).** Standards of internal control supporting the CSA process should be updated to reflect the results of corrective action plans.

ETHICS AND "TONE AT THE TOP"

The connection between fraud and the tone at the top of an organization has received a great deal of attention over the last few years. "Tone at the top" refers to the ethical atmosphere that is created in the workplace by the organization's leadership. Whatever tone management sets will have a trickle-down effect on employees of the company. If the tone set by managers upholds ethics and integrity, employees will be more inclined to uphold those same values.

As a best practice, many organizations integrate ethics and compliance requirements into all business processes. Companies need to ensure that an environment of ethics and compliance is embedded within their areas of responsibility. Additionally, a business process owner plays a key role in managing all internal control initiatives in private and public companies. These initiatives usually include the deployment of ethical standards or a code of conduct for the organization.

What is "tone at the top"?

The tone at the top establishes the integrity of a company and directs how employees, shareholders, and stakeholders of a company will behave. A tone at the top focused on personal salary and greed, or that supports and overlooks fraudulent activities, results in a company that may behave the same way. A tone at the top that is focused on doing the right thing for employees, shareholders, and stakeholders results in a company that has an environment of openness and honesty.

What are the components of an effective ethics policy?

1. Communicates an organization's ethical values, standards, and commitments to stakeholders that will underpin the way that it does business
2. Confirms leadership commitment to the above
3. Describes how this will be achieved and monitored through an ethics program
4. Identifies the main ethical issues faced by the organization
5. Identifies other policies and documents that support and detail aspects of the ethics policy—such as a code of ethics, a speak-up policy, a bullying and harassment policy, a gifts and hospitality policy, an environment policy, etc.

What are the components of a well-defined code of conduct?

As a best practice, companies and organizations of all sizes have implemented a code of conduct to support their "tone at the top" message. The Institute of Business Ethics suggests that a code of conduct include the following components:

- How we compete
- Bribery and facilitation payments
- Gifts and entertainment
- Conflicts of interest
- Use of company assets
- Safeguarding important information
- Political involvement and contributions
- The application of human rights standards in our business
- Our environmental responsibilities
- Timely payments of suppliers
- Other issues

What are examples of poor "tone at the top"?

According to the AICPA, the following list provides examples of poor tone at the top and establishes a negative work environment for an employee who is vulnerable to a fraudster. These examples or symptoms also support the Fraud Triangle concept in which there must be: (1) Need, (2) Rationalization, and (3) Opportunity for an individual to commit fraud.

- Top management apparently not caring about or rewarding appropriate behavior
- Lack of recognition for proper job performance
- Negative feedback
- Perceived organizational inequities
- Autocratic management rather than participative management
- Unreasonable budget expectations or other financial targets
- Low organizational loyalty
- Fear of delivering "bad news" to supervisors and/or management
- Less-than-competitive compensation
- Poor training and promotional opportunities
- Unfair, unequal, or unclear organizational responsibilities
- Poor communication practices or methods within the organization

CODE OF CONDUCT CONSIDERATIONS

An environment of internal control in any size organization begins with the tone at the top, which is reflected in the company's code of conduct. A code of conduct establishes the organization's commitment to internal controls, which can help protect the company against fraud. Fraud can occur in organizations of all sizes and in all industries. Controllers and business process owners have the responsibility to ensure that the accounting staff exhibits the highest ethical behavior possible. Negative ethical behavior usually shows up in accounting processes where payments are made, such as accounts payable and payroll.

The following three types of fraud are examples of violations of tone at the top:

1. **Internal fraud:** One or more employees facilitate the activity by using false entries to cover the action. The activity can be concealed for a length of time so that fraud is not easily recognized.
2. **External fraud:** Someone outside of the accounts payable department is able to gain access to company assets through fraudulent means. As a result, funds are misappropriated or extorted from the company.
3. **Conspiracy fraud or collusion:** This is a combination of both internal and external fraud in which an employee conspires with someone outside of the company such as a vendor or an ex-employee to commit a fraudulent activity.

ENTITY-LEVEL CONTROLS

Entity-level controls have a pervasive influence throughout all organizations. If they are weak, inadequate, or nonexistent, they can impact material weaknesses relating to an audit of internal control. Week entity-level controls can also lead to material misstatements in the financial statements of the company. The presence of material misstatements could result in receiving an adverse opinion on internal controls and a qualified opinion on the financial statements.

Entity-level controls should be included in the internal controls programs for all companies and organizations, no matter how large or small. In a January 11, 2010, article, "Taking Control: Public Company Auditors Use Internal Controls to Measure Effectiveness," published by the AICPA's *CPA Insider*, it was noted that entity-level controls (also called top-level controls or management review controls) can provide effectiveness for all controls.

"Entity-level controls are often related to the monitoring process and financial close and reporting cycle—although small companies may not refer to them in those words," explains Wayne Kerr, senior consultant with Thomson Reuters. Kerr says that these top-level controls are items such as weekly or monthly top management reviews of financial information; approval of large transactions, such as payments or sales; and reviews of bank reconciliations.

"Smaller companies rely on these types of controls, in part, because they often lack the resources or capacity to incorporate separation of duties and other 'prevent' controls into their processes," he adds.

Benefits for Entity-Level Controls

There are several benefits to implementing an effective entity-level controls program that are applicable to all types of organizations. These benefits include:

- Reduction of the likelihood of a negative risk event by establishing and reinforcing the infrastructure that sets the control consciousness of the organization.
- For companies conducting evaluations of internal controls, the presence of effective entity-level controls can contribute to a more effective and efficient evaluation strategy.
- Increased effectiveness and efficiency of management's risk assessment and controls evaluation.
- Enforcing the adherence to an internal controls framework.
- An assessment of entity-level controls can highlight potential problems that require a revision of existing internal controls programs at the activity level.

"Tone at the Top"

This is a subjective analysis on the emphasis and seriousness that senior management displays toward internal controls and compliance. This can be quite easy to determine based on the results of the tests mentioned above, but can also be supported by reviewing the following:

- Has the company implemented the appropriate internal control framework?
- Does the company have the requisite amount of independence in the audit, finance, and other functional areas as evidenced by the organizational chart?
- Are meeting minutes documented for each board of directors meeting?
- Do the CEO and president participate in the follow-through and implementation of internal control reviews, gaps, and remediation? Is this documented?

Depending upon the complexity of the organization, there are additional considerations to include in the evaluation of entity-level controls:

- Controls Over Management Override
- The Company's Risk Assessment Process
- Centralized Processing and Controls, Including Shared Service Environments
- Controls to Monitor Results of Operations
- Controls to Monitor Other Controls, Including Activities of the Internal Audit Function, the Audit Committee, and Self-Assessment Programs
- Controls Over the Period-End Financial Reporting Process
- Policies That Address Significant Business Control and Risk Management Practices
- Internal Audit
- Ethics Hotline
- Code of Conduct
- IT Environment and Organizations
- Self-Assessment
- Disclosure Committee
- Oversight by the Board or Senior Management
- Policies and Procedures Manual
- Variance Analysis Reporting
- Remediation Mechanism
- Management Triggers Embedded Within IT Systems
- Internal Communication and Performance Reporting
- Tone at the Top

- Board and Audit Committee Reporting
- External Communication
- Segregation of Duties
- Account Reconciliations
- System Balancing and Exception Reporting
- Change Management
- Risk Assessment Methodology
- Corporate Governance
- Delegation of Authority Policies
- Hiring and Retention Practices
- Fraud Prevention/Detection Controls and Analytical Procedures

 ## ROLES AND RESPONSIBILITIES FOR INTERNAL CONTROL

Internal control over financial reporting continues to be a major area of importance in the governance of an organization. The table presented in this section was developed to provide a template to suggest the roles and responsibilities for the specific components of an organization's system of internal controls that can be used in both public and privately held companies. The roles and responsibilities include those of the Employees, Board of Directors, Audit Committee, Chief Executive Officer and Executive Management Team, Controller and Chief Financial Officer (CFO), Internal Controls Team, Assertion Team, SOX 404 Steering Committee, Internal Auditors, and External Auditors.

Key Point: Ownership of internal controls is critical for all levels of organization. Management directives must be:

- Developed and documented
- Communicated
- Understood (existence, meaning, and use) by appropriate people
- Supported by processes to ensure compliance
- Supported by management

Responsibilities	Definition of Responsibilities
Employees	■ Employees support the organization's internal control program and adhere to the organization's code of conduct and tone at the top. ■ The internal control system is only as effective as the employees throughout the organization who must comply with it. Employees throughout the organization should understand their role in internal control and the importance of supporting the system through their own actions and encouraging respect for the system by their colleagues throughout the organization.
Audit Committee	■ Boards of directors and audit committees have responsibility for making sure the internal control system within the organization is adequate. ■ This responsibility includes determining the extent to which internal controls are to be evaluated.
Chief Executive Officer (CEO) and Executive Management Team of the Organization	■ The chief executive officer is ultimately responsible and should assume ownership of the system. ■ More than any other individual, the chief executive sets the tone at the top that affects integrity and ethics and other factors of a positive control environment. ■ Senior managers in turn assign responsibility for establishment of more specific internal control policies and procedures to personnel responsible for the unit's functions. ■ In a smaller entity, the influence of the chief executive, often an owner-manager, is usually more direct. In any event, in a cascading responsibility, a manager is effectively a chief executive of his or her sphere of responsibility. ■ In a large company, the chief executive fulfills this duty by providing leadership and direction to senior managers and reviewing the way they're controlling the business. ■ As an indication of management's responsibility, top management at a publicly owned organization will include, in the organization's annual financial report to the shareholders, a statement indicating that management has established a system of internal control management believes is effective. The statement may also provide specific details about the organization's internal control system. ■ The primary responsibility for the development and maintenance of internal control rests with an organization's management. With increased significance placed on the control environment, the focus of internal control has changed from policies and procedures to an overriding philosophy and operating style within the organization. ■ Emphasis on these intangible aspects highlights the importance of top management's involvement in the internal control system. If internal control is not a priority for management, then it will not be one for people within the organization, either.

Responsibilities	Definition of Responsibilities
Controller and Chief Financial Officer (CFO)	■ Controllers and CFOs are usually responsible for the development and implementation of internal controls programs for their companies. ■ Controllers and CFOs are also responsible for the results of the effectiveness of the organization's internal controls programs, which means that controls must be updated to reflect current system and operational environments. ■ They are required to ensure that all accounting practices impacting financial results are properly controlled. ■ Controllers and CFOs also drive the assertion process required by Sarbanes-Oxley (SOX) 404. They may lead an Internal Controls Team with Assertion Teams to facilitate this effort as described below. ■ A controller and CFO may also enlist the efforts of a Sarbanes-Oxley (SOX) Steering Committee to help with the governance of the internal controls program and assertion process. This approach is also described below.
Internal Controls Team (Public Company Example)	The VP of Internal Controls, along with the Internal Controls Team, is responsible for implementing the requirements of Sarbanes-Oxley (SOX) 404, by which the organization's internal controls are documented and evaluated. This requirement includes implementing the foundational direction for the organization's internal controls program. Specific responsibilities of the Internal Controls Team include: **Project Management** ■ Primary liaison to impacted organizations and external service providers and escalate project-wide issues to management and Steering Committee for resolution. **Tactical Project Focus** ■ Interact with controls and procedures owners. ■ Ensure delivery of all tasks assigned to the specific work stream. ■ Report to the Internal Controls Project Manager to obtain scope approval. ■ Assist with issue escalation and provide milestone progress updates. ■ Responsible for day-to-day work effort in areas of ownership. ■ Working for the Internal Controls Project Manager, complete assigned workload with designees from control and procedures owners. **Disclosure Committee, Audit Committee, and SEC Reporting (10Q and 10K)** ■ The VP of Internal Controls attends each Disclosure Committee meeting and presents significant controls issues that impact the organization's key controls. ■ The VP of Internal Controls attends each Audit Committee meeting and provides SOX 404 project updates and presents significant control issues. ■ The VP of Internal Controls develops the response for the evaluation of internal controls for the 10Q and 10K reports.

Responsibilities	Definition of Responsibilities
Assertion Team (Public Company Example)	As part of the structure for the SOX 404 project, and to establish the foundational structure control environment, Assertion Teams are established to represent each accounting cycle, process, and/or business area. The Assertion Team is responsible for: ■ Providing input and signoff on the scope of the SOX 404 project ■ Participating in workshops, and providing access to subject matter experts (SMEs) ■ Completing assertion packages with the Internal Controls team ■ Approving deliverables ■ Providing input into testing effort during planning, execution, and results remediation stages ■ Addressing remediation actions ■ Accepting responsibility for ongoing maintenance of controls and documentation
SOX 404 Steering Committee (Public Company Example)	The SOX 404 Steering Committee has the following responsibilities: ■ The SOX 404 Steering Committee will provide written certification to support the organization's Section 404 assertion on internal controls on an annual basis. This effort is supported by the sub-certification process at the detailed process-owner level and the deliverable acceptance in individual process areas. ■ The SOX 404 Steering Committee will review sensitive policies required for SOX 404 compliance, including: Segregation of Duties, Delegation of Authority changes, and remediation and resolution of other enterprise-wide issues. ■ The SOX 404 Steering Committee will provide visible sponsorship of project and commitment of skilled resources from all represented areas, and committee members play an important role in reviewing and understanding the project scope, approach, and risks.
Internal Auditors	■ Internal auditors' responsibilities typically include ensuring the adequacy of the system of internal control, the reliability of data, and the efficient use of the organization's resources. Internal auditors identify control problems and develop solutions for improving and strengthening internal controls. ■ Internal auditors are concerned with the entire range of an organization's internal controls, including operational, financial, and compliance controls.
External Auditors	■ Internal controls will also be evaluated by the external auditors. External auditors assess the effectiveness of internal control within an organization to plan the financial statement audit. ■ In contrast to internal auditors, external auditors focus primarily on controls that affect financial reporting. External auditors have a responsibility to report internal control weaknesses (as well as reportable conditions about internal control) to the audit committee of the board of directors.

CHAPTER TWO

The Order to Cash (O2C) Process

 INTRODUCTION

The O2C process includes the sub-processes of acquiring and accepting customer orders; writing sales contracts; granting customer credit; shipping or otherwise delivering products or services; billing and recording sales and lease transactions; maintaining and monitoring accounts receivable; instituting effective collection procedures; recording and controlling cash receipts; establishing pricing and promotional activities; and properly valuing receivable balances.

Order to cash (O2C) and AR are important business processes within a corporation. AR is one of a series of accounting transactions dealing with the billing of a customer for goods and services received. In most business entities this function is typically done by generating an invoice and mailing or electronically delivering it to the customer, who in turn must pay it within an established timeframe called credit or payment terms. Terms of payment are established in the customer contract.

 PROCESS OVERVIEW

The diagram below suggests that the foundational elements for the O2C process are internal controls and compliance, ERP systems, and O2C automation solutions.

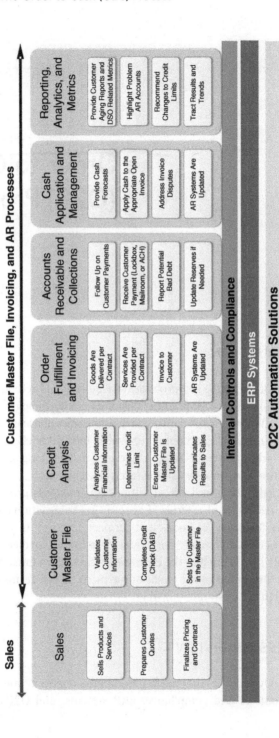

Customer Master File, Invoicing, and AR Processes

Sales

Sales
- Sells Products and Services
- Prepares Customer Quotes
- Finalizes Pricing and Contract

Customer Master File
- Validates Customer Information
- Completes Credit Check (D&B)
- Sets Up Customer in the Master File

Credit Analysis
- Analyzes Customer Financial Information
- Determines Credit Limit
- Ensures Customer Master File Is Updated
- Communicates Results to Sales

Order Fulfillment and Invoicing
- Goods Are Delivered per Contract
- Services Are Provided per Contract
- Invoice to Customer
- AR Systems Are Updated

Accounts Receivable and Collections
- Follow Up on Customer Payments
- Receive Customer Payment (Lockbox, Mailroom, or ACH)
- Report Potential Bad Debt
- Update Reserves if Needed

Cash Application and Management
- Provide Cash Forecasts
- Apply Cash to the Appropriate Open Invoice
- Address Invoice Disputes
- AR Systems Are Updated

Reporting, Analytics, and Metrics
- Provide Customer Aging Reports and DSO Related Metrics
- Highlight Problem AR Accounts
- Recommend Changes to Credit Limits
- Tract Results and Trends

Internal Controls and Compliance

ERP Systems

O2C Automation Solutions

APPLICATION OF INTERNAL CONTROLS

In management's selection of procedures and techniques of control, the degree of control implemented is a matter of reasonable business judgment. The common guideline used in determining the degree of internal controls implementation is that the cost of a control should not exceed the benefit derived. However, there is a minimum set of controls that should exist in a normal business environment. The internal control standards listed here represent the minimum controls to be implemented for the revenue process. In some cases, the requirements of the U.S. government exceed these minimum controls.

 ## METRICS

Table of Metrics

- **Accounts Receivable Aging**—Independently age accounts receivable on invoice date. Identify all open accounts receivable transactions as of a specified date (but default to the current date) and report the aging of accounts receivable transactions by client and for all clients together in predetermined aging categories, based on invoice/billing date.

- **Number of Duplicate Customers (Same Name or Address)**—Ensure all customers are valid and created only once. Identify all sales orders by customers where more than one occurrence of the same Customer Name or Customer Address exists in the customer database under different customer ID.

- **Customer Data Validity**—Ensure transaction validity by identifying transactions where critical data elements deviate from expected values and formats. For each sales order transaction, test that critical transactional and customer master data is present.

- **Invalid Customer Prices**—Ensure all sales prices are authorized. Identify all Sales Orders by customer where the price on the master file differs from the price on the sales order by more than the percentage variance or the threshold amount variance.

- **Sales Process Kick-Back**—Ensure all transactions are valid and to highlight potentially fraudulent activity. Identify Customers with any Sales orders with (1) unusually high sales discounts; unusually high credit terms/credit limits; or (2) unusually frequent credit memos to the same customer.

- **Non-Compliant Customer**—Verify that customers are not listed in the GSA-EPLS and SAM list. Also, check the customer master for KYC, OFAC, OIG, and FCPA compliance. Identify all Sales Orders where the customer name matches names found in the GSA-EPLS list.

Table of Metrics

■ **Valid Credit Limits**—Ensure all credit limits assigned to customers adhere to company polices. Identify all sales orders by customers where the total sales order + AR balance are greater than the customer's credit limit.

■ **Unauthorized Price Changes**—Verify that prices in the price master file are authorized and valid. Identify all sales orders where the individual who entered/modified prices in the price master has the proper systems access.

■ **AR Billing Status and Review**—Monitor the AR transactions, specifically billing and adjustment type transactions, per customer, to identify clients with a high adjustment ratio. This information can help uncover the manipulation of client records, and ultimately assets such as inventory. Examine the AR transactions file (billing and adjustments) with the objective of profiling clients who appear to have a high number of adjustments, write-offs when compared to their charges.

■ **Days Sales Outstanding (DSO)**—Ensure all billings are within a timely manner. Identify all Invoices where the corresponding sales order was entered greater than the <<Aging Period>> number of days before the invoice.

■ **True DSO Calculation**—True DSO calculates the actual number of days credit sales are unpaid by tracking individual invoices to the month of sale.

■ **Best Possible DSO**—Best Possible DSO utilizes only your current (non-delinquent) receivables to calculate the best length of time you can achieve in turning over receivables. It should be compared to the standard calculation above, and be close to your terms of sale.

■ **Delinquent DSO (Average Days Delinquent) Calculation**—Delinquent DSO or Average Days Delinquent (ADD) calculates the average days invoices are past due. This provides a snapshot to evaluate individuals, subgroups, or overall collection performance.

■ **Countback DSO Calculation**—The Countback Method of calculating takes into account sales fluctuations. Giving more weight to the current month's sales, it reflects the correct assumption that most of the A/R balance will be from current, as opposed to previous, sales. It also takes into account the real effect of the actual difference in the number of days per month (e.g. 28 in February vs. 30 in April, June, September, and November vs. 31 the rest of the months).

■ **Sales Weighted DSO Calculation**—Sales Weighted DSO, as with the regular DSO calculation, measures the average time that receivables are outstanding. However, some consider it an improvement over other methods of calculating DSO because it attempts to smooth out the bias of credit sales and terms of sale.

■ **Collection Effectiveness Index (CEI)**—The Collection Effective Index, also known as CEI, is a calculation of a company's ability to retrieve their accounts receivable from customers. CEI measures the amount collected during a time period to the amount of receivables in the same time period. In comparison, the collection effectiveness index is slightly more accurate than daily sales outstanding (DSO) because of the time period.

SUB-PROCESSES

The sub-processes included in the O2C process are:

2.1 Order Entry/Edit

2.2 Export Controls

2.3 Sales Contracts

2.4 Credit

2.5 Shipping

2.6 Revenue Recognition/Billing

2.7 Accounts Receivable

2.8 Collection

2.9 Cash Receipts and Application

2.10 Price Establishment

2.11 Promotional Activities

 2.1 ORDER ENTRY/EDIT

Introduction

Customer and product master data must be accurate, timely, with the appropriate safeguards to ensure the data is secured. Orders/contracts must be properly documented and fully edited before they are released to production and/or shipping, as appropriate.

Standard of Internal Control

2.1.1 **Master Data.** All modifications to the database must be approved by the appropriate member of management prior to data entry.
Refer to risks: A-2, A-4, A-5, A-7, A-8, A-10

2.1.2 **Order Evidence.** All orders must be supported by an authorized customer purchase order or other evidence supporting the customer's initiation of the order.
Refer to risks: A-1, A-2, A-3

2.1.3 **Access to Orders.** Customer order information must be safeguarded from unauthorized access.
Refer to risk: A-8

2.1.4 **Credit Review.** New customers who do not remit a payment in advance at the time of order or delivery must be reviewed for creditworthiness prior to the acceptance and/or shipment of customer orders.
Refer to risk: A-4

2.1.5 **Order Fulfillment.** Orders must be evaluated to ensure the customer's expected fulfillment date is possible prior to accepting the order.
Refer to risks: A-11, A-13

2.1.6 **Order Acceptance.** Formal acknowledgment of order acceptance must be sent to the customer on a timely basis, unless reasonable business practice dictates otherwise.
Refer to risk: A-5

2.1.7 **Sales Contracts.** As a standard practice, a signed contract should be approved by the applicable financial and operational boards or management teams for all customer product and service prior to execution.
Refer to risks: A-1, A-2, A-10

2.1.8 **Order Documentation.** Items to be reviewed include existence of appropriate contract forms, purchase order terms and conditions, shipping and payment terms, credit approvals, order receipt date, applicable tax documentation/calculations, prices, extensions, product compatibility, and compliance with applicable federal, state, and local government laws/regulations and export control requirements.
Refer to risks: A-1, A-2, A-4, A-6, A-7, A-11, A-14

2.1.9 **Open Order Review.** Open order status must be reviewed periodically for backorders, canceled, and partially filled orders. Backorders and partially filled orders must be researched and resolved.
Refer to risk: A-9

2.1.10 **Sales Subject to Financing.** When selling product subject to financing, policies and procedures must be established and documented to ensure the third-party lease/conditional sales contract has been approved by the customer and is acceptable to the company prior to order acceptance.
Refer to risks: A-1, A-10, A-14, A-15

2.1.11 **Order Processing.** Orders must be processed expeditiously. Metrics should be established and monitored to measure average time to process and number of items greater than a certain number of days.
Refer to risks: A-12, A-13, A-15

2.1.12 **Order Terms.** Order administration should ensure orders being processed are consistent with corporate standards (margin, risk, payment terms, project milestones, etc.).
Refer to risk: A-7

Risk If Standard Is Not Implemented

A-1 Products may be manufactured and shipped or services performed without a valid customer commitment.

A-2 The products, quantity, selling price, payment terms, sales tax, or shipping address included on the manufacturing order may be incorrect.

A-3 Commission credit may be processed for an invalid invoice.

A-4 Products or services may be sold to an unauthorized customer or to an unacceptable credit risk, resulting in uncollectible accounts.

A-5 Errors in the manufacturing order (e.g. products, quantity, and price) may not be identified and corrected prior to manufacture and shipment.

A-6 Non-compliance with government regulations may result in substantial fines, penalties, delays in collection, and/or loss of exporting privileges.

A-7 Orders may be accepted and processed at prices and/or terms and conditions that are not acceptable to management.

A-8 Sales/orders may be lost, destroyed, or altered.

A-9 Confidential information may be used to the detriment of the company.

A-10 Sales and lease contracts may not be acceptable to management regarding pricing, terms, penalty clauses, or credit risk.

A-11 Customers may not make payments to the company and/or issue fines or penalties resulting from unmet milestones.

A-12 Untimely pricing and inventory information may result.

A-13 Customer dissatisfaction may result.

A-14 Product may be manufactured or shipped prior to finalization of payment arrangement with customer.

A-15 Loss of revenue.

2.2 EXPORT CONTROLS

Introduction

The U.S. government controls exports of sensitive equipment, software, and technology as a means to promote our national security interests and foreign policy objectives.

Through this export control system, the U.S. government can effectively:

- Provide for national security by limiting access to the most sensitive U.S. technology and weapons.
- Promote regional stability.
- Take into account human rights considerations.
- Prevent proliferation of weapons and technologies, including of weapons of mass destruction, to problem end-users and supporters of international terrorism.
- Comply with international commitments (e.g. nonproliferation regimes and UN Security Council sanctions and UNSC resolution 1540.

Under the current export control system, three different USG agencies have the authority to issue export licenses: the Departments of State, Commerce, and the Treasury. In 2009, licensing agencies within these departments processed over 130,000 applications. In 2010 alone, the Department of Commerce processed approximately 22,000 applications. In some cases, exporters were required to apply for multiple licenses from separate departments.

The goal of the ECR Initiative is to create a Single Licensing Agency (SLA), which would act as a "one-stop shop" for businesses seeking an export license and for the USG to coordinate review of license applications. The result will be a licensing process that is transparent, predictable, and timely.

The United States controls lists correspond directly with the lists maintained by the various multinational export control regimes, but are augmented by unilateral controls when necessary to ensure national security and foreign policy imperatives.

The three major lists of export-controlled items are the Commerce Control List (CCL), the United States Munitions List (USML), and the Nuclear Regulatory Commission Controls (NRCC).

The CCL includes the following:

- Items on Wassenaar Arrangement Dual-Use List
- Nuclear-related dual-use commodities (compiled in the Nuclear Suppliers Group's Nuclear Referral List)
- Dual-use items on Missile Technology Control Regime List
- CW Precursors, biological organisms and toxins, and CBW-related equipment on the Australia Group lists
- Items controlled in furtherance of U.S. foreign policy and other objectives, including anti-terrorism, crime control, Firearms Convention, regional stability, UN sanctions, and short supply reasons
- Unlisted items when destined for specified end-uses or end-users (catchall controls)

The regulations emphasize a company's responsibility for knowing the destination of its products and technical data. The regulations apply to all non-U.S. sales, and additionally, certain requirements apply to sales within the United States. The regulations typically require licensing of exports. In the United States, to export Commerce Control List items the most commonly used licenses are general and individual validated licenses.[1]

Application of Internal Controls

It is corporate policy to comply with export regulations worldwide. The export or re-export of products will not be carried out except in compliance with these regulations. It is the responsibility of each Company operating unit in the United States as well as each company international order processing location to understand the regulations and have a working knowledge of U.S. Export Regulations. All company managers must consult with internal resources responsible for corporate trade for assistance in identifying those trade control legal requirements specifically applicable to their business operations, which must be integrated within the internal controls program. Mistakes in the procedural application and/or omissions and failures to implement appropriate processes for compliance with any of these Trade control requirements may

---

[1]U.S. Department of State, "A Resource on Strategic Trade Management and Export Controls," accessed January 5, 2019, https://www.state.gov/strategictrade/overview/.

result in regulatory violations and the imposition of government monetary penalties and other sanctions, including the loss or suspension of exporting privileges.

Standard of Internal Control

2.2.1 **Export Control Assessment.** In consultation with the Trade organization, all company operating units must assess the character and scope of their business activities to determine which export control requirements, if any, will apply to those activities. Once identified, a written export control program must be developed and implemented to ensure that (a) all required controls are in place, (b) such controls provide a reasonable assurance of continuing satisfactory compliance, and (c) they are adequately documented for audit purposes.
Refer to risks: B-1, B-2, B-3

2.2.2 **Elements of the Export Control Program.** An export control program should incorporate the following elements:
   a. A clear statement of management's awareness of, commitment to and expectation of employee compliance with applicable export controls.
   Refer to risk: B-2
   b. Company hardware, software, technical data, and technical assistance, and that of third parties, transferred by any means or method, both internally and externally, across national boundaries must be assessed or "classified" by the trade organization for its technology characteristics and specifications. This is necessary to ensure that any required non-U.S. and/or U.S. government export authorization is correctly identified and cited in shipping documentation or is made available to fulfill other regulatory requirements. The export of products and services without a required export authorization is a violation of the law.
   Refer to risks: B-1, B-2, B-3
   c. Appropriate documentation must be created and retained in conformity with national export control administration requirements.
   Refer to risks: B-1, B-2
   d. All company transactions must be assessed for the appearance of factors identified in the profile of technology "diversion risk indicators" or other suspicious or unreasonable circumstances that might indicate a potential for illegal technology diversion.
   Refer to risks: B-1, B-2, B-3

e. Unless subject to specific proliferation screening exemption, all transactions must be screened for the appearance of factors suggesting a prohibited weapons of mass destruction "proliferation" nuclear, missile, chemical-biological end-use or end user.

Refer to risks: B-1, B-2, B-3

f. A process must be established to evaluate, select, and then utilize the correct license requirements necessary authorizing any export and to correctly fulfill all accompanying administrative requirements.

Refer to risks: B-1, B-2

g. A high level of vigilance must be exercised in all transactions to detect the appearance of prohibited verbal or written boycott related language and terms.

Refer to risks: B-1, B-2

h. The country content of products must be assessed in order to satisfy the certification processes of the United States and/or other countries required to qualify for certain national government purchasing and procurement programs.

Refer to risks: B-1, B-2

i. There is an evolving worldwide Trade requirement for information identifying the country(ies) of origin in the manufacture or assembly of products. This is a necessary requirement to satisfy certain government contract compliance, importation, and funding program requirements.

Refer to risks: B-1, B-2

j. A process must be established to detect, in any transaction, the appearance of product or services having technical characteristics that are classified for export purposes as "munitions" products or services which are subject to stringent control required by the International Traffic in Arms Regulations (ITAR).

Refer to risks: B-1, B-2, B-3

k. Opportunities must be provided for the periodic presentation to employees of appropriate training in export controls awareness, comprehension, and procedural administration.

Refer to risk: B-2

l. Appropriate processes must be implemented to ensure that an effective self-testing program exists for measuring compliance with the individual elements of a function's export control program.

Refer to risk: B-2

2.2.3 **Notifications.** To ensure that all controlled materials/products purchased by customers are not sold or re-exported in violation of export regulations, the following notifications must be present when required:
   a. The Destination Control Statement is a legal statement required by the Export Administration Regulations (EAR) and the International Traffic in Arms Regulations (ITAR) stating that the goods you are exporting are destined for the country indicated in all the shipping documents.
   b. Contracts with distributors or other resellers must contain a statement to indicate that they have agreed not to violate any applicable export regulations.
   Refer to risks: B-1, B-3

2.2.4 **Self-Audits.** All worldwide operating unit managers will ensure that their respective self-audit programs will include periodic reviews of their export licensing control programs to assure compliance with U.S. and local regulations.
   Refer to risk: B-2

Risk If Standard Is Not Implemented

B-1 Noncompliance with the regulations may result in license denial, shipment seizures, substantial civil fines, criminal penalties, and/or loss of exporting privileges. Penalties are often severe but vary by country and seriousness of violation.

B-2 Internal controls may be circumvented or may not be executed.

B-3 Inaction may adversely impact U.S. national security and foreign policy.

2.3 SALES CONTRACTS

Introduction

Sales contracts may be in, but are not limited to, these forms:

a. An accepted customer quote
b. A purchase order with terms and conditions which are different from the company's standard terms and conditions, or a formal document

Standard of Internal Control

2.3.1 **Enforceable Contracts.** Sales contracts should be standardized, clearly written, and legally enforceable, with the terms of the sale completely documented. The contracts should be financially and operationally sound (achievable) and strategically aligned. Authorization to draft, modify, approve, and sign contracts must be clearly defined and in accordance with the company's policy on delegation of authority with appropriate segregation of duties controls. Legal counsel must review contracts where appropriate to assure that the company is entering into a correct and appropriate contract and that it is not assuming liability for the negligence, errors, or omissions of another party.
Refer to risks: C-1, C-2, C-3, C-5, C-6

2.3.2 **Feasible Contracts.** All sales contracts must be reviewed for product availability and administrative, financial, and performance feasibility and communicated to those responsible for implementation and follow-up (e.g. pricing, terms and conditions, etc.).
Refer to risks: C-1, C-2, C-3

2.3.3 **Contract Storage.** All sales contracts must be filed and safeguarded appropriately.
Refer to risks: C-1, C-2, C-4

2.3.4 **Contract Reviews.** Compliance reviews must be performed periodically so potential losses are recognized.
Refer to risk: C-8

2.3.5 **Contract Renewals.** Contracts are renewed in a timely fashion before delivering product or providing services.
Refer to risks: C-1, C-8

2.3.6 **Oral/Side Agreements.** Oral/side agreements in lieu of a sales contract should not be made.
Refer to risks: C-1, C-3, C-7, C-8

Risk If Standard Is Not Implemented

C-1 Customer dissatisfaction may result.

C-2 Assessment of fines and/or penalties may result.

C-3 Different prices of product to similar customers could create pricing difficulties locally and possibly globally. In addition, different prices for the same product to similar customers may be illegal and result in penalties to the company.

C-4 Lost, incorrectly recorded, and/or misappropriated sales contracts may not be identified and corrected in a timely manner.

C-5 The company could be held responsible for the negligence, errors, or omissions of another party, resulting in financial loss to our shareholders.

C-6 If the contract is not consistent regarding liability provisions, it can be unenforceable.

C-7 Inability to deliver product or service.

C-8 Financial losses may occur.

 ## 2.4 CREDIT

Introduction

Formal, written credit procedures (e.g. establishment of credit terms, reserves for bad debt, promissory notes, direct loans, indemnified transactions) should be established and implemented for each operating unit and be consistent with policy established by the corporate controller.

Credit limits must be established for each customer with established payment terms. Credit limits must be recorded in an information system (e.g. customer master) that is used for managing the shipment of orders to customers. A review of approved credit limits and the current receivable balance must be made before additional customer orders are accepted and/or shipped. The review should consider all regional and business units' leasing or direct sales resulting in the global receivable balance.

Standard of Internal Control

2.4.1 **Credit Policies.** Formal, written credit procedures (e.g. establishment of credit terms, reserves for bad debt, promissory notes, direct loans, indemnified transactions) should be established and implemented for each operating unit and be consistent with policy established by the corporate controller.
Refer to risks: D-1, D-2, D-4

2.4.2 **Credit Limits.** Credit limits must be established for each customer. Credit limits must be recorded in an information system (e.g. customer master) that is used for managing the shipment of orders to customers. Credit limits must be based on a review of the customer's ability to

pay and should be balanced between the local and global credit position. Reliable outside sources of information must be used to establish such limits.
Refer to risks: D-2, D-4

2.4.3 **Credit Limit Exceptions.** Credit management approval is required before credit is extended in excess of approved limits. When extended credit is granted, a timeline should be established with criteria for an extension/reduction process when period expires or criteria are not met.
Refer to risks: D-2, D-4

2.4.4 **Credit Limit Reviews.** Established customer credit limits must be documented, filed, and reviewed for adequacy at least annually. Where appropriate, adjustments to credit limits must be made in accordance with approved corporate policies/procedures. Customer credit history must be maintained.
Refer to risks: D-2, D-4

2.4.5 **Past Due Customers.** Customers must be assigned "refer to credit" designation whenever undisputed past due balances exist on their accounts. All orders placed by these customers must be approved by Credit prior to being released for shipment.
Refer to risks: D-2, D-4

2.4.6 **Terms of Sale.** Standard terms of sale must be extended to all customers or classes of customers. Exceptions to standard terms of sale must only be made in concert with custom product delivery and custom services delivery and approved by appropriate level of management.
Refer to risks: D-2, D-4

2.4.7 **Segregation of Duties.** Credit administration must be independent of the order entry, billing, general ledger, and sales functions.
Refer to risks: D-2, D-3

2.4.8 **System Access.** Individuals with system capability to make entries in the accounts receivable subsidiary ledger (e.g. cash application, account write-offs, sales concessions, and sales discounts) must not have system capability to invoice customers, issue credit memos, or adjust the general ledger. If this separation is not possible due to limited staff size, compensating controls must be documented, implemented, and followed.
Refer to risk: D-2, D-3, D-5

2.4.9 **Cash Rebates.** Where rebates are not processed as credits, a process is established to ensure the account is current. Cash rebates should be initiated by credit, authorized by finance, paid by accounts payable, and reconciled by finance.
Refer to risk: D-3, D-6

2.4.10 **Cash Deductions.** Customer deductions (debit memos) are created by credit, approved by region finance, and applied by appropriate finance function.
Refer to risk: D-3

2.4.11 **Disputes and Concessions.** Guidelines must be developed and monitored for dispute detection, tracing, and resolution. Criteria and approval for concession must be developed and monitored.
Refer to risks: D-4, D-6

Risk If Standard Is Not Implemented

D-1 Inconsistent and/or inadequate credit review may be completed.

D-2 Products or services may be sold to an unauthorized customer or to an unacceptable credit risk, resulting in uncollectible accounts.

D-3 Intentional alteration of receivable records/invoices could occur.

D-4 Revenue may be lost due to poor credit decisions.

D-5 Company funds may be disbursed to customers with past due balances.

D-6 Customer dissatisfaction may result if resolution is not performed in a timely manner.

 ## 2.5 SHIPPING

Introduction

Numerically controlled shipping transactions must be prepared for all goods shipped. Evidence of shipment must be transmitted to accounting or billing module in a timely manner, generally within 24 hours. Sales cut-off requirements for revenue recognition purposes will be followed by the shipping department.

Standard of Internal Control

2.5.1 **Authorized Shipments.** Proper written authorization with an appropriate business need is required for all products shipped from company premises.
Refer to risks: E-1, E-2, E-3, E-4

2.5.2 **Accounting for Shipments.** Sales orders or shipping authorizations must be accounted for on a periodic basis by someone independent of the order processing and shipping functions. This will include ensuring all product shipments have been billed and are accurately reflected in the inventory records.
Refer to risks: E-3, E-5, E-9, E-10

2.5.3 **Documented Shipments.** Accurate documentation that meets legal and contractual requirements must be prepared for all shipments.
Refer to risks: E-1, E-2

2.5.4 **Shipping Records.** Shipping documents must be pre-numbered where the integrity of sequencing is not computer controlled. Missing documents must be investigated.
Refer to risks: E-3, E-7, E-8

2.5.5 **Product Transfers.** Evidence of shipment, such as a signed bill of lading, must be obtained from the carrier to establish the physical and legal transfer of products. Such documents must always reflect the actual date of shipment.
Refer to risks: E-3, E-6, E-7

2.5.6 **Quantity and Product Verification.** A person independent of the shipping function must verify the types and quantities of products to be shipped on at least a test basis. Some form of validation of quantity/type should be obtained from carrier.
Refer to risks: E-2, E-4

2.5.7 **Warehouse Layout.** The Shipping department must be physically segregated from the production and receiving facilities, as dictated by good business practices. Returned product must be segregated from inventory available for sale.
Refer to risk: E-4

2.5.8 **Warehouse Access.** Admittance to the shipping area must be restricted to authorized personnel only.
Refer to risks: E-4, E-10

2.5.9 **Sales Cutoff.** There will be no deviations from the company's sales cutoff policy.
Refer to risk: E-7

2.5.10 **Blank Shipping Forms.** Blank shipping authorizations, numerically controlled shipping documents, and bills of lading must be safeguarded from unauthorized access and use.
Refer to risks: E-8, E-10

2.5.11 **Segregation of Duties.** The shipping function must be independent of the physical inventory count, order entry, billing, accounts receivable, and general ledger functions.
Refer to risks: E-3, E-10

2.5.12 **Complaints.** Customer correspondence (billing and shipping complaints, service problems, etc.) must be investigated and resolved in a timely manner.
Refer to risks: E-4, E-8, E-10, E-11

2.5.13 **Drop Shipments.** Locations involved with domestic and international drop shipments must have documented procedures that are enforced.
Refer to risks: E-1, E-2, E-3, E-7

Risk If Standard Is Not Implemented

E-1 Shipments may be made to incorrect or unauthorized customers or to incorrect customer locations.

E-2 Incorrect products or quantities may be shipped, or products may be shipped early, late, or in violation of export control and/or customs requirements.

E-3 Products may have been shipped but not billed or recorded.

E-4 Customer shipments may be lost, misplaced, or misappropriated.

E-5 Products that have been authorized for shipment may not have been shipped.

E-6 The company may not recover for products lost by the carrier.

E-7 Revenues and related cost of sales may be recorded in the wrong accounting period, as complete and accurate information may not be forwarded to accounting/billing.

E-8 Accountability over products shipped may be lost. Unbilled and/or misappropriated shipments may not be identified.

E-9   Backorders or lost sales orders may not be identified and resolved on a timely basis.

E-10   Intentional errors or misappropriation of assets could occur.

E-11   Customer dissatisfaction may result.

2.6 REVENUE RECOGNITION/BILLING

Introduction

According to International Finance Reporting Standards (IFRS) criteria, for revenue to be recognized, the following conditions must be satisfied:

1. Risks and rewards have been transferred from the seller to the buyer.
2. The seller does not have control over the goods sold.
3. The collection of payment from goods or services is reasonably assured.
4. The amount of revenue can be reasonably measured.
5. Costs of revenue can be reasonably measured.

An explanation for each condition is provided below.

- Conditions (1) and (2) are referred to as Performance. Regarding performance, it occurs when the seller has done what is to be expected to be entitled to payment.
- Condition (3) is referred to as Collectibility. The seller must have a reasonable expectation that he or she will be paid for the performance.
- Conditions (4) and (5) are referred to as Measurability. Due to the accounting guideline of the matching principle, the seller must be able to match the revenues to the expenses. Hence, both revenues and expenses should be able to be reasonably measured.

IFRS 15, revenue from contracts with customers, establishes the specific steps for revenue recognition. It is important to note that there are exclusions from IFRS 15 such as:

- Lease contracts (IAS 17)
- Insurance contracts (IFRS 4)
- Financial instruments (IFRS 9)[2]

---

[2]Corporate Finance Institute (CFI), "Revenue Recognition," accessed January 1, 2019, https://corporatefinanceinstitute.com/resources/knowledge/accounting/revenue-recognition/.

Standard of Internal Control

2.6.1 **Responsibilities.** The ultimate decision regarding how revenue is recognized is a financial responsibility and may not be delegated to other functional areas.
Refer to risks: F-1, F-2

2.6.2 **Recorded Sales Transactions.** Accounting for sales transactions is a financial responsibility and must not be delegated to other functional areas. Local Finance/operational management must ensure invoice preparation is adequately controlled.
Refer to risks: F-3, F-4, F-5, F-6

2.6.3 **Non-Standard Sales Transactions.** Unusual or non-standard sales transactions should be reviewed by finance to determine proper revenue recognition. Examples of non-standard transactions could include: custom product, custom services, return rights, upgrades, maintenance installation, acceptance, will-call sales, delayed billings, leasing transactions, pre-paids, and consignment or no-release inventory.
Refer to risks: F-1, F-2

2.6.4 **Revenue Reversal.** Revenue reversal must be recognized when termination of business, product recalls, or product withdrawals decisions are made.
Refer to risks: F-1, F-2

2.6.5 **Product Returns.** Sales with a substantial right of return should be avoided. However, should such sales occur, appropriate reserves should be established, and revenue should not be recognized until the sales can be reviewed by an appropriate level of financial management to determine the appropriate timing for revenue recognition.
Refer to risks: F-1, F-2, F-7

2.6.6 **Contract Reviews.** Contracts must be periodically reviewed to ensure profits and losses are recognized when identified. An estimate needs to be made for total contract revenue, total contract costs, and percentage of completion to ensure appropriate revenue is recognized, contract losses are accrued, and margin equalization occurs.
Refer to risks: F-1, F-2

2.6.7 **Reserves.** Appropriate reserves should be established to cover estimated warranty expenses, customer returns, or other customer allowances. These reserves must be periodically reviewed for adequacy.
Refer to risks: F-1, F-2

2.6.8 **Price Protection.** An appropriate reserve must be established for approved pricing reductions and associated outstanding claims. The reserve should be released upon expiration of submission period, provided a claim has been submitted or pending resubmission. Non-standard price protection terms must be approved according to the Delegation of Authority policy.
Refer to risks: F-1, F-2, F-3, F-7, F-8

2.6.9 **Account Reviews.** Deferred revenue, accruals, and deferred asset accounts must be reviewed and reconciled on a timely basis to ensure the accounts are current, complete and accurate, and supported by the appropriate documentation.
Refer to risks: F-1, F-2, F-3

2.6.10 **Segregation of Duties.** The billing function must be independent of the shipping and accounts receivable functions.
Refer to risk: F-4, F-5, F-6

2.6.11 **Billing Transactions.** All billing transactions must be prepared in a timely manner on the basis of authorized master data and supporting shipping documentation, service delivery, and acceptance criteria. All invoices must be pre-numbered where the integrity of sequencing is not computer controlled.
Refer to risks: F-1, F-2, F-3, F-4, F-6, F-8

2.6.12 **Accrued Revenue.** Where accruals have been made for unbilled accounts receivable, a procedure must be established to ensure that when subsequent billings are generated, revenue is not recorded twice.
Refer to risks: F-4, F-6

2.6.13 **Deferred Revenue.** A procedure must be established to ensure amounts billed have in fact been earned. Where revenue has been deferred, a process must be established to ensure the deferred revenue is relieved when it is earned.
Refer to risks: F-4, F-6

2.6.14 **Cash Advance.** A procedure must be established to ensure that cash advances received from customers are accrued to the extent that they have not been earned. When cash advances have been earned, revenue should be recognized and the liability for cash advances received should be relieved.
Refer to risks: F-4, F-6

2.6.15 **Accurate Invoices.** Invoices must accurately reflect the items shipped or services provided. Invoices, both manual and computer generated, should be reviewed for accuracy on a test basis.
Refer to risks: F-3, F-4, F-6, F-9, F-12

2.6.16 **Taxes.** Sales, use, and/or value-added taxes must be billed in accordance with local laws. Where tax is not billed, supporting documentation is required to support the customer's tax-exempt status. This documentation must be obtained and filed.
Refer to risk: F-10

2.6.17 **"Zero-Dollar" Invoices.** All invoices or other billing documents containing "zero-dollar" or "no charge" items must have written approval by local Finance and Marketing management (according to their respective authorization levels).
Refer to risk: F-11

2.6.18 **Partial Shipments.** Where partial shipments are not accepted by a customer, billing should be in agreement with the customer's PO.
Refer to risk: F-6

2.6.19 **Invoice Delivery.** Invoices must be sent directly to the customer upon product shipment or service completion and must not be returned to the Credit department for revision.
Refer to risk: F-13

2.6.20 **Approved Exceptions.** All billing exceptions, such as no charge invoices/line items, billing price overrides, credits and adjustments, and change orders must be properly approved and within the individual's level of authority.
Refer to risks: F-12, F-16

2.6.21 **Credits and Adjustments.** Credits and adjustments associated with returns, short shipments, promotional programs, or discounts of product must only be processed when the claim has been investigated, proper documentation has been prepared, and authorization has been obtained from appropriate Sales and Marketing, Finance, Operating Unit, and Supply Chain Management depending on the nature of the adjustment. All discrepancies (e.g. unmatched documents) must be resolved in a timely manner.
Refer to risks: F-5, F-14, F-15

2.6.22 **Numerically Controlled Credit Memos.** Credit memo transactions must be numerically controlled, and they should be accounted for with their value properly accrued. Credit memos must be pre-numbered where the integrity of sequencing is not computer controlled.
Refer to risks: F-6, F-15

2.6.23 **Blank Paper Stock.** Blank invoice and credit memo stock must be safeguarded.
Refer to risk: F-16

2.6.24 **Will-Call Orders.** A documented procedure for will-call orders must be established and enforced.
Refer to risks: F-3, F-4, F-5, F-10

2.6.25 **Cost of Goods Sold.** The quantity of units sold or the percentage of completion in the billing system should be compared for reasonableness to the quantity or percentage of completion used to compute the Cost of Goods Sold.
Refer to risks: F-1, F-6

Risk If Standard Is Not Implemented

F-1   Information contained in the corporate accounting records may be inaccurate, and the financial statements may not be fairly stated.

F-2   Financial decisions made by the company management may be erroneous due to the use of inaccurate or inconsistent financial data.

F-3   Sales transactions may be incorrectly prepared, and/or billings and other terms may be misstated.

F-4   Sales transactions may have occurred but may not have been billed and/or recorded.

F-5   Misappropriation of assets or intentional errors could occur. Examples include the following:
a. Products or services may be shipped or provided but not billed.
b. Shipments or services provided may be billed but not recorded in the accounting records.
c. Products or services may be billed and recorded but not shipped or provided.

F-6   Revenues and cost of sales may be incorrectly recorded and/or recorded in the wrong accounting period.

F-7   Billing errors may cause cash flow not to be maximized, and certain accounts may become uncollectible.

F-8   Cash flow may not be maximized due to untimely billings, and the amount may be uncollectible.

F-9   Export requirements may be violated. The company may be exposed to litigation from external sources for misrepresentation of invoices.

F-10   The company will be liable for unbilled sales tax or value-added tax where adequate documentation verifying tax-exempt status is not on file.

F-11   "No charge" transactions may not be properly recorded in the accounting records. Related-party transactions may not be identified.

F-12   The company may be assisting the customer in circumventing the customer's internal control system.

F-13   Intentional alteration of the invoice and/or receivable records could occur.

F-14   Credit transactions may not reflect the proper accounting treatment or may conflict with good business practices.

F-15   All credit transactions may not be included in the accounting records.

F-16   Unauthorized use of the documents may occur, resulting in a loss of revenues or an adverse effect on the company's reputation.

2.7 ACCOUNTS RECEIVABLE (AR)

Introduction

AR represents an integral portion of a company's income-generating process and requires special attention in ensuring monies owed it are accurately monitored, collected, and reported. Controllers and AR professionals need to be able to apply their skills and understanding to companies of all sizes—small owner/operator companies, mid-level companies, and Fortune 500 firms.

A mid-level company may have an electronic or computer-based invoicing system that will allow the company to know when invoices were issued so as to age amounts due. However, the company may not utilize such a system but rely on defined processes and a paper trail. Such a company could employ as few as one person who is responsible for AR, or as many as four or five.

A large Fortune 500 company may have an entire division dedicated to management of AR. Processes may include computer systems tied directly to sales and credit departments. Invoices may include multiple products and multiple shipments with varying terms. Staffing may vary depending on experience and backgrounds, all needing to be managed in such a way as to maximize revenue generation with as little corresponding cost as possible.

Standard of Internal Control

2.7.1 **Segregation of Duties.** The accounts receivable function must be separate from credit, collections, billing, and cash remittance functions.
Refer to risk: G-1

2.7.2 **Billing and Remittance Inputs.** Input to the detailed accounts receivable subsidiary ledger must be based upon valid customer billing records and remittances. Procedures must be established to ensure the accurate and timely recording of billings.
Refer to risks: G-2, G-3, G-6

2.7.3 **General Ledger Reconciliations.** The detailed accounts receivable subsidiary ledger must be reconciled (contents are known and status is current) to the general ledger monthly and any differences researched and resolved. The next appropriate level of Finance management must approve the reconciliation.
Refer to risks: G-4, G-6

2.7.4 **Aging.** An aging of the accounts receivable detail must be reviewed monthly by operating unit management for any unusual or seriously delinquent items. The aging must be accurate and not distorted by customer liabilities (e.g. customer advances, down payments, milestone payments, or unapplied cash or credits).
Refer to risks: G-3, G-5

2.7.5 **Aging Adjustments.** Aging of accounts receivable should not be altered. Financial management must approve any changes to the aging of a specific invoice.
Refer to risks: G-9, G-10

2.7.6 **Balance Adjustments.** All accounts receivable journal entry adjustments must be approved in accordance with the appropriate corporate policy (or appropriate local/operating unit policy if

more restrictive) and recorded in the accounting period the adjustment was determined.
Refer to risks: G-6, G-7, G-8

2.7.7 **Management Reporting.** Operating unit and Finance management must implement a system of management reporting and review to assist in managing the accounts receivable balance. The internal reports should include days sales outstanding (DSO), aging of accounts, listing of delinquent accounts, potential write-offs, adequacy of collection efforts, dispute tracking, etc.
Refer to risks: G-3, G-12

2.7.8 **Reserves.** Using corporate policy as a minimum guideline, a valuation reserve must be established by Finance management to record receivables at their net realizable value.
Refer to risk: G-5

2.7.9 **Reserve Reviews.** Consistent with corporate policy, valuation reserves must be reviewed by Finance management at least quarterly for adequacy and reasonableness with adjustments made to the reserves as required.
Refer to risk: G-5

2.7.10 **Credit Memos.** Resolution of a disputed customer's receivable balance must be documented via a credit memo.
Refer to risks: G-3, G-7, G-8

2.7.11 **Safeguarded Records.** Detailed accounts receivable information must be safeguarded from loss, destruction, or unauthorized access.
Refer to risks: G-9, G-10

2.7.12 **Employee Accounts.** Accounts receivable from employees, including travel advances, must be maintained independently from the customer accounts receivable ledger and must be reviewed and reconciled on a monthly basis. A procedure to settle employee accounts prior to termination must be established and enforced.
Refer to risks: G-3, G-4, G-6, G-11

Risk If Standard Is Not Implemented

G-1 Intentional errors or misappropriation of assets could occur. Examples include:

a. Sales are invoiced but not recorded. Upon receipt, cash is misappropriated.
b. Cash receipts are incorrectly applied to customer accounts and/or are misappropriated or diverted.

G-2 The subsidiary ledger may be inaccurate as invoices and/or cash receipts may not be recorded, may be incorrectly recorded, or may be recorded in the wrong accounting period.

G-3 Inefficient collection activities may occur, and/or incorrect aging may result in delinquent customer remittances or the write-off of delinquent accounts.

G-4 Errors in either the general or subsidiary ledgers may not be identified and corrected on a timely basis.

G-5 The accounts receivable valuation reserves may be incorrectly calculated. Net receivables and the related financial statements may be misstated.

G-6 The financial records and financial statements may be misstated.

G-7 Adjustments processed may not reflect good business practices, or adjustment errors may not be detected.

G-8 Collectible accounts receivable may be written off, and/or cash receipts may be misappropriated.

G-9 Loss, destruction, or alteration of accounts receivable records may result in the inability to collect outstanding balances.

G-10 Unauthorized use of customer receivable information could adversely affect the company's competitive position or reputation.

G-11 Receivables may not be collected from terminated employees.

G-12 Errors and omissions, poor receivable management practices, and inappropriate concentration of risk may not be detected and corrected on a timely basis.

 ## 2.8 COLLECTION

Introduction

Formal, written collection procedures must be developed and implemented by each operating unit that controls accounts receivable balances.

Standard of Internal Control

2.8.1 **Documented Procedures.** These procedures, which define collection as well as the frequency of contact and reporting, must be appropriately reviewed and approved and should comply with relevant corporate policy.
Refer to risk: H-1

2.8.2 **Accounts Receivable Balance Reviews.** The Collection department must review the customer's outstanding balances (both debits and credits) regularly and initiate collection efforts on all accounts outstanding. Collection efforts must be adequately documented in the customer credit files.
Refer to risks: H-2, H-3, H-5

2.8.3 **Complaints.** Customer correspondence (billing/shipping complaints, service problems, etc.) must be investigated and resolved in a timely manner.
Refer to risks: H-3, H-4, H-5

2.8.4 **Write-offs.** Customer account write-offs must be adequately documented and approved.
Refer to risks: H-3, H-4, H-6

Risk If Standard Is Not Implemented

H-1 Inadequate or inconsistent collection policies and procedures may be implemented, which could result in inadequate/inefficient collection efforts.

H-2 Delinquent accounts may have to be written off due to inadequate collection efforts.

H-3 Misapplication or misappropriation of cash receipts may not be identified and corrected in a timely manner.

H-4 Customer dissatisfaction may result in loss of the customer.

H-5 Cash flow may not be maximized.

H-6 The company may lose valuable tax deductions.

2.9 CASH RECEIPTS AND APPLICATION

Introduction

All remittances must be applied to the specific customer account level within a specified time (e.g. 72 hours). Credit cards, checks, electronic funds transfer, and electronic data interchange receipts must be considered to be cash, and the same standards associated with cash receipts must be followed. Cash receipts must be logged and deposited in the bank daily or as dictated by good business practice.

Standard of Internal Control

2.9.1 **Cash.** Credit cards, checks, electronic funds transfer, and electronic data interchange receipts must be considered to be cash, and the same standards associated with cash receipts must be followed.
Refer to risks: I-1, I-2, I-3, I-4, I-5, I-6, I-7

2.9.2 **Restrictive Endorsements.** All checks must be restrictively endorsed for deposit only and secured immediately upon receipt or becoming negotiable (e.g. post-dated checks).
Refer to risk: I-1

2.9.3 **Deposits.** The cash receipts log must be compared to bank statements and posted to the general ledger periodically by someone independent of the cash receipt function.
Refer to risks: I-2, I-3, I-7

2.9.4 **Segregation of Duties.** Control and responsibility for receiving and depositing cash must be assigned to an individual who is not responsible for:
a. Recording to the accounts receivable subsidiary ledger;
b. Recording to the general ledger;
c. Collecting receivables;
d. Authorizing bad debt write-offs;
e. Authorizing credit memos, discounts, allowances, or customer returns; and
f. Preparing billing documents.
g. This individual should be bonded.
Refer to risks: I-1, I-2, I-3, I-4, I-5, I-6, I-7

2.9.5 **Depository Accounts.** Where practical, all customers should be encouraged to remit payments directly to depository accounts or other automated payment systems at established company banking facilities.
Refer to risks: I-1, I-3, I-7

2.9.6 **Posting.** All customer remittances must be posted to accounts receivable subsidiary records or customer advances within 24 hours. Where post-dated checks are accepted, the checks must be safeguarded and posted the first day after they become negotiable.
Refer to risks: I-2, I-4, I-5, I-6, I-7

2.9.7 **Application.** Unless otherwise approved by the customer, payments must be applied to specific invoices. Where customer advances are accepted, the advances cannot be used to clear an account balance until they are earned.
Refer to risks: I-2, I-4, I-5, I-6, I-7

2.9.8 **Cutoff Procedures.** Monthly customer remittance cutoff procedures must be established and enforced.
Refer to risks: I-5, I-6

2.9.9 **Miscellaneous Remittances.** Adequate control procedures must be established over miscellaneous remittances received on site. Appropriate local financial management must approve these procedures.
Refer to risks: I-1, I-2, I-7

2.9.10 **Checks with Insufficient Funds.** A procedure for handling checks returned for insufficient funds must be established by local financial management to ensure that the open item file is updated and appropriate refer-to-credit action is initiated.
Refer to risks: I-1, I-3, I-4, I-5

Risk If Standard Is Not Implemented

I-1 Cash receipts may be lost and/or misappropriated.

I-2 Lost, incorrectly recorded, and/or misappropriated cash receipts may not be identified and corrected timely.

I-3 Cash flow may not be maximized.

I-4 Inefficient collection activities may occur due to inaccurate customer account balances.

I-5 The receivable balance and/or aging of receivables included in internal receivable management reporting may not be accurate.

I-6 The financial records and financial statements may be misstated.

I-7 Customer dissatisfaction could result if order fulfillment fails to correctly apply cash payments.

 ## 2.10 PRICE ESTABLISHMENT

Introduction

A documented pricing policy as well as specific pricing actions must be approved by global business unit and local business unit management and reviewed with finance for administrative feasibility. Pricing strategies must be consistent in determining global market prices and pre-established minimum margin targets for all products.

Standard of Internal Control

2.10.1 **Approved Pricing.** Local legal staff must review for compliance with local pricing regulations and global pricing strategies (price discrimination, parallel trade, etc.). Where relevant, pricing must be viewed along with promotional programs, terms and conditions, etc. to ensure overall offering to customer is appropriate.
Refer to risks: J-1, J-2, J-3

2.10.2 **Pricing Strategies.** Pricing strategies must be consistent in determining global market prices and pre-established minimum margin targets for all products. Where relevant, pricing must be viewed along with promotional programs, terms and conditions, etc. to ensure overall offering to customer is appropriate.
Refer to risks: J-1, J-2, J-3

2.10.3 **Established Prices.** A price must be set for each product with a clear set of price discounts established for each customer or well-defined customer group. Authorization and processes to establish or change pricing must be clearly defined with appropriate segregation of duties. Controllers should collectively review material list price moves and decide on material pricing actions at their weekly meetings.

Where pricing is dependent on meeting volume commitments, the local legal staff must be consulted.
Refer to risks: J-1, J-2, J-3

2.10.4 **Tax Compliance.** Domestic pricing must be consistent with local tax laws. International pricing [exit pricing to foreign trade customers (export to trade) and transfer pricing to foreign company subsidiaries (export to subsidiaries), etc.] must comply with domestic and international tax guidelines as well as corporate policy.
Refer to risks: J-1, J-2, J-3, J-4

2.10.5 **"Most Favored Customer Pricing."** "Most favored customer pricing" should be avoided where possible. Where this is required (e.g. global accounts, major accounts, etc.), there must be legal review. Appropriate administrative processes must be established to prevent violations. Additionally, appropriate operating unit and Region approval must be obtained in accordance with the appropriate level of authority.
Refer to risks: J-1, J-2, J-3, J-4

2.10.6 **Price Discounts.** Sales/Marketing and Finance management approval, documented via special bid letters, must be obtained prior to order shipment for discounts or allowances in excess of amounts defined by operating unit and region management.
Refer to risks: J-1, J-2, J-3

2.10.7 **Payment Terms.** Standard payment terms by operating unit by country must be extended to customers or classes of customers. Exceptions to standard payment terms must only be made in concert with individual customer pricing decisions, including compliance with local laws (e.g. Robinson-Patman Act) and impact to the operating unit global pricing strategy. Changes or exceptions to standard terms require the approval according to the delegation of authority policy.
Refer to risk: J-1, J-2, J-3, J-5

2.10.8 **"Special Bid" Pricing.** Where "special bid" pricing is practiced, local legal counsel should be consulted to ensure the practice is sanctioned by local laws and regulations and to ensure appropriate records of such pricing are generated and maintained.
Refer to risk: J-1, J-2, J-3, J-5

2.10.9 **Sales Goal Structure.** Sales goal structure must not encourage end-of-period discounts. End-of-period discounts should be limited in use.
Refer to risk: J-6

Risk If Standard Is Not Implemented

J-1 Customer dissatisfaction may result.

J-2 Assessment of fines and/or penalties may result.

J-3 Different prices of product to similar customers could create pricing difficulties locally and possibly globally. In addition, different prices for the same product to similar customers may be illegal and result in penalties to the company.

J-4 The company may incur additional tax costs.

J-5 Net revenue per unit may decrease unnecessarily, and marketing may be able to provide an alternative strategy [e.g. customer may be willing to pay a higher price for company product versus the competition if the customer understands that the company provides more services (benefiting the customer and included in the product price) than the competition].

J-6 Buying habits may become cyclical in nature, and may avoid buying when margins are higher.

 ## 2.11 PROMOTIONAL ACTIVITIES

Introduction

Pricing and promotional activities may include, but are not limited to, the following:

a. Volume rebates
b. Coupons
c. Premium items
d. Product giveaways
e. Allowances
f. Cooperative advertising
g. Cash rebates
h. Meet-competition/tactical payments
i. Third-party (end-user) rebates
j. Special performance incentive funds
k. Off-invoice discounts

Standard of Internal Control

2.11.1 **Policies and Procedures.** Formal, written policies and procedures must be established and developed to ensure that promotional payments are processed properly and in a timely manner.
Refer to risks: K-3, K-7

2.11.2 **Approved Promotional Programs.** Promotional programs must be approved by global and local operating unit management and reviewed with finance for administrative feasibility. Local legal staff must review for compliance with local pricing regulations, and global pricing strategies (price discrimination, parallel trade, etc.) prior to implementation by the field sales force.
   a. Maximum discount levels must be pre-established on a global level for each product class.
   b. Only a limited amount of promotional programs may be executed simultaneously. Programs must have global objectives and centralized program ownership.
   c. Promotional programs must be routinely evaluated to ensure cost/benefit maximization and all corporate contra-revenue policy requirements are met.
Refer to risks: K-1, K-2, K-4, K-5, K-6

2.11.3 **Accruals.** Appropriate accruals with respect to amount and timing must be made for pricing and promotional activities. Promotion-to-date payments for all programs must be reconciled and balanced regularly based on materiality and complexity. Accruals must be adjusted as appropriate during programs and closed at the end of programs.
Refer to risks: K-2, K-3

2.11.4 **Payment Requirements.** Payments (checks, credits, free product, etc.) must only be made when there is:
   a. An approved marketing program,
   b. Documentation supporting that performance commitments have been met (e.g. valid customer numbers, program identification codes, product codes, media samples, original proofs of performance, photographs of displays, etc.), and
   c. Appropriate approval has been obtained.
      The request for payment and the appropriate documentation must be filed and retained in accordance with record-retention policies.
Refer to risk: K-2

2.11.5 **Approved Exceptions.** An approval hierarchy must be established and enforced to ensure that individuals approve exceptions only within their level of authority.
Refer to risks: K-1, K-8

2.11.6 **Segregation of Duties.** Price creation, authorization, and administration responsibilities must be clearly defined and appropriately segregated. Administration of pricing and promotional activities must be independent of the selling function and subject to review and approval by finance.
Refer to risks: K-1, K-8

2.11.7 **Non-Customer Payments.** Where payments are made to other than customers (e.g. repayment of media expenses), policies on such payments must be established and documented and must be in accordance with local legal and regulatory requirements.
Refer to risk: K-6

2.11.8 **Accounting Treatment.** All payments must be properly accounted for in accordance with the appropriate corporate policy (e.g. treated as expense or as a reduction from sales).
Refer to risk: K-2

2.11.9 **Approved Check Requisitions.** Check requisitions must be approved by someone independent of the claim processing function.
Refer to risks: K-1, K-8

2.11.10 **Information Access.** Only authorized individuals must be granted access to customer-specific accrual and payment information. Customer-specific accrual and payment data must be subject to periodic independent reviews.
Refer to risks: K-1, K-8

2.11.11 **Asset Protection.** Premium items, blank check stocks, and bearer drafts must be appropriately stored, safeguarded, and accounted for.
Refer to risk: K-8

2.11.12 **Net Revenues.** The difference between gross and net revenues should be reflected in the operating unit's annual forecast, monitored, and managed.
Refer to risk: K-9

Risk If Standard Is Not Implemented

K-1 Unauthorized promotional funds may be spent which may not be recoverable and may violate fair pricing laws and regulations.

K-2 Sales revenue and/or expense could be misstated in the financial statements.

K-3 Customer dissatisfaction may result.

K-4 Additional labor and mailing expense may be incurred.

K-5 Customers may not respond in the manner in which the marketing program was designed to drive them.

K-6 Assessment of fines and/or penalties may result.

K-7 Potential overstatement of accounts receivable may occur.

K-8 Inappropriate payments could be made.

K-9 The company's cash flow may not be maximized.

CHAPTER THREE

Treasury Process

 ## INTRODUCTION

The Treasury process includes the functions associated with determining company's cash requirements, investment management, foreign exchange management, the investigation and selection of appropriate forms of financing and monitoring compliance with financing agreements, the issuance and redemption of capital stock, and the payment of dividends.

For the Treasury process, financial investments and equity investments are defined as follows:

- Financial investments result from the purchase of financial instruments (deposit certificates, money market funds, marketable securities, medium term notes, etc.) for the sole purpose of generating a financial return.
- Equity investments are company investments in common or preferred equity investments in unrelated companies and joint ventures for marketing and strategic reasons.

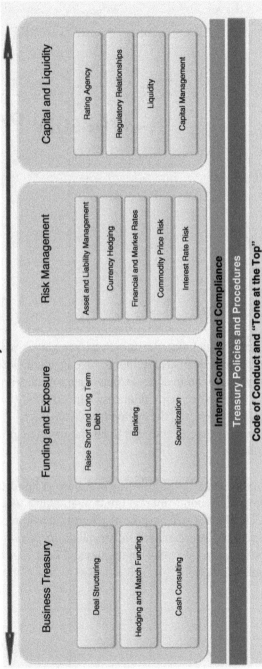

PROCESS OVERVIEW

The diagram below suggests that the foundational elements for the Treasury process are Internal Controls and Compliance, Treasury Policies and Procedures, and Code of Conduct, and "Tone at the Top."

METRICS

Table of Metrics

- **Accuracy of Cash Forecasts**—Actual cash balance minus forecasted cash balance)/forecasted cash balance.
- **Accuracy of Forecasted Investment Income**—Actual interest investment income minus forecasted investment income)/forecasted investment income.
- **Accuracy of Forecasted Interest Expense**—Actual interest expense minus forecasted interest expense/forecasted interest expense.
- **Accuracy of Trustee/Issuing, Paying Agent Fees**—Actual fees minus forecasted fees)/forecasted fees.
- **Percentage of Payments Containing Errors**—(1) Number of payments by type containing errors/total number of payments by type. (2) Number of payments containing errors/number of payments.
- **Percentage of Payments Released on Time**—Total number of payments released on time/total number of released payments.
- **Percentage of Daily Cash Balances vs. Forecast**—Sum of daily cash balances/forecasted total cash balances.
- **Days Cash Available**—Total available cash/average value of payments per day.
- **Percentage of Committed Credit**—Total principal value of committed credit facilities/total principal value of all credit facilities.
- **Credit Available**—Total principal value of drawn credit/total principal value of all credit facilities.
- **Portfolio Credit Rating**—Weighted average of issuer credit ratings vs. stated policy benchmark.

APPLICATION OF INTERNAL CONTROLS

In management's selection of procedures and techniques of control, the degree of control implemented is a matter of reasonable business judgment. The common guideline that should be used in determining the degree of internal controls implementation is that the cost of a control should not exceed the benefit derived. However, there is minimum set of controls that should exist in a normal business environment. The internal control standards listed here represent the minimum controls to be implemented within the Treasury process.

 ## SUB-PROCESSES

The sub-processes functions of the Treasury process are:

3.1   General Treasury Controls

3.2   Financing Operations

3.3   Investment of Available Funds

3.4   Foreign Exchange

 ## 3.1 GENERAL TREASURY CONTROLS

Introduction

Policies are implemented for all aspects of the Treasury function to ensure that segregation of duties, controls, and reconciliation processes are in place to mitigate risk for the company. Financing, financial investment, foreign exchange, capital stock, and equity transactions must be promptly recorded and properly classified to facilitate the reporting and required disclosure of external financial information. All recorded balances must be reconciled monthly to the supporting detail (e.g. bank account reconciliations, revolving credit lines, investment sub-ledgers, capital stock, ownership records, etc.).

Standard of Internal Control

3.1.1 **Segregation of Duties.** Policies and procedures for the treasury functions ensure:

    a. The financial investment decisions and actual investment activity must be separated from accounting and custodial responsibilities.

    b. The payments of interest and dividend payments must be separated from accounting for debt and equity securities.

    c. The access to cash receipts must be separated from the accounting for the related cash receipts.

    d. The processing and the review of borrowings must be separated from financial investment transactions.

    e. Foreign exchange trades, foreign exchange confirmations, and foreign exchange accounting activities must be adequately segregated.

    Refer to risks: A-1, A-2, A-4, A-6

3.1.2 **Banking Requirements.** Procedures on opening, maintaining, and closing bank accounts must be established. At a minimum, the procedures must cover required approvals, signature authority and limits, and documentation standards.

    Refer to risks: A-1, A-2

3.1.3 **Records and Reconciliations.** Financing, financial investment, foreign exchange, capital stock, and equity transactions must be promptly recorded and properly classified to facilitate the reporting and required disclosure of external financial information. All recorded balances must be reconciled monthly to the supporting detail (e.g. bank account reconciliations, revolving credit lines, investment sub-ledgers, capital stock, ownership records, etc.). Such reconciliations (contents are known and status is current) must be performed by employees not involved in cash or custodial activities.

    Refer to risks: A-1, A-3, A-4, A-5

3.1.4 **Safeguarding of Records and Securities.** Access to cash, debt, equity, financial investment, and capital stock records and securities must be restricted.

    Refer to risks: A-1, A-2, A-4

3.1.5 **Accounting for Company Securities.** Banks, brokers, independent registrars, transfer agents, or other approved third parties are to be used to account for changes in ownership of the company's issued and unissued shares, the change in the company's debt instruments, and the changes in its financial and publicly traded equity investments.

    Refer to risks: A-2, A-3, A-4, A-5

3.1.6 **Foreign Exchange Transactions.** Procedures must be established for approving foreign exchange transactions and ensuring the transactions are properly documented and recorded in the proper accounts.

    Refer to risks: A-5, A-6

3.1.7 **Financial Risk Management.** Procedures must be established to monitor counterparty exposure and market risk related to financing, investing, and foreign exchange activities.
Refer to risk: A-7

3.1.8 **Counter-trade/Offset.** Procedures must be established to ensure that counter-trade/offset obligations are executed in accordance with corporate policy.
Refer to risks: A-8, A-9

3.1.9 **Cash Pooling.** Procedures must be established to ensure that all cash pooling and netting arrangements involving more than one company/legal entity are executed in accordance with corporate policy.
Refer to risk: A-10

Risk If Standard Is Not Implemented

A-1 Cash or securities may be lost, stolen, destroyed, or temporarily diverted.

A-2 Records may be misused or altered by unauthorized personnel to the detriment of the company, its owners, or its creditors.

A-3 Reports may not be accurate, and critical decisions may then be based upon erroneous information.

A-4 Errors and omissions in physical safeguarding, authorization, and transaction processing may not be detected and corrected.

A-5 Financial statements and records may be misstated due to improper cutoff or valuation, omission of certain financial data, or inaccurate recording or classification.

A-6 Transactions made may not be consistent with the currency requirements of the company.

A-7 Financing and investing activities may expose the company to unacceptable levels of counterparty and market risk.

A-8 The countertrade/offset arrangement may be illegal or in violation of corporate policy and considers the company code of conduct.

A-9 Failure to meet and fulfill countertrade/offset obligations may result in penalties, liquidated damages, potential litigation in foreign countries, and other possible sanctions by foreign governments.

A-10 Transactions may result in undesirable legal and/or tax implications.

3.2 FINANCING OPERATIONS

Introduction

The following items and activities must be approved by the board of directors of the company and must be documented in minutes of their meetings: banking resolutions and the assigned delegation of authority, borrowing resolutions and delegations of authority, all significant debt financing arrangements and financing leases.

Standard of Internal Control

3.2.1 **Board Approvals.** Total company financing activity must be periodically reviewed with the board of directors.
Refer to risks: B-1, B-2, B-3

3.2.2 **Delegations and Authorizations.** Delegations of signing and authorization limits must be approved by the appropriate chief financial officer of the legal entity. All financing resolutions and authorizations must be reviewed with the appropriate financial institutions periodically or whenever changed.
Refer to risks: B-1, B-2, B-3, B-4

3.2.3 **Treasury Approvals.** Financing arrangements must be reviewed with corporate legal and approved by corporate treasury management. These include: customer financing agreements, debt financing agreements, guarantees and loans in support of third parties, lease and rental of capital assets, programs for factoring or discounting receivables, subsidiary capital stock changes, and interest and foreign currency derivatives.
Refer to risks: B-1, B-2, B-3

3.2.4 **Capital Transactions.** All capital transactions such as the issuance of stock, stock splits, stock or cash dividends, employee stock options, etc., must be approved by the company's board of directors.
Refer to risks: B-1, B-2, B-3, B-5

3.2.5 **Compliance with Agreements.** All financing arrangements and foreign exchange contracts must be monitored for compliance to terms, covenants, and underlying obligations.
Refer to risk: B-3

3.2.6 **Cancellation of Instruments.** All financing instruments must be appropriately canceled, or accounted for as canceled by the custodian, upon completion of repayment.
Refer to risk: B-5

3.2.7 **Management Review.** All financial and equity investment transactions must be reviewed for reasonableness and proper approval, be compared to transaction advices or other documentation, and be promptly recorded in the general ledger account.
Refer to risks: B-5, B-6, B-7

3.2.8 **Stockholder Information.** For public companies, all stockholder information is confidential. Such information must be maintained so as to account for authorized, issued, and outstanding shares, transfers of issued shares, dividends, exercising of employee stock options, and treasury stock.
Refer to risks: B-3, B-5, B-6, B-7

Risk If Standard Is Not Implemented

B-1 Financing funds may be obtained at unauthorized costs or terms. Excessive financing costs and/or unnecessarily restrictive covenants may be incurred.

B-2 Financing may be illegal or in violation of corporate policy. Fines, penalties, litigation, or a loss of integrity in financial markets may occur.

B-3 Legal or loan restrictions and covenants may be violated.

B-4 Financing requirements may not be satisfied.

B-5 Cash or dividend payments may be duplicated or improperly or fraudulently disbursed.

B-6 Financial statements and records may be misstated due to improper cutoffs or valuation, omission of certain financial data, or inaccurate recording or classification.

B-7 Reports may not be accurate, and critical decisions may then be based upon erroneous information.

 ## 3.3 INVESTMENT OF AVAILABLE FUNDS

Introduction

Financial investment policies and procedures must exist and be approved in advance by the company treasurer or designee and must specify, at a minimum: type, credit quality, and maturity of instruments, approved counterparties, counterparty exposure guidelines, and personnel authorized.

Standard of Internal Control

3.3.1 **Investment Policies.** Any investments outside of policy must be approved individually and in advance by company's treasurer.
Refer to risks: C-1, C-2

3.3.2 **Safeguarding of Securities.** Where possible, purchased securities must be registered in the name of the company or an appropriate legal subsidiary. Where bearer securities are purchased, appropriate confirmation advices must be received. All securities must be held in safekeeping by the appropriate financial institution, in an in-house safe, or by a company-designated custodian.
Refer to risk: C-3

3.3.3 **Record keeping.** Detailed records of financial and equity investments must be maintained and safeguarded to protect essential information regarding ownership and anticipated income. These records must be kept independent from the custodian and must be reconciled to the securities on hand on a periodic basis.
Refer to risks: C-3, C-4, C-5

3.3.4 **Investment Transaction Requirements.** All investment transactions, either financial or equity, must have prior approval, be properly documented, and be promptly recorded in the proper accounts.
Refer to risks: C-2, C-3, C-5, C-6, C-7

3.3.5 **Valuation of Investments.** Methods of valuation of financial and equity investments, including those within the pension plans, must be developed in accordance with finance policies established by the corporate controller and requirements of governmental reporting bodies. Write-offs and adjustments to the investment accounts must be properly reviewed, evaluated as to worth, and approved by the director of corporate finance in accordance with finance policy.
Refer to risks: C-3, C-5, C-6

Risk If Standard Is Not Implemented

C-1 Legal or loan restrictions and covenants may be violated.

C-2 Investments may be made illegally or in violation of corporate policy, resulting in fines, penalties, and/or investment losses.

C-3 Cash or securities may be stolen, lost, destroyed, or temporarily diverted.

C-4 Records may be lost or destroyed.

C-5 Financial statements and records may be misstated due to improper cut-offs or valuations, omission of certain financial data, or inaccurate recording or classification.

C-6 Reports may not be accurate, and critical decisions may then be based upon erroneous information.

C-7 Transactions may result in undesirable legal and/or tax implications.

3.4 FOREIGN EXCHANGE

Introduction

The corporate treasurer is solely responsible for managing the company's foreign currency risk. Foreign currency "spot" transactions as defined as the purchase and/or sale of foreign currency to satisfy payment obligations due in the next one to three business days are not "hedging" but require the establishment of operating procedures and controls that must be approved by the corporate treasurer or designee.

Standard of Internal Control

3.4.1 **Hedging Strategies and Transactions.** Hedging strategies and transactions (vehicles used to manage foreign currency risk) can only be executed with the explicit approval of the corporate treasurer.
Refer to risks: D-1, D-2, D-3

3.4.2 **Procedures for Spot Transactions.** Foreign currency "spot" transactions, as defined as the purchase and/or sale of foreign currency to satisfy payment obligations due in the next one to three business days, are not "hedging" but require the establishment of operating procedures and controls that must be approved by the corporate treasurer or designee.
Refer to risks: D-1, D-2, D-3

3.4.3 **Operating Procedures.** Operating procedures for purchase and/or sale of foreign currency must include the selection and rotation of counterparties, specification of authority and limits for the trading process and trade execution, and responsibilities for settlement, confirmation, and recording of transactions.
Refer to risks: D-4, D-5, D-6, D-7

3.4.4 **Netting of Exposures.** When feasible, foreign currency obligations between company operating units and designated third parties are to be settled through a company intercompany netting process. Foreign currency contracts between company operating units and designated third parties must be priced, recorded, and accounted for as if they were (independent) third-party contracts.

Refer to risks: D-1, D-2, D-3

3.4.5 **Hedging Procedures.** Operating procedures for "hedged" transactions are the same as those designed for "spot" transactions in 3.4.2 and 3.4.3 above. Additionally, any "hedged" transaction, irrespective of accounting treatment, must be "marked to market" on a regular basis, at least quarterly.

Refer to risks: D-1, D-2, D-3, D-4, D-5, D-6, D-7

Risk If Standard Is Not Implemented

D-1 The company may be exposed to increased risk, increased cost, and/or potential financial loss.

D-2 Transactions may not be consistent with the currency requirements and risk parameters of the company.

D-3 Inconsistent actions may occur, resulting in the company increasing its exposure to foreign exchange risk rather than mitigating its exposure.

D-4 Errors and omissions in physical safeguarding, authorization, and transaction processing may not be detected and corrected.

D-5 Reports may not be accurate, and critical decisions may then be based upon erroneous information.

D-6 Financial statements and records may be misstated due to improper cutoffs or valuation, omission of certain financial data, or inaccurate recording or classification.

D-7 Inaccurate classification may have tax and external reporting consequences.

CHAPTER FOUR

Procure to Pay (P2P) Process

INTRODUCTION

The P2P process includes the functions of securing and qualifying sources of supply; initiating requests for materials, equipment, merchandise, supplies, or services; obtaining information as to availability and pricing from approved suppliers; placing orders for goods or services; receiving and inspecting or otherwise accepting the material or merchandise; accounting for the proper amounts due to suppliers; and processing payments in a controlled and efficient manner. In this toolkit, research and product development is included in the P2P process.

CONSIDER AUTOMATION TO MITIGATE RISK IN THE P2P PROCESS

How does a P2P leader anticipate, plan for, and mitigate a potential risk? In this chapter we'll address how 10 P2P Automation Solutions can be used to help mitigate risk. We'll only identify the specific risks that are mitigated by implementing the solution.

1. **Supplier Portals**—Supplier portals can be used to validate supplier information before it is entered into the supplier master file. Supplier information can be validated against the Office of Foreign Asset Control (OFAC), Office of Inspector General (OIG), and other compliance lists. W8 and W9 forms can also be validated with IRS and tax authorities. Lastly, clients can request additional records to support the validity of the supplier and the supplier management process.

   Risks Mitigated
   - Suppliers are automatically validated before they are entered into the supplier master file.
   - "Scam" and "at risk" suppliers can be spotted with validation rules contained in supplier portals.
   - Compliance checks and W8 and W9 validation reduce the risk of fines and incorrect tax information, which could result in penalties.
   - A sound upfront supplier validation process reduces the risk of an employee intending to act as a supplier.
   - Documentation supporting the validation of the supplier is obtained within the onboarding process. Besides tax forms, insurance forms, e-payment information, diversity, and supplier profile information can be gathered in a single process.

2. **E-Procurement**—The E-Procurement solution includes the ability to issue Purchase Order Requests and Purchase Orders and build a corresponding approval chain electronically. This eliminates the extra work of needing to manually circulate a PO from one approver to the other. With an E-Procurement solution that is integrated with an ERP system, the master supplier master file, chart of accounts, and other variables are used to support the three-way matching process within the accounting module. This facilitates greater accountability and reconciliation of orders, invoices, and high organizational and supplier spend for accurate and timely decision making.

   Risks Mitigated
   - Requisitions and Purchase Orders are created electronically, removing the risk of errors made in the manual data entry process.
   - Direct integration with an ERP system supports the three-way matching process and removes the risk of any clearing account reconciliation issues.

3. **E-Invoicing**—E-invoices make the process of handling supplier invoices easier, faster, and more productive. E-invoicing is one of the key enablers of a fully automated accounts payable function. Companies around the world are adopting e-invoices to streamline their operations, eliminate waste, and unlock the working capital value of innovative payment strategies.

Risks Mitigated

- E-invoicing eliminates the risk of processing a duplicate invoice, paying an incorrect amount, or paying the invoice to an incorrect supplier.
- It removes possible financial exposure for the company since invoices are paid more accurately.
- It also reduces the risk of fraud and builds in Segregation of Duties (SoD) controls.

4. **PO to Invoice Conversion**—This technology allows a buying organization to send a purchase order electronically to a supplier and then allows the selling organization to convert the purchase order into an electronic invoice. The seller can then submit the invoice immediately back to the accounts payable organization. The resulting invoice will be a duplicate of the original purchase order.

   Risks Mitigated

   - Eliminates the risk of processing a duplicate invoice, paying an incorrect amount, or paying the invoice to an incorrect supplier.
   - This automation solution also reduces the risk of fraud and builds in Segregation of Duties (SoD) controls.
   - Speeds up the approval time and can improve working capital management since there are now more opportunities for early payment discount.
   - The approval status of an invoice can be shared with a supplier as part of this automation solution. This alleviates the need for supplier inquires and can improve supplier satisfaction.

5. **Document Management, Invoice Scan, and Data Capture**—A document management system is used to track and store electronic documents and/or images of paper documents. It is usually also capable of keeping track of the different versions modified by different users. The term has some overlap with the concepts of content management systems. It is often viewed as a component of enterprise content management (ECM) systems.

   Risks Mitigated

   - Eliminates the risk of processing a duplicate invoice, paying an incorrect amount, or paying the invoice to an incorrect supplier.
   - This automation solution also reduces the risk of fraud and builds in Segregation of Duties (SoD) controls.

6. **Automated Matching**—Automated three-way matching provides an immediate match of the invoice, purchase order, and receipt when using related accounts payable automation solution. The user establishes specific business rules for the matching process and reviews

resulting audit trails to ensure the process is working. The user is also responsible for resolving any exceptions that may occur to determine if violation of business rules needs to be addressed.

Risks Mitigated

- Automated matching performs the three-way with no human intervention, reducing the risk of error and improper matches.
- Reduces the risk of paying an erroneous or duplicate payment.
- Improves the invoice cycle time process and reduces processing costs.
- Provides data accuracy based on user-defined matching rules.

7. **Automated Workflow Approvals**—In an automated workflow approval process, the invoice approval process is linked to your company's Delegation of Authority (DoA) policy. The invoice approval process is completely automated based on defined rules via workflow. The workflow determines if an invoice needs approval; who the appropriate approvers are; and in what order approvers should approve payment of the invoice. The workflow then sequentially asks each approver in the approval list to approve invoices online. For example, you can define a rule so invoices over $100,000 (or a specific amount designated in your DoA policy) require CFO approval and then CEO approval.

Risks Mitigated

- An automated workflow can be linked to the employee master file in which approval levels are automatically updated when an approval moves to another department and is promoted.
- Reduces the risk of fraud since there is no opportunity for manual manipulation.
- Escalation processes can be built into the workflow to link to the Delegation of Authority (DoA) policy and tables.

8. **E-Payment**—If your company is paying more than 50% of invoices by check, it's way too many. I suggest paying your invoices by ACH or P-Card. Consider the cost of issuing the check, postage fees, resource fees, reconciliation costs, and the risk of check fraud. The e-payment process also includes the use of ACH supplier remittances rather than issue a separate manual remittance for an invoice payment. Additionally, if your accounts payable department is faced with ongoing escheatment issues due to uncashed suppler checks, besides looking into ACH and P-Cards for your payment process, consider outsourcing your payments process.

Risks Mitigated

- The E-payment process reduces risk and enhances internal control for the P2P process.

- The use of e-payment reduces check fraud, check reconciliation issues, and escheatment process challenges.
- The use of ACH remittance in the P2P process ensures that the invoice details are properly applied.
- Besides obtaining significant rebates as more suppliers settle with P-Cards, one of the advantages to using a P-Card is that the buyer is making a deferred payment.
- Accounts payable can pay their supplier using a P-Card at any point during the payment term and settle with the card issuer 30 to 60 days later.

9. **Systems Access Verification Tools**—Systems Access Verification tools can provide real-time monitoring and proactive enforcement of Segregation of Duties (SoD) policies. Such tools can anticipate a system access conflict before it arises and can even prevent an assignment of a role within an application that could compromise the P2P or put the company at risk.

   Risks Mitigated

   - Systems Access Verification tools can prevent a fraudulent transaction from being processed within the P2P process. As an example, an individual cannot set up a supplier in the supplier master file, pay that supplier, and void the transaction with proper system access controls in place. These are referred to as "intra" SoD controls.
   - These tools can also catch an "extra" SoD conflict in which an employee from another department may attempt to process an unrelated transaction. An employee in accounts receivable may try to process a fraudulent accounts payable transaction.

10. **Accounts Payable Self-Audit Tools**—The goal of any accounts payable department is to pay a supplier "once and only once." Rather than have a third party or external audit firm identify a control weakness, many companies have worked with a solution provider to implement a self-assessment process that identifies a possible duplicate payment before the payment is initiated. This software considers "fuzzy" logic algorithms that flag a potential duplicate or erroneous payment.

    Risks Mitigated

    - A self-audit tool can often be included in a company's internal control program as a continuous control monitoring (CCM) initiative.
    - Duplicate and erroneous payments are prevented before the cash is disbursed, improving the company's working capital and cash flow position.
    - Process improvements and improvements to internal control programs can be made in a real-time environment.

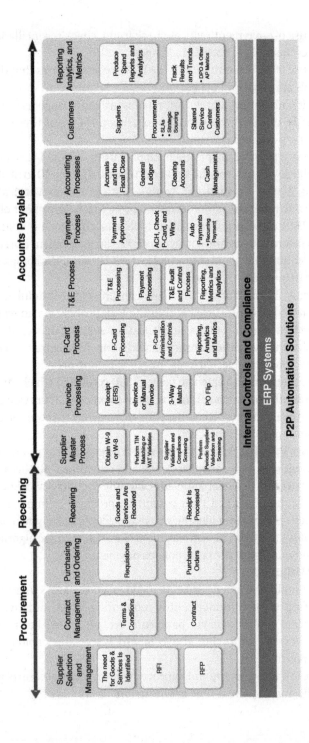

PROCESS OVERVIEW

The diagram below suggests that the foundational elements for the P2P process are Internal Controls and Compliance, ERP Systems, and P2P Automation Solutions.

APPLICATION OF INTERNAL CONTROLS

In management's selection of procedures and techniques of control, the degree of control implemented is a matter of reasonable business judgment. The common guideline that should be used in determining the degree of internal controls implementation is that the cost of a control should not exceed the benefit derived. The internal control standards listed here represent the minimum controls to be implemented within the P2P process.

METRICS

Table of Metrics

Functional Metrics

- Total Cost of the Total P2P Function as a Percentage of Revenue
- Total Cost of the Procurement Function as a Percentage of Revenue
- Total Cost of the Accounts Payable Function as a Percentage of Revenue
- Number of FTEs in the Total P2P Function
- Number of FTEs in the Procurement Functions
- Number of FTEs in the Accounts Payable Function

Procurement Cost and Process Metrics

- Cost per RFP
- Cost per Contract
- Cost per Purchase Order
- Strategic Sourcing Cost Savings
- Purchase Order Workflow Defects
- Unapproved Items in Purchase Order Workflow
- Non-Purchase Order Invoices
- Cost per P-Card Transaction

Table of Metrics

- Suppliers Using eProcurement
- Suppliers Using Supplier Portals Onboarding Invoice Status

Accounts Payable Cost and Process Metrics

- Cost per Invoice
- Cost per Invoice Line Item
- Percentage of First-Time Payment Matches
- Supplier Payments with Errors
- Number of Duplicate Payments (Identified Pre-Payment Run) Number
- Duplicate Payments (Identified Post-Payment Run)
- Percentage of Payment Recoveries (Post Payment)
- Percentage of Recoveries by Check (Post Payment)
- Percentage of Recoveries by Credit Memo (Payment)
- Percentage Use of Electronic Invoicing (eInvoicing)
- Percentage Use of Electronic Payments (ePayment)
- Invoices Paid Within Specified Terms
- Value of Supplier Discounts Taken
- Number of Manual Checks Issued per Period
- Invoice Payment Cycle Time
- Number of Invoices Processed Monthly
- Goods Receipt/Invoice Receipt Balance (Clearing Account)
- Goods Receipt/Invoice Receipt Balance Aging
- Goods Receipt/Invoice Receipt Balance Aging by Root Cause
- Invoices Paid Early
- Customer Service Cost per Inquiry
- Customer Service Response Time
- Blocked Payments—Number of Invoices
- Blocked Payments—Dollars
- Blocked Payments—Aging
- Blocked Payments—By Business Unit
- Number of Voided Checks
- Number of Reissued Checks
- Percentage of Checks vs. ACH
- Returned Checks

Table of Metrics

- Customer Inquiries by Reason
- External vs. Internal Customer Inquiries
- Top Five Inquiry Reasons
- Number of Suppliers
- Percentage of One-Time Suppliers
- Percentage of Foreign Suppliers
- Debt Balance Totals by Month
- Debit Balance Aging
- Percentage of Suppliers with Debit Balances

Internal Controls and Compliance

- Number of TIN Matching Issues
- Number of Regulatory Compliance Issues
- Regulatory Compliance Issues by Type
  - OFAC of Foreign Asset Control (OFAC)
  - Bureau of Industry and Security (BIS)
  - Office of the Inspector General (OIG)
  - Foreign Corrupt Practices Act (FCPA)
- Number of Pricing Issues
- Number of Internal Control Issues
- Aging of Internal Control Issues
- Number of Self-Assessments Completed
- Cycle Time for Remediation of an Internal Control Issue
- Internal Control Issues by Type
  - Delegation of Authority Errors
  - Segregation of Duties Errors
  - Coding the Invoice to an Incorrect Supplier
  - Percentage of Currency Errors (Wrong Currency Paid)
  - Duplicate Supplier on the Supplier Master File
  - Credit Memo Paid as Invoice
  - Invoice Already Paid on a P-Card
- Number of Suspicious or Fraudulent Suppliers
- Number of Control Issues Reported (Positive Pay, Positive Payee, ACH Debit Block, or Filter)

SUB-PROCESSES

The specific sub-processes included in the P2P process are:

4.1 Supplier Selection and Management

4.2 Purchasing/Ordering

4.3 Import Controls

4.4 Receiving

4.5 Accounts Payable

4.6 The Payment Process– General

4.7 The Payment Process—Travel and Entertainment

4.8 Research and Product Development

4.9 Procurement Cards (P-Cards)

 4.1 SUPPLIER SELECTION AND MANAGEMENT

Introduction

Purchases must be made from an approved supplier database/list in accordance with local procedures. A formal process should be in place to approve purchases from suppliers not on the approved database or on a government watch-list such as the Office of Foreign Assets (OFAC) and the Office of Inspector General (OIG). Suppliers need to be screened to ensure that foreign officials and politically exposed persons (PEPs) are not included on the supplier master file and the Foreign Corrupt Practices Act (FCPA) is not violated. Noncompliance with any of these screening processes noted could result in significant fines and damage to the company's reputation.

Standard of Internal Control

4.1.1 **Purchasing Strategies.** Sourcing strategies, supplier selections, and contract negotiation processes should be developed and documented. **Refer to risks: A-1, A-2, A-3, A-4**

4.1.2 **Documented Supplier Selection.** Purchasing has established and follows documented policies and procedures to qualify and evaluate

vendors based on established criteria prior to becoming approved suppliers. Compliance screening is conducted for all suppliers and a W-9 form is obtained for all domestic suppliers with the validation of the tax identification number (TIN) against IRS records. A W-8 is obtained for all foreign (non-U.S.) suppliers and the value-added tax information is validated accordingly.
Refer to risks: A-1, A-2, A-3, A-4, A-6

4.1.3 **Purchasing from Approved Suppliers.** The supplier master file must be reviewed, updated, and purged of inactive suppliers (e.g. suppliers with no activity for 18–24 months) at least annually. Suppliers should be added to the supplier database upon completion of supplier selection process and financial review.
Refer to risks: A-1, A-2, A-3, A-4

4.1.4 **Global and Regional Contracts.** Where global, regional, or geographic contracts are in place (e.g. information technology), that contract will be leveraged by all affected operating units.
Refer to risks: A-1, A-2, A-3, A-4

4.1.5 **Business Interruption Contingency Plans.** Supplier and sourcing strategies must take into consideration contingency plans to address or minimize risk of business interruption. These plans should be regularly reviewed and simulated.
Refer to risk: A-6

4.1.6 **Supplier Performance Monitoring.** Suppliers must be periodically monitored in accordance with Business Unit policy to ensure that actual performance meets quality, cost, and service expectations.
Refer to risks: A-3, A-6, A-7

4.1.7 **Supplier Master Ownership and Updates.** The actual update and maintenance of the supplier master must be performed by individuals not involved in supplier selection process.
Refer to risks: A-1, A-2, A-3, A-5

Risk If Standard Is Not Implemented

A-1 A purchase may be made from an unapproved supplier.

A-2 Export control violations, related-party transactions, or conflict-of-interest situations may occur. The potential for errors and irregularities is substantially increased.

A-3 Goods purchased may not meet quality standards. Unauthorized prices or terms may be accepted.

A-5 Records may be misused or altered by unauthorized personnel to the detriment of the company and its suppliers.

A-6 Materials may be received early or late, resulting in business interruption or excess levels of inventory.

A-7 Lose opportunity to revise supplier base to better meet the needs of the company.

4.2 PURCHASING/ORDERING

Introduction

To reduce company and supplier risk for the purchasing and ordering process, all ordering responsibilities must be segregated from accounts payable/payment, receiving, and accounting activities. Responsibilities should be clearly defined and system access is validated on a regular basis.

Standard of Internal Control

4.2.1 **Segregation of Duties.** All purchasing (ordering) responsibilities must be segregated from accounts payable/payment, receiving, and accounting activities.
Refer to risks: B-1, B-2, B-5, B-6, B-7, B-9, B-11, B-12

4.2.2 **Written Purchasing Policies.** Purchasing policies and procedures are established, communicated, and followed.
Refer to risks: B-1, B-2, B-4, B-6, B-7, B-9, B-10, B-11

4.2.3 **Access Controls.** All purchase orders or access to input screens must be safeguarded and internal control procedures for processing and approval must be in place to prevent unauthorized use.
Refer to risks: B-1, B-2, B-4, B-5, B-6, B-9, B-10, B-12

4.2.4 **Purchase Price Negotiation.** To assure the company's competitive advantage, prices will be negotiated through cost analysis (e.g. target costing), bidding, or industry cost benchmarking.
Refer to risks: B-2, B-5, B-7

4.2.5 **Conduct Prior to Vendor Selection Process.** Oral or written contracts, memorandums of understanding, and statements of intent that

may financially obligate the company must not be done prior to the completion of the selection process without proper approvals.
Refer to risks: B-1, B-2, B-5, B-6, B-7, B-9, B-10

4.2.6 **Advance Payments.** Payment in advance should be avoided if possible. A procedure should be established and followed when it is necessary to make payments in advance of the shipment or receipt of material to prevent overpayment. No advance payments can be made unless they are part of the purchase order terms.
Refer to risks: B-6, B-9, B-11

4.2.7 **Order Audit Trail.** All orders/transactions must be uniquely identifiable and traceable and periodically accounted for.
Refer to risks: B-3, B-4, B-5, B-6, B-9, B-10, B-11, B-12

4.2.8 **Invoice Forwarding.** Purchase orders/transactions must instruct suppliers to forward their billings directly to accounts payable.
Refer to risks: B-3, B-4, B-5, B-6, B-9, B-10, B-11

4.2.9 **Purchase Order Distribution.** Purchase order information must be made available to the receiving and accounts payable departments. Accounts payable and receiving must be notified of changed or canceled purchase orders immediately.
Refer to risks: B-3, B-5, B-6, B-7, B-8, B-9, B-11, B-12, B-14

4.2.10 **Product Return Procedures.** Procedures must be established to ensure proper approval, recording, and follow-up of all return items (due to poor quality, improper specifications, etc.).
Refer to risks: B-4, B-5, B-7, B-9, B-10, B-11, B-12

4.2.11 **Evaluation of Purchasing Process.** Purchasing process should be evaluated consistent with the supply management.
Refer to risks: B-7, B-8

4.2.12 **Safeguarding Intellectual Property.** Procedures governing the review and approval of contracts should address the safeguarding of the company's intellectual property, including patents and trademarks.
Refer to risks: B-4, B-5, B-10, B-12, B-13

4.2.13 **Blanket Purchase Orders.** A "not to exceed" limit and duration must be specified on each blanket purchase order.
Refer to risk: B-8

4.2.14 **Independence Within the Purchasing Process.** Independence between purchasing agent/buyer and supplier must be maintained.

This can be accomplished through periodic buyer rotation, or participation in corporate contracts, or use of commodity teams. The company's code of conduct should be distributed to all suppliers.

Refer to risks: B-1, B-2, B-3, B-4, B-5, B-7, B-11

4.2.15 **Requisitioning Procedures.** Purchase requirements (e.g. purchase orders, blanket orders, contracts, etc.) must be initiated by the requesting department and be properly approved, within approver's limits, before a purchase request is made. Purchase orders must not be split to circumvent approval limits.

Refer to risks: B-1, B-2, B-3, B-5, B-11

4.2.16 **Low-Value Requisitions.** Authorization limits must be established for individuals making low-value purchases through special procurement processes (e.g. credit cards, catalogs, procurement cards, etc.).

Refer to risks: B-1, B-3, B-5, B-11

4.2.17 **Purchase Order Revisions.** Purchase order revisions for price or quantity that cause increases that exceed buyer's approval level must be approved in compliance with local procedures.

Refer to risks: B-1, B-2, B-3, B-5, B-7, B-8

4.2.18 **After-the-Fact Purchase Orders.** After-the-Fact POs are identified, tracked, and addressed regularly. The After-the-Fact Purchase PO is typically used when a requisition and purchase order are being issued after the transaction has occurred and when the transaction doesn't fit the limited requirements of a payment request form.

Refer to risks: B-1, B-3, B-5, B-7, B-8

Risk If Standard Is Not Implemented

B-1   A purchase order may be:
  a. Unauthorized or improperly authorized
  b. Made from an unauthorized supplier
  c. Ordered and received by an unauthorized individual

B-2   Import and export control violations, related-party transactions, or conflict-of-interest situations may occur. The potential for errors and irregularities is substantially increased.

B-3   Rather than being returned or refused, the following items may be received and ultimately paid for:
  a. Unordered goods or services
  b. Excessive quantities or incorrect items
  c. Canceled or duplicated orders

B-4   Records may be lost or destroyed.

B-5   Records may be misused or altered by unauthorized personnel to the detriment of the company and its suppliers.

B-6   Goods and services may be received but not reported or reported inaccurately. Unrecorded liabilities and misstated inventory and cost of sales may occur.

B-7   Goods purchased may not meet quality standards. Unauthorized prices or terms may be accepted.

B-8   Materials may be received early or late, resulting in business interruption or excess levels of inventory

B-9   Duplicate payments may occur, or payments may be made for the wrong amount or to unauthorized or nonexistent suppliers.

B-10 Records may not be available for external legal, tax, or audit purposes.

B-11 Purchases and/or payments may be recorded at the incorrect amount, to the wrong account, or in the wrong period.

B-12 Payment may be made for goods or services never received.

B-13 Loss of intellectual property.

B-14 A purchase order may be received by an unauthorized individual.

 ## 4.3 IMPORT CONTROLS

Introduction

Both the customs border patrol (CBP) and the importing/exporting community have a shared responsibility to maximize compliance with laws and regulations. In carrying out this task, CBP encourages importers/exporters to become familiar with applicable laws and regulations.[1]

Generally, the customs authority of each country is part of the treasury/revenue department or ministry and has the primary responsibility of ensuring not only that duties and taxes are collected on imports but also that imports meet all their domestic laws and regulations. Such laws and regulations pertain to the health and welfare of its citizens and trade policies. Therefore, the primary role of a customs authority is border enforcement rather than trade

---

[1]U.S. Customs and Border Patrol, "Basic Importing and Exporting," accessed January 5, 2019, https://www.cbp.gov/trade/basic-import-export.

facilitation. Customs authorities have a broad and potent enforcement power such as search and seizure, and can impose heavy civil and criminal penalties, including the suspension of import privileges and imposition of jail terms when customs laws are violated.

The company and its subsidiaries import finished products, raw materials, and components in varying degrees for production support and distribution in local markets. In order to ensure continued timely release of imports from customs custody, the company will operate in full compliance with all laws and regulations applicable to our imports and will promptly address financial obligations and inquiries from customs authorities.

Standard of Internal Control

4.3.1 **Documented Procedures.** Each operating unit must have written procedures in place to ensure compliance with applicable laws and regulations pertaining to imports, including the valuation and classification of products.

Refer to risks: C-1, C-2, C-3, C-4, C-5, C-6

4.3.2 **Customs Brokers.** All importing units, including those which utilize certified customs brokers for import purposes, must establish written instructions and authorizations to ensure compliance with applicable laws and regulations.

Refer to risks: C-1, C-2, C-3

4.3.3 **Timely Responses to Inquiries.** All inquiries from customs authorities and financial obligations to customs authorities must be addressed in a timely manner.

Refer to risks: C-1, C-2, C-3, C-5, C-6

4.3.4 **Trade Preference Programs.** All operating units participating in trade preference programs must document the eligibility requirements of their participating products to ensure compliance with applicable laws and regulations.

Refer to risks: C-1, C-2, C-4, C-6

4.3.5 **Origin Declarations and Certifications.** All origin declarations and certifications for preferential and non-preferential purposes are the responsibility of the origin (exporting) unit and must be reviewed for accuracy and compliance by the receiving operating unit's Import Administration organization.

Refer to risks: C-1, C-2, C-4, C-6

4.3.6 **Duty Management.** Duty refund and deferral programs (e.g. duty drawback, foreign trade zone management, and other special-duty programs) must be administered in accordance with applicable regulations.
Refer to risks: C-1, C-2, C-6

4.3.7 **Records Management.** All importing entities must establish and maintain adequate records retention systems to ensure compliance with the company statement of corporate policy on records management.
Refer to risks: C-1, C-2, C-3, C-6

Risk If Standard Is Not Implemented

C-1 Governmental and/or customs regulations may be violated.

C-2 Civil and criminal penalties against the company and/or individual employees may occur.

C-3 Import privileges may be lost.

C-4 The company as a whole may lose preferential tariff rates.

C-5 Inaction may adversely impact the timely release of goods from customs custody.

C-6 Incorrect documentation may result in significant financial exposure to the company.

 ## 4.4 RECEIVING

Introduction

To ensure proper segregation of duties, the receiving department should be physically segregated from the production facilities and shipping. As a key component of the procure to pay (P2P) process, receiving is responsible for the recording of all company receipts. The accurate receipt of good and services drives the three-way matching process in which the purchase order (PO), invoice, and receiving document are validated for the correct pricing, quantities, and price.

Standard of Internal Control

4.4.1 **Physical Segregation of Receiving Department.** The receiving department should be physically segregated from the production facilities and shipping. Where segregation is not feasible, compensating controls must be established.
Refer to risks: D-1, D-2, D-3

4.4.2 **Segregation of Duties.** The receiving function must be separated from the buying function, invoice processing, accounts payable, and general ledger functions.
Refer to risks: D-1, D-2, D-3, D-5, D-6, D-7, D-8

4.4.3 **Access to Receiving Department.** Access to the receiving department must be restricted to authorized personnel only.
Refer to risks: D-1, D-2, D-3, D-4, D-5, D-6

4.4.4 **Receiving Policy.** All incoming material, merchandise, and supplies must be processed by the designated receiving location at each facility, unless otherwise arranged and approved in accordance with local policy.
Refer to risks: D-1, D-2, D-4, D-5

4.4.5 **Acceptance of Goods Received.** The receiving location will accept only those goods with an approved purchase order or when its equivalent has been prepared. All other receipts should be returned to the supplier or investigated for propriety in a timely manner.
Refer to risks: D-3, D-4, D-5, D-6, D-7

4.4.6 **Receipt Documentation.** Each designated receiving location must account for and provide evidence of a receiving transaction for all material, merchandise, or supplies accepted by the receiving location. Evidence must exist of goods returned or moved to other areas.
Refer to risks: D-2, D-6, D-7

4.4.7 **Receipt Recording.** Receiving transactions will not be generated without actual receipt of goods or services and adequate proof of delivery.
Refer to risks: D-3, D-6

4.4.8 **Receiving Procedures.** In the absence of an effective supplier qualification and performance-monitoring program, incoming goods must be evaluated for damage and shortages. Goods must be counted, weighed, or measured on a sample basis to determine the accuracy of supplier's

shipments. All discrepancies and damage must be documented, tracked, and appropriately resolved with the supplier.
Refer to risks: D-2, D-3, D-4, D-6, D-7

4.4.9 **Receiving Information.** Receiving transaction information and copies of documentation (BOL, packing slip, etc.) must be maintained in the receiving department and made available to purchasing and accounts payable for supplier payment processing on a timely basis.
Refer to risks: D-2, D-6, D-7

4.4.10 **Supply Chain Inspection.** In the absence of an effective supplier qualification and performance-monitoring program, incoming goods must be promptly inspected and tested for damage, quality characteristics, product specifications, etc. by the appropriate supply chain personnel.
Refer to risks: D-4, D-7

4.4.11 **Safeguarding Receiving Information.** Receiving transaction information must be adequately safeguarded from theft, destruction, or unauthorized use. Receiving transactions must be uniquely identifiable, traceable, and accounted for periodically. Access to the receiving system must be controlled and password protected.
Refer to risks: D-1, D-2, D-4, D-5

4.4.12 **Safeguarding of Received Goods.** Incoming goods must be secured and safeguarded upon receipt. High-value parts, such as microprocessors, must be safeguarded during the receiving process.
Refer to risk: D-1

4.4.13 **Changes to Receiving Records.** Changes required to correct errors in original receiving transactions may be generated only by authorized personnel as specified by local policy.
Refer to risks: D-1, D-2, D-4, D-5, D-6, D-7, D-8

Risk If Standard Is Not Implemented

D-1 A purchase may be:
   a. Unauthorized or improperly authorized
   b. Made from an unauthorized supplier
   c. Ordered and received by an unauthorized individual

D-2 Related-party transactions or conflict-of-interest situations may occur. The potential for errors and irregularities is substantially increased.

D-3 Rather than being returned or refused, the following items may be received and ultimately paid for:
   a. Unordered goods or services
   b. Excessive quantities or incorrect items
   c. Canceled or duplicated orders

D-4 Records may be lost or destroyed.

D-5 Records may be misused or altered by unauthorized personnel to the detriment of the company and its suppliers.

D-6 Goods and services may be received but not reported or reported inaccurately. Unrecorded liabilities and misstated inventory and cost of sales may occur.

D-7 Goods purchased may not meet quality standards. Unauthorized prices or terms may be accepted.

D-8 Purchases and/or payments may be recorded at the incorrect amount, to the wrong account, or in the wrong period.

4.5 ACCOUNTS PAYABLE

Introduction

The AP process or function is immensely important since it involves nearly all of a company's payments outside of payroll. Regardless of the company's size, the mission of AP is to pay only the company's bills and invoices that are legitimate and accurate. This means that before a supplier's invoice is entered into the accounting records and scheduled for payment, the invoice must reflect:

- What the company had ordered
- What the company has received
- The proper unit costs, calculations, totals, and terms

Standard of Internal Control

4.5.1 **Segregation of Duties.** The accounts payable function must be segregated from the following functions:
   a. Receiving
   b. Purchasing
   c. Disbursing cash or its equivalent
   Refer to risks: E-1, E-2

4.5.2 **Invoice Accuracy.** Prior to payment, supplier's invoices must be reviewed for receipt of material or services, checked for accuracy (price, quantity, mathematical extension, currency, proper freight charges, sales tax, etc.) and account classification and distribution, and agreed to the PO/contract terms. Invoices with a discrepancy exceeding the tolerance limits or lacking reference information (PO quantity/ amount) must be resolved before payment is made.
Refer to risks: E-2, E-4, E-5, E-6, E-7, E-8

4.5.3 **Alternative Processes.** If alternative processes are used, such as pay on receipt, Evaluated Receipt Settlement (ERS), consignment inventories, or Electronic Data Interchange (EDI), the procedures in place to ensure correct pricing and received quantities are documented and approved by local operating and financial management.
Refer to risks: E-1, E-3, E-4, E-5, E-7, E-8

4.5.4 **Invoice Approval.** Invoices without a purchase order or receiving report (e.g. non-production services, lease payments, check requests, one-time purchases, etc.) must be approved by authorized personnel in accordance with their approval limits before payment.
Refer to risks: E-2, E-3, E-7, E-9

4.5.5 **Original Invoices.** Original invoices or approved electronic invoices should be used as the basis for payment. Where the original invoice is not available, a copy can be used only if it is properly identified as a duplicate. A facsimile document can be used to expedite payment only when a process is in place to match the facsimile with the original document in a timely manner.
Refer to risks: E-5, E-6, E-7

4.5.6 **Duplicate Payments.** A process must be in place to detect and prevent duplicate payments. Supporting documents for the payments must be originals and must be effectively canceled after payment to prevent accidental or intentional reuse. No payments should be based upon a statement unless the supplier has been pre-approved for such.
Refer to risks: E-7, E-9

4.5.7 **Goods Receipt—Invoice Receipt (GR/IR) Clearing Account Reconciliation.** Aged, unmatched purchase orders, receiving transactions, and invoices must be periodically reviewed, investigated, and resolved.
Refer to risks: E-2, E-4

4.5.8 **Supplier Statements.** Supplier statements must be regularly reviewed for past-due items and open credits, to be resolved in a timely manner. The currency used for statements and invoices should be consistent.
Refer to risks: E-2, E-4, E-7, E-8, and E-9

4.5.9 **Reconciliations.** Items forwarded to payments should be reconciled (contents are known and status is current) monthly with payments actually made and recorded in the general ledger. The accounts payable trial balance should also be reconciled (contents are known and status is current) with the general ledger each month. All differences must be resolved on a timely basis.
Refer to risks: E-8, E-9

4.5.10 **Debit Balance Accounts.** Accounts payable should review debit balance accounts at least quarterly and request remittance on debit amounts outstanding for over 90 days. Any significant debit balance should be classified as an account receivable.
Refer to risks: E-6, E-7

4.5.11 **Debit and Credit Memos.** Debit and credit memos issued to supplier accounts must be documented, recorded, controlled, and approved by authorized personnel in accordance with their approval limits.
Refer to risks: E-6, E-7, E-9

4.5.12 **Debit and Credit Memo Audit Trails.** Debit and credit memos must be uniquely identifiable and traceable. Company-generated hardcopy documents must be pre-numbered for security control.
Refer to risk: E-9

4.5.13 **Established Suppliers.** Prior to the payment, accounts payable must ensure the supplier is established on the approved supplier master file. Suppliers not on the approved supplier masterfile must be validated independent of the originating source.
Refer to risks: E-4, E-7, E-9

4.5.14 **Liability Accruals.** Procedures and mechanisms must be in place to identify and capture all items and services that have been billed but not yet received and received but not yet billed to ensure that financial results are accurately stated. These items must receive proper treatment in the accounting records.
Refer to risks: E-1, E-2, E-6

Risk If Standard Is Not Implemented

E-1 Purchases may be stolen, lost, destroyed, or temporarily diverted. The potential for errors and irregularities is substantially increased.

E-2 Purchases may be received but never reported, or reported inaccurately.

E-3 Purchases or services may be ordered and received by an unauthorized individual.

E-4 Rather than being returned or refused, the following goods or services may be received and ultimately paid for:
  a. Unordered goods or services
  b. Inventory that does not meet quality standards
  c. Excessive quantities or incorrect items

E-5 Materials may be received too early or too late for production. Business interruption or excessive levels (quantity and/or $$) or inventory may occur.

E-6 Payment may be made for goods or services not received and/or in advance of receipt.

E-7 Payments to suppliers may be duplicated, incorrect, or fraudulent.

E-8 Records may be lost or destroyed.

E-9 Records may be misused or altered to the detriment of the company or its suppliers.

 ## 4.6 THE PAYMENT PROCESS—GENERAL

Introduction

Once company expenditures are approved for payment, the actual payment process commences, which leads to the exchange of funds between the purchasing company and its supplier. Personnel involved in the payment process must adhere to policies and procedures designed to ensure accurate, timely, and secure payments initiation using the appropriate payment method for each payment.

Standard of Internal Control

4.6.1 **Segregation of Duties.** The function of disbursing cash or its equivalent must be segregated from the following functions:
  a. Receiving
  b. Purchasing
  c. Invoice processing
  d. Accounts payable
  e. General ledger reconciliation
  f. Payee master data setups and changes
  Refer to risks: F-1, F-2, F-3, F-7

4.6.2 **Payment Reconciliations.** All payments and other payment activities must be traceable, uniquely identifiable, and reconciled (contents are known and status is current) with general ledger and bank statements on a monthly basis.
  Refer to risks: F-1, F-4

4.6.3 **Supporting Documentation.** Requests for checks, electronic funds transfers, and bank transfers must be supported by approved purchase orders, receiving transactions, or original invoices. This documentation will be provided to the signers for their review as part of the approval process.
  Refer to risks: F-2, F-3, F-4, F-7

4.6.4 **Payment Approval.** Approved payments must be aged and made in accordance with corporate policy or within the agreed-upon company and supplier terms.
  Refer to risk: F-8

4.6.5 **Supplier Discounts.** All eligible supplier discounts should be taken whenever favorable to the company.
  Refer to risks: F-5, F-9

4.6.6 **Recording in Accounting Records.** All payments must be recorded in the period payment was made. Expenses must be properly and accurately recorded in the accounting period in which the liability was incurred.
  Refer to risks: F-3, F-5, F-6, F-9

4.6.7 **Bearer Checks.** Checks must not be made payable to cash or bearer.
  Refer to risks: F-1, F-3, F-7

4.6.8 **Blank Check Storage.** Blank checks must be safeguarded from destruction or unauthorized use. The supply of blank checks must be numerically controlled and regularly accounted for as issued, voided, or unused. Employees that have access to unissued checks must be independent of the check signing and voucher preparation functions.
Refer to risks: F-l, F-3, F-4, F-7

4.6.9 **Voided and Canceled Checks.** Spoiled, voided, and canceled checks must be altered or voided immediately. These checks must be accounted for and protected. They may be destroyed, provided the destruction is witnessed, and documented by an additional individual.
Refer to risks: F-1, F-7

4.6.10 **Bank Account Limits.** Specific limits of signing authority for checks, promissory notes, and bank transfers must be established and approved according to an appropriate board of directors banking resolution and communicated to the disbursing entity and the appropriate bank(s).
Refer to risks: F-1, F-3, F-7

4.6.11 **Positive Pay Controls.** Checking accounts must be provided with "match pay" or "positive pay" controls that permit a preview of checks presented to the bank for payment to ensure that both the payment amount and payee have not been altered. If such controls are not practical, bank accounts must be subject to activity limits and dual signatory controls.
Refer to risks: F-1, F-4, F-7

4.6.12 **Signatures.** The signatures of authorized signers must be on file within the company and at the bank.
Refer to risks: F-1, F-2, F-6, F-9

4.6.13 **Records Management.** Documents or electronic data supporting expenditures must be safeguarded from loss or destruction and must be in a retrievable format. Such records must be retained and maintained in accordance with the company's policy on records management.
Refer to risks: F-5, F-10

4.6.14 **Check Delivery.** All checks should be mailed. In those cases where this is not possible, prior arrangements should be made for check delivery. When the check is picked up in person, proper identification must be provided and delivery of the check must be documented via their signature.
Refer to risk: F-1

4.6.15 **ACH Payments and Wire Transfers.** Payments by ACH and wire transfer must be made only to pre-established and validated bank accounts. Where practical, recurring wire payments should be established as repetitive payments within the wire transfer system. Non-repetitive wires require independent review and approval.
Refer to risks: F-1, F-4, F-6, F-7, F-8

4.6.16 **Petty Cash.** Payments made from petty cash must be supported by a receipt and approved by authorized personnel in accordance with their approval limits. In general, the use of petty cash should be avoided and a procurement card (P-Card) or other corporate credit cards should be used.
Refer to risks: F-4, F-6, F-7

4.6.17 **Custody and Security of Check-Signing Equipment.** Where check-signing equipment and facsimile signature plates or digitized signature images are utilized, the equipment and plates must be secured, and custody of the check-signing equipment and the signature plates or digitized signature image files must be segregated. In addition, a reconciliation (contents are known and status is current) should be made of checks written and checks authorized to the check-signing machine totals.
Refer to risks: F-1, F-5

Risk If Standard Is Not Implemented

F-1 Controls may be bypassed allowing the potential for theft or error.

F-2 Purchases or services may be ordered and received by an unauthorized individual.

F-3 Items or services may be received but not reported, or reported inaccurately. Unrecorded liabilities, misstated inventories, and over-/underpayments to suppliers may result.

F-4 Duplicate payments may occur, or payments may be made for the wrong amount or to unauthorized or nonexistent suppliers.

F-5 Financial statements, records, and operating reports may be misstated. Critical decisions may be based upon erroneous information.

F-6 Purchases or services may be unauthorized, recorded for the wrong amount or in the wrong period, and/or payment made to the wrong person.

F-7 Items may be recorded and payment made for goods or services not received.

F-8 Operations may be adversely affected as suppliers may refuse future business with the company.

F-9 Cash utilization may not be optimized or may be misappropriated.

F-10 Fines or penalties may be imposed if required supporting documents are not available.

4.7 THE PAYMENT PROCESS—TRAVEL AND ENTERTAINMENT

Introduction

T&E expenses are "incurred when an employee conducts business away from home or the company's offices. For example, if one must travel to another location to conduct a meeting with an important client, any lodging, meals, or transportation costs usually count as travel expenses. One may deduct travel expenses from one's taxable income, provided they are in fact directly related to business. For this reason, travel expenses are somewhat controversial; some companies, for example, toolkit a business meeting at a major resort and deduct the entire cost. Whether this is an actual travel expense is a matter for debate."[2]

- Divide up your policy into sections: air travel, hotel lodging, dining, entertainment expenses, and car rental.
- Provide a section that clearly states what is not reimbursable.
- Let employees know what enforcement measures will be taken to ensure policy compliance.
- Include a guideline around traveling with spouses or significant others. What if an employee chooses to stay over extra days? Or over a weekend?
- Who is responsible for travel charges if the employee cancels a reservation or is a "no-show"?
- What is your policy about home offices? Can employees be reimbursed for Internet and/or phone charges? What about office supplies or office furniture?

---

[2]*Farlex Financial Dictionary*, © 2011 Farlex, Inc. All Rights Reserved.

- What's your company's policy about consuming alcohol at meals with clients? If alcohol is permitted, what is your policy about paying for an alternative ride back home or to a hotel if the employee can't drive?
- If a receipt is missing, let employees know all is not lost. Ask for an explanation of the expense, business need, and date of the expense, supplier, location, and dollar amount. You might also consider calling the supplier for a duplicate receipt if possible.
- Update your mileage reimbursement rate. Should employees start the mileage count from your company's headquarters? Or from home? (One company automatically deducts 20 miles when an employee submits a mileage expense form—even when the employee works from home.)
- Are credit card statements an acceptable form of receipt? Or do you require itemization and a store receipt along with a credit card slip?
- Also, be sure to fit the current mode of your company growth. Are you in growth mode or cost-cutting mode? Are you a smaller company or larger? How high in the management structure do expenses need to be approved?

4.7.1 **Corporate Credit Card.** Employees must obtain and use a credit card in accordance with the appropriate corporate policy.
Refer to risk: G-4

4.7.2 **Reimbursable Expenses.** Reimbursed expenditures must be actual, necessary, reasonable, and consistent with the appropriate corporate policy. Any expenditures that appear to be excessive should be investigated.
Refer to risk: G-2

4.7.3 **Timely Completion of Expense Reports.** Expense reports should be completed, approved, and forwarded to the proper accounting department in a timely fashion in accordance with corporate policy. Any balance due the employee should be settled at that time.
Refer to risks: G-1, G-2

4.7.4 **Supporting Documentation.** Original receipts as required by policy should be attached to business expense reports for all expenses over $25 or the dollar amount specified by the company's travel policy.
Refer to risks: G-1, G-2, G-3, G-5

4.7.5 **Approved Expenditures.** Employee expenditures should be approved by the employee's supervisor. In the absence of the supervisor, expenditures should be forwarded to an equal or next higher level of supervision for approval. The authorizing signature must be authentic (e.g. administrative assistants cannot sign in lieu of supervisors).
Refer to risks: G-1, G-2, G-3

Risk If Standard Is Not Implemented

G-1 Controls may be bypassed, allowing the potential for theft or error.

G-2 Expenditures or services may be ordered and received by an unauthorized individual.

G-3 Duplicate payments may occur, or payments may be made for the wrong amount.

G-4 Cash utilization may not be optimized.

G-5 Valuable tax deductions may be lost.

 ## 4.8 RESEARCH AND PRODUCT DEVELOPMENT

Introduction

Concurrent and integrated market research and product development should be performed to analyze the need and help define customer requirements and expectations. Organization and assignments of the research and product development teams should include functional and cross-functional teaming to ensure that the company process is consistent.

Standard of Internal Control

4.8.1 **Plan/Manage Development Process.** Develop standards, procedures, and resource requirements for product design, testing, and production. This plan must be managed, periodically evaluated, and reengineered to meet the operating unit's objectives.
Refer to risks: H-1, H-2, H-3, H-5, H-8

4.8.2 **Responsibilities.** Quality and production process owners should be involved at the beginning of the process.
Refer to risks: H-1, H-5, H-6, H-9

4.8.3 **Risk Assessment.** Risk assessment procedures should be developed to ensure product risks are analyzed and documented. Regulatory requirements should also be identified and appropriately addressed.
Refer to risks: H-2, H-3, H-7, H-8

4.8.4 **Market Research.** Concurrent and integrated market research and product development should be performed to analyze the need and help define customer requirements and expectations.
Refer to risks: H-3, H-7

4.8.5 **Information Management Systems and Tools.** Up-to-date systems that support product development should be evaluated and implemented (e.g. CAD tools, simulation tools, etc.).
Refer to risk: H-6

4.8.6 **Safeguarding Intellectual Property.** Confidentiality is critical to the research and product development functionalities. Confidentiality agreements should be executed between all pertinent parties in the research and product development process.
Refer to risk: H-4

4.8.7 **Nonstandard Solutions.** Efforts to reduce nonstandard solutions should be made. The use of nonstandard solutions should be approved by appropriate management.
Refer to risks: H-3, H-7, H-8

4.8.8 **Supplier Relationships.** Suppliers should be involved as early in the process as possible. Monitor supplier agreements regarding partnering, bonuses, or penalties for quality, costs, and timely deliveries. Consider incentives for suppliers proposing optimized solutions. For supplier selection controls and risks, refer to Section 4.1.
Refer to risks: H-1, H-5, H-9

4.8.9 **Testing.** Design tests, quality tests, and customer beta tests should be performed consistently. Prototype and testing procedures should be communicated and followed. To the extent possible, customers should be involved as early in the process as possible.
Refer to risks: H-1, H-7, H-9

4.8.10 **Monitor and Track Performance.** Consistent monitoring of performance in all phases of a project should be completed and evaluated. Aspects that should be monitored include, but are not limited to:
a. Strict adherence to design, testing, and project plans, including the participation of all team members
b. Cycle times
c. Problems reported by customers and compared with industry standards and company objectives (customer feedback mechanism)
d. Development and testing costs
e. Actions taken as a result of feedback from consumers and production teams
f. Customer service and support P&L trends
Refer to risks: H-1, H-2, H-3, H-6, H-7, H-8, H-9

4.8.11 **Supporting Documentation.** Documentation of engineering specifications, drawings, vendor drawings and other specifications should be maintained in accordance with corporate document retention policies. Modifications during the development process should be documented; as changes are approved, all engineering drawings should be updated. **Refer to risks: H-6, H-9**

Risk If Standard Is Not Implemented

H-1 Quality products are not designed, developed, and sold to the customers.

H-2 Time-to-market is not minimized. Process times are too long. Long development lead times, resulting in obsolete products being marketed; competitor beats the company to the market.

H-3 Product is more expensive than customers are willing to bear.

H-4 Loss of intellectual property.

H-5 Product does not meet the design criteria.

H-6 Personnel do not have adequate information, tools, training and/or skills to perform the necessary functions.

H-7 Market expectations are not met, leading to customer dissatisfaction.

H-8 Product is not profitable for the corporation.

H-9 Product cannot be manufactured as specified by the design team (i.e. may require purchase of special, expensive, or custom tools to manufacture product).

 ## 4.9 PROCUREMENT CARDS (P-CARDS)

Introduction

According to the Professional Association for the Commercial Card and Payment Industry (NAPCP), P-Cards provide a means for streamlining the procure-to-pay process, allowing organizations to procure goods and services in a timely manner, reduce transaction costs, track expenses, take advantage of supplier discounts, reduce or redirect staff in the purchasing and/or AP departments, reduce or eliminate petty cash, and more. Originally, P-Cards were targeted for such low-value transactions as supplies and maintenance, repair and operations (MRO), where their use eliminated purchase orders and invoicing. Over the years, their use has expanded to higher-value transactions as the industry has grown and greater controls have been introduced.

Standard of Internal Control

4.9.1 **SoD and System Access.** Access to the card-issuance area and system access for P-Card activity is limited to employees of the organization. On a quarterly basis, the P-Card system access table is reviewed. The access table is reviewed to ensure that recent system access changes that result from employee changes in job responsibility are properly reflected. Administrator reviews for appropriate level of access based on the job function and appropriate segregation of duties within the organization. The P-Card Administrator only has access to reports from the financial institution. The function of processing and disbursing travel and expense claims must be segregated from the following functions:
- Receiving
- Purchasing
- AP invoice processing
- Vendor file maintenance
- General ledger reconciliation
- AP invoice approval

Refer to risks: I-1, I-2, I-3, I-4, I-5, 1-6

4.9.2 **Cardholder Statements.** The cardholder submits periodic statements with supporting documentation for each transaction according to P-Card policies and procedures to the P-Card Administrator.
Refer to risks: I-1, I-2, I-3, I-4, I-5, 1-6

4.9.3 **Management Responsibilities.** Management with Delegation of Authority (DoA) is responsible for 100% audit of cardholder's statement and supporting documentation/receipts. Management DoA signature approval is required on cardholder's statement (DoA applies to each transaction on the statement, not the statement total).
Refer to risks: I-1, I-2, I-3, I-4, I-5, 1-6

4.9.4 **Review Spend Activity.** Review of spend activity in credit card is conducted through an online recording and reporting system is conducted.
Refer to risks: I-1, I-2, I-3, I-4, I-5, 1-6

4.9.5 **Statement Review Process.** Every statement is reviewed upon receipt:
- Date stamped with date received in A/P
- Verified for appropriate management Delegation of Authority (DoA)

Refer to risks: I-1, I-2, I-3, I-4, I-5, 1-6

4.9.6 **Statement Tracking.** The P-Card Administrator tracks statements on P-Card audit log:
- Use to monitor submission of statements.
- Follow up on outstanding statements.
- Document audit activity.

Refer to risks: I-1, I-2, I-3, I-4, I-5, 1-6

4.9.7 **P-Card Random Audit Process.** A minimum of 10% of statements, with an average of 20% to 30% of random statements, must be audited sporadically to review the following:
- Supplier review—appropriateness of purchase
- Misuse of card—personal purchases
- Justification for unusual purchases and pre-approvals if applicable

Refer to risks: I-1, I-2, I-3, I-4, I-5, 1-6

4.9.8 **P-Card Targeted Audits (in addition to random audits).** Specific to cardholder and/or object account spend, audits should include the following:
- Preferred supplier spending data on office supplies
- Charitable contributions
- Review of 100% of statements for retail or restaurant spending to identify misuse or unusual purchases
- Credit card online reporting tool reports to assist with audit and review spend activity

Refer to risks: I-1, I-2, I-3, I-4, I-5, 1-6

4.9.9 **P-Card Controls Monitoring.** Monitor P-Card audit tracking log monitors tracking and audits performed by the program administrator.

Refer to risks: I-1, I-2, I-3, I-4, I-5, 1-6

4.9.10 **Spending Level Reports.** As an example, a company may receive an over-$15K report that reflects any individual transaction over $15K, which should be reviewed to ensure that approval levels are correct. Review P-Card spending via reporting and metrics processes.

Refer to risks: I-1, I-2, I-3, I-4, I-5, 1-6

4.9.11 **Spending Limit Changes.** Any temporary or permanent change spreadsheets or support must be approved by management who holds DoA with supporting reason for increase in limit.

Refer to risks: I-1, I-2, I-3, I-4, I-5, 1-6

4.9.12 **Transaction Detail Report.** Review transaction volumes by site to look for any unusual spending patterns.
Refer to risks: I-1, I-2, I-3, I-4, I-5, 1-6

4.9.13 **Supplier Controls.** Block suppliers from vouchering to a P-Card supplier. P-Card suppliers cannot also be paid via a check or an ACH payment.
Refer to risks: I-1, I-2, I-3, I-4, I-5, 1-6

4.9.14 **P-Card Management Review.** Verify 100% of A/P P-Card statements have supporting documentation and DoA approval on support.
Refer to risks: I-1, I-2, I-3, I-4, I-5, 1-6

4.9.15 **Bank Payment Verification.** The file feed is validated against statement from the issuing bank by the P-Card Administrator.
Refer to risks: I-1, I-2, I-3, I-4, I-5, 1-6

4.9.16 **P-Card Accruals.** Review and analyze any accrued activity incurred but not included in the cycle-cut of the current month file.
Refer to risks: I-1, I-2, I-3, I-4, I-5, 1-6

4.9.17 **Review Cardholder Listing.** Conduct a cardholder listing and spending limit review to reassess limits and/or business need for card.
Refer to risks: I-1, I-2, I-3, I-4, I-5, 1-6

4.9.18 **P-Card Cardholder Agreement.** Ensure that all P-Card cardholders and their managers have signed a cardholder agreement that specifies requirements for the use of the card and clearly defines the responsibilities of the employee and manager. The cardholder agreement should also clearly define and specify the repercussions of both card abuse and misuse.
Refer to risks: I-1, I-2, I-3, I-4, I-5, 1-6

Risk If Standard Is Not Implemented

I-1 Improper SoD and system access. The lack of good segregation of duties and system access controls may result in incorrect payments and accounting data. Incorrect payments may be undetected for a lengthy period, and payments that are too high may be unrecoverable.

I-2 Violation of P-Card policies. Policies may be violated, leading to duplicate, erroneous, or fraudulent payments to suppliers.

I-3 Poor visibility or errors during the review process. The lack of a timely review process may cause errors to be undetected and incorrect payments to be made.

I-4 Unclear and undefined roles and responsibilities. Unclear responsibilities for the cardholder and management may result in P-Card abuse and inappropriate payments.

I-5 Payment activity payment errors. The lack of attention to the P-Card process may result in incorrect payments to the issuing financial institution and duplicate payments to suppliers.

I-6 Misstatement of financial results. Financial statements, records, and operating reports may be misstated. Critical decisions may be based upon erroneous information, resulting in the misstatement of financial results.

CHAPTER FIVE

Hire to Retire (H2R) Process

 INTRODUCTION

Hire to Retire (H2R) is a human resources process that includes everything that needs to be done over the course of an employee's career with a company. The following are high-level process steps.

- **Human Resources Planning:** Human resource management planning such as work design
- **Recruiting:** Recruiting processes such as relationship building, employer branding, job posting, job fairs and interviewing
- **Employee Management:** Everything that is required to manage an employee, such as onboarding, performance management, training and development, and benefits and compensation processes
- **Redeploy:** The processes related to an employee being redeployed, such as foreign work assignments
- **Payroll:** The control and delivery of payroll
- **Retire:** The processes related to an employee leaving such as exit interviews and retirement benefits

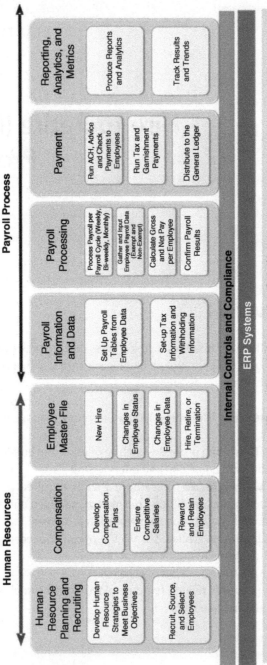

PROCESS OVERVIEW

The diagram below suggests that the foundational elements for the H2R process are Internal Controls and Compliance, ERP Systems, and HR and Payroll Automation Solutions.

 ## METRICS

Table of Metrics

- **Number and Value of Payroll Payment Issues and Errors Identified and Mitigated**
- **Number of New Hires**
- **Number of Hiring Violations Identified**
- **Number of Transfers**—The number of employee transfers within the company.
- **Number of Terminations**—The number of employee terminations.
- **Attrition Rate**—Reflects the number of employees departing from a company.
- **Employee Satisfaction Rating**—Determines the level of employee satisfaction.
- **Percentage of Performance Reviews Completed**—Reports the percentage of employee performance reviews completed.
- **Number of Hiring and Discriminatory Issues Reported**—Discriminatory issues reported by new employees.
- **Number and Value of Employee Benefit Issues Identified and Mitigated**—Benefit problems reported and resolved.
- **Number of Controls Self-Assessment Performed**—Number of self-assessments performed per period.
- **Number and Value of Compliance Fines Incurred**—Number and value of fines reported.
- **Number and Value of Payroll Exceptions Identified**—Number and value of payroll exceptions.
- **Number of Special Payments Paid per Period**—Number of special payroll payments.
- **Cost to Process Payroll Results**—The cost to process payroll.
- **Cycle Time for Each Payroll Process**—The cycle time to complete the payroll process.
- **Number and Value of Pre-Close and Post Close Adjustments for the Payroll Process**—Number and value of closing adjustments.
- **Value of Variances Reported in Payroll Bank Accounts**—Value of payroll payment account variances.

Table of Metrics
■ **Aging of Variances Reported in Payroll Bank Accounts**—Aging of variances in payroll payment account variances.
■ **Number and Value of Unclaimed Wages (by State)**—Used to report unclaimed wages by state.

 ## APPLICATION OF INTERNAL CONTROLS

In management's selection of procedures and techniques of control, the degree of control implemented is a matter of reasonable business judgment. The common guideline that should be used in determining the degree of internal controls implementation is that the cost of a control should not exceed the benefit derived. However, a minimum set of controls should exist in a normal business environment. The internal control standards listed here represent the minimum controls to be implemented within the payroll process. The term *checks* in this chapter is generically used to describe all forms (electronic, bank transfer, etc.) of payroll payments to employees.

Within the hire-to-retire process, human resources includes the functions involved in hiring employees and determining their proper classification and compensation; defining skills requirements; training, developing, and maintaining employees; ensuring employee communications; providing employee services; reporting hours worked, attendance, and compensatory absence entitlements; and ensuring the confidentiality and physical security of personnel information.

Human resources are the people who work in an organization. It is also the name of the department that exists to serve the needs of those people. William R. Tracey, in *The Human Resources Glossary*,[1] defines human resources as "the people that staff and operate an organization . . . as contrasted with the financial and material resources of an organization."

Human resources are the people who work for an organization in jobs that produce the products or services of the business or organization.

In the past, these people, also known as employees, staff members, co-workers, colleagues, team members, or workers in organizations and workplaces, were called *personnel*. In some organizations, they are still called personnel,

---

[1] William R. Tracey, *The Human Resources Glossary: The Complete Desk Reference for HR Executives, Managers, and Practitioners*, CRC Press, April 19, 2016.

manpower, operators, or workmen—names that are generally no longer used in more evolved and modern workplaces. *Human resources* evolved from these older terms as the functions of the field moved beyond paying employees and managing employee benefits. The evolution of the HR function gave credence to the fact that people are an organization's most important resources.

THE HEALTH INSURANCE PORTABILITY AND ACCOUNTABILITY ACT (HIPAA) SECURITY RULE

The HIPAA Security Rule (HSR) establishes national standards to protect individuals' electronic personal health information that is created, received, used, or maintained by a covered entity. The Security Rule requires appropriate administrative, physical, and technical safeguards to ensure the confidentiality, integrity, and security of electronic protected health information.[2] All employee records need to be protected under this requirement.

The National Institute of Standards and Technology (NIST) HIPAA Security Toolkit Application is a self-assessment survey intended to help organizations better understand the requirements of the HIPAA Security Rule (HSR), implement those requirements, and assess those implementations in their operational environment.

SUB-PROCESSES

The specific sub-processes included in the H2R process are:

5.1 Payroll Preparation and Security

5.2 Payroll Payment Controls

5.3 Distribution of Payroll

5.4 Compensation and Benefits

5.5 Hiring and Termination

5.6 Education, Training, and Development

5.7 Contingent Workforce

---

[2]U.S. Department of Health & Human Services, HIPAA Health Information Privacy, "The Security Rule," accessed January 13, 2019, https://www.hhs.gov/hipaa/for-professionals/security/index.html.

5.1 PAYROLL PREPARATION AND SECURITY

Introduction

The payroll process includes the processes involved in preparing payroll checks in a controlled and accurate manner which ensures the accurate accounting for payroll costs, deductions, employee benefits, and other adjustments; distributing checks to employees; and ensuring the confidentiality and physical security of payroll and personnel information.

A payroll master file (database) must be maintained which includes all employees of the company. Procedures must be established to physically secure and protect master file information and ensure that the HIPAA security rule is not violated. Employees must, where required by local laws, submit, on a timely basis, approved time reporting and attendance records before payroll processing is performed. Payroll results must be prepared from the payroll master file and the approved time reporting records.

Standard of Internal Control

5.1.1 **Payroll Master File.** The file must contain all information concerning current pay rates, withholding deductions, tax codes, etc.
Refer to risk: A-1

5.1.2 **Security of Payroll Master File.** Changes should be restricted to properly documented and authorized additions, deletions, and modifications.
Refer to risk: A-2

5.1.3 **Security of Payroll Records.** Access to payroll records must be restricted to authorized personnel to ensure that the HIPAA security rule is not violated.
Refer to risk: A-2

5.1.4 **Employee Termination or Transfer.** The payroll department must be promptly and formally notified of the termination or transfer of any employee or of payroll changes so that payroll records can be promptly adjusted. The payroll department will establish the necessary procedures to facilitate this notification.
Refer to risks: A-3, A-5, A-6

5.1.5 **Approved Time Reporting Records.** The payroll department will establish the necessary procedures to facilitate this notification.
Refer to risks: A-4, A-6, A-7

5.1.6 **Reconciliation of Payroll Earnings Records.** Paychecks, payroll registers, and employee earnings records should be prepared from the same database of information. Where system constraints prohibit the use of the same database, a reconciliation (contents are known and status is current) of the payroll earnings records and the payroll (check) register must be completed.
Refer to risks: A-4, A-5, A-6, A-7

5.1.7 **Controls over Payroll Source Data.** Controls must be maintained, with sufficient edits, to ensure all payroll source data within the employee master is valid and properly input. Controls must also be established to ensure that only current authorized payroll source data is used.
Refer to risks: A-5, A-6, A-7, A-8

5.1.8 **Time Reporting Records.** Department management staff is responsible to ensure time reporting records are authorized. A comparison of actual salary, benefits, and other payments to budgeted costs needs to occur in order to determine reasonableness.
Refer to risk: A-9

5.1.9 **Payroll Withholdings.** Payroll withholdings must be controlled to ensure the propriety of amounts, compliance with applicable governmental requirements, timely remittance to the appropriate entity, and timely reconciliation (contents are known and status is current) to the general ledger accounts.
Refer to risks: A-7, A-10, A-12

5.1.10 **Documentation of Payroll Procedures.** Departmental procedures should be clearly documented for all key payroll functions and cutoff procedures.
Refer to risks: A-5, A-7, A-11, A-12

5.1.11 **Government/Regulatory Requirements.** Annual summaries of employee wages and withholdings must be prepared and mailed directly to all employees in accordance with applicable governmental requirements. In addition, summaries of employee wages must be reconciled (contents are known and status is current) to payments made to the statutory government agencies.
Refer to risk: A-12

5.1.12 **Special Payments.** All other/special payments processed by the payroll department (e.g. relocation, education, bonuses, patent awards, advances, adjustments, etc.) must be properly authorized independent of payroll and human resources, approved, and documented before payment and must be in accordance with applicable tax requirements.
Refer to risk: A-6

5.1.13 **Segregation of Duties.** Payroll preparation responsibilities must be segregated from payroll authorization, the human resource department, check signing, and check distribution responsibilities.
Refer to risk: A-13

5.1.14 **Payroll Expense Distribution.** Payroll expenses must be completely and accurately distributed to the appropriate department or cost center.
Refer to risks: A-5, A-7, A-8

Risk If Standard Is Not Implemented

A-1 Incorrect information in the payroll master file could result in incorrect payments. Withholdings of earned wages may be incorrect and can result in incorrect reporting and violation of the HIPAA security rule.

A-2 Inadequate security over the payroll department and its records may result in:
    a. Destruction or loss of payroll records, including the payroll master file;
    b. Unauthorized review and/or disclosure of confidential payroll information; and/or
    c. The processing of unauthorized changes to the payroll master file. This in turn may result in the following:
        ■ Misappropriation of company assets
        ■ Misstatement of accruals such as pensions

A-3 Employees may be incorrectly paid or paid for services not received, and collection of overpayments to terminated employees may require legal action. Employee withholdings may also be incorrect.

A-4 Employees may be erroneously paid for hours not worked or may not be paid for hours actually worked. Charges to the wrong department may not be detected.

A-5 Management reports and employee earnings records may be inaccurate.

A-6 Unauthorized payments may be made, and funds may be misappropriated.

A-7 Inaccurate information may be input into the general ledger. The financial statements may be misstated.

A-8 The processing of payroll may be incomplete and/or inaccurate. There is an increased opportunity for intentional or unintentional processing errors to go undetected.

A-9 Errors that would not be detected during routine edits (e.g. ineligible or unauthorized employees) may not be detected and corrected.

A-10 Detailed withholdings and payments may not agree to the recorded withholdings and payments.

A-11 Consistent procedures may not be followed, resulting in the incorrect, incomplete, or untimely processing of payroll information and potential errors in earned wages paid to employees.

A-12 Noncompliance and/or calculation errors may result in fines and penalties being assessed by the government.

A-13 Unauthorized transactions may be processed and remain undetected, resulting in the misappropriation or temporary diversion of assets.

 ## 5.2 PAYROLL PAYMENT CONTROLS

Introduction

There are several important components of the payroll process. The processing of an employee's earned pay from gross to net amount must be done in a strict yet varying regulatory environment. The environment varies because the process is controlled by several entities on both the federal and state levels. A controller and business process owner must be aware of the regulations which must be followed to ensure compliance that will prevent audit exceptions potentially resulting in penalties, fines, and interest.

Some of the process such as determining gross pay is regulated by either the Federal Department of Labor (DoL) or the state's equivalent, depending on which one favors the employee, while others such as when an employee must be paid are governed strictly on the state level. Still other processes such as determining taxable gross wages are controlled by the Internal Revenue Service (IRS). The employer is responsible for determining the correct regulation to follow for each process and the controller is responsible for ensuring the appropriate payroll controls are in place.

Payroll includes the processes involved in preparing payroll payments in a controlled and accurate manner, which ensures accurate accounting for payroll costs, deductions, employee benefits, and other adjustments; distributing checks, initiating direct deposits, or issuing prepaid cards to employees; and ensuring the confidentiality and physical security of payroll and personnel information.

Standard of Internal Control

5.2.1 **Payment Bank Accounts.** For payroll payments, management should consider using an impress or zero balance bank account where available.
Refer to risk: B-1

5.2.2 **Account Reconciliations.** All payroll bank accounts and general ledger payment accounts must be reconciled (contents are known and status is current) on a monthly basis.
Refer to risk: B-1

5.2.3 **Payroll Payments.** All payroll payments must be traceable and uniquely identifiable.
Refer to risks: B-2, B-3, B-7

5.2.4 **Security of Blank Payroll Checks.** Blank check stock used, identifying the company or its financial institutions, must be safeguarded. All payroll checks must be periodically accounted for as being issued, voided, or unused.
Refer to risk: B-3

5.2.5 **Voided Check Procedures.** Spoiled, voided, and/or canceled checks must be accounted for and destroyed or clearly stamped void.
Refer to risk: B-3

5.2.6 **Security of Payroll Checks.** Company approved (signed) payroll checks and direct deposit advices must be secured until distributed to employees.
Refer to risks: B-4, B-5

5.2.7 **Segregation of Duties.** Payroll check signatories must be individuals having no payroll authorization or preparation responsibilities, access to the unused checks, or check distribution responsibilities.
Refer to risks: B-3, B-4

5.2.8 **Approval of Payroll Records.** Completed payroll registers, journal reports, and requests for payroll account reimbursement (or similar documents to support the amounts being paid) must be reviewed and approved by appropriate management in a timely manner.
Refer to risk: B-6

5.2.9 **Issuance of Payroll Checks.** Formal authorization procedures must be established and adhered to in the signing of payroll checks.
Refer to risk: B-3

5.2.10 **Custody and Security of Check-Signing Equipment.** Where check-signing equipment and facsimile signature plates or digitized signature images are utilized, the equipment and plates must be secured, and custody of the check-signing equipment and the signature plates or digitized signature image files must be segregated. In addition, a reconciliation (contents are known and status is current) should be made of checks written and checks authorized to the check-signing machine totals.
Refer to risks: B-2, B-3

Risk If Standard Is Not Implemented

B-1 Errors and omissions in the safeguarding, authorization, and processing of checks may not be detected and corrected. The financial statements may be misstated.

B-2 Checks may be issued which have not been recorded, resulting in incorrect financial statements.

B-3 Unauthorized use or issuance of payroll checks may occur, and any misappropriation of cash may go undetected.

B-4 Checks may be diverted and cashed by unauthorized persons.

B-5 Confidential payroll information may be reviewed and/or disclosed by unauthorized persons to the detriment of the company or its employees.

B-6 Significant payroll errors or unauthorized transactions may not be detected prior to payroll distribution.

B-7 Duplicate check numbers may be assigned or check numbers may be omitted.

5.3 DISTRIBUTION OF PAYROLL

Introduction

This section provides the standards required for the distribution of payroll, unclaimed wages, and non-wage payments.

Standard of Internal Control

5.3.1 **Segregation of Duties.** Persons responsible for the distribution of payroll checks must not approve labor hours, time cards, or special payments.
Refer to risk: C-1

5.3.2 **Payroll Check Distribution.** Within each facility, signed receipts must be obtained from individuals who receive payroll checks/advices for distribution.
Refer to risk: C-2

5.3.3 **Unclaimed Wages.** Unclaimed wages not disbursed in a reasonable timeframe, and after a reasonable attempt to redirect funds to employees, are to be returned to the company. Unclaimed wages must be remitted to the appropriate government authorities when required by law. Payments of unclaimed wages should be made only upon proper employee identification.
Refer to risk: C-4

5.3.4 **Non-Wage Payments.** Payments processed by the payroll department that are not related to wages earned (e.g. special recognition) must be included in the regular paycheck or direct deposit and distributed following normal distribution channels.
Refer to risk: C-3

Risk If Standard Is Not Implemented

C-1 Funds may be misappropriated as improper changes/additions could be made to the master file or incorrect hours may be submitted for payment.

C-2 An audit trail is not created to assess responsibility for lost or diverted checks.

C-3 Distribution may be made to unauthorized employees and remain undetected.

C-4 Misappropriation of the unclaimed checks, loss of checks, irreconcilable bank statements, and/or noncompliance with government regulations could result.

5.4 COMPENSATION AND BENEFITS

Introduction

Human resources (HR) management must establish and maintain policies and guidelines for the hiring, promotion, compensation, transfer, relocation, and termination of employees. Designated HR management must be responsible for the administration of the employee benefit plans. The plans must be administered in accordance with corporate policy and defined plan procedures.

Standard of Internal Control

5.4.1 **Human Resource Policies.** The policies and guidelines should be clearly defined by HR management in the form of specific criteria and procedures.
Refer to risks: D-2, D-3, D-4, D-10, D-11, D-12

5.4.2 **Employee Benefits.** Policies for major employee benefits, such as profit sharing, pension, vacations, and insurance, must be reviewed and approved by management. Rules, criteria, procedures, etc. for all benefits must be documented and approved by HR management and secured under the HIPAA security rule.
Refer to risks: D-2, D-3, D-4, D-10, D-11, D-12

5.4.3 **Compensation.** Compensation (base pay, variable pay, sales commissions, recognition awards, etc.) to employees should be made at appropriate authorized rates and in the proper job classifications for the services rendered. Department management must properly authorize changes to compensation.
Refer to risks: D-2, D-4, D-10, D-11, D-12

5.4.4 **Records Management.** All compensation and benefit records must be properly and accurately maintained by HR and company management in accordance with corporate employee plans. HR documentation should, at a minimum, include properly executed employment data, authorized classification, and pay rates.
Refer to risk: D-4

5.4.5 **Authorized Transactions.** Formal procedures, along with correctly authorized documentation, must be maintained to ensure that only authorized additions, deletions, or changes to employee information are allowed. Procedures must be in place to ensure key payroll elements agree

with HR documentation. The payroll department must be promptly notified of additions, deletions, or changes to employee information.
Refer to risks: D-2, D-4, D-5, D-6, D-7

5.4.6 **Administration of Employee Benefit Plans.** Benefit payments to employees must be made in accordance with the terms and conditions of the plans and must be adequately documented and properly approved.
Refer to risks: D-2, D-3, D-4, D-6

5.4.7 **Segregation of Duties.** HR responsibilities, including payroll authorization (such as adding and terminating an employee, changing pay rates, and changing the master payroll data), must be segregated from payroll processing, distribution, and recording responsibilities.
Refer to risk: D-8

5.4.8 **Confidentiality.** Confidentiality of payroll and human resource information should be maintained and restricted to authorized personnel to ensure that HIPAA security rules are adhered to.
Refer to risk: D-9

Risk If Standard Is Not Implemented

D-1 Individuals may be employed who do not meet company's hiring criteria, resulting in an inadequate workforce in terms of numbers and/or quality.

D-2 Incorrect payment amounts may subsequently be disbursed to employees.

D-3 Accruals for benefits, such as profit sharing, pension, vacation, and insurance, may be incorrectly calculated, resulting in misstated liabilities.

D-4 Laws and governmental regulations may be violated, resulting in fines, penalties, lawsuits, or contingent liabilities.

D-5 Payroll payments and payroll tax accounts may be misstated.

D-6 Unauthorized transactions may be processed, resulting in improper payments and/or payments to fictitious employees.

D-7 Improper payments may not be detected and corrected.

D-8 Unauthorized transactions may be processed and remain undetected, resulting in the misappropriation or temporary diversion of funds.

D-9 Human resource records are not subject to proper security procedures and confidential information may be accessed and/or disclosed to the detriment of the company and its employees and be in violation of the HIPAA security rule.

D-10 Compensation and benefits are less than that offered by comparable companies.

D-11 Employees may not feel their efforts are noticed or appreciated.

D-12 Employee turnover rate is higher than optimal.

 ## 5.5 HIRING AND TERMINATION

Introduction

Before employees are hired, HR and staffing groups along with the potential employee's departmental supervisor must ensure that the specific criteria are established.

Standard of Internal Control

5.5.1 **Employee Hiring Procedures.** Before employees are hired, HR/staffing groups along with the potential employee's departmental supervisor must ensure that the following criteria are met:

  a. Appropriate candidate identification, screening, and hiring practices are documented and maintained.

  b. The skill requirements for the position identified are defined and documented.

  c. Reasonable attempts are made to investigate and review internal candidates; however, both internal and external recruiting will begin at the same time.

  d. Adequate job descriptions with skill requirements and hiring criteria are identified and can be used to measure and compare candidates' qualifications.

  e. Staffing plan requirements are developed and reviewed as part of the ongoing business planning process. This will be done on a yearly basis or as business dictates.

  f. New employees receive an employee orientation and are exposed to an onboarding process.

  Refer to risks: E-1, E-2, E-3

5.5.2 **Employee Termination/Resignation Procedures.** Upon notification of an employee's termination or resignation, the employee's supervisor notifies Human Resources and together they must ensure:

  a. All outstanding cash advances and expense statements have been completed and cleared.

b. All company credit cards (e.g. American Express, telephone cards, procurement cards, air travel cards) have been returned and cut up.

c. Notification is made to the Information Services group to have all computer and telephone accounts canceled.

d. All company property (such as computers, etc.), proprietary information, employee badges, and security passes or keys have been returned.

e. Third-party vendors are notified to eliminate any authority to conduct company business (e.g. authority to sign checks, contracts) by terminating employee.

f. An exit interview is conducted by the HR department to ensure all final business is taken care of and there is an understanding of the reason for departure if the termination is voluntary.

Refer to risks: E-4, E-5, E-6

5.5.3 **Labor Arrangements.** It is important to continually be aware of the morale of employees and their work arrangements to identify any hostile work situations. Reasonable steps should be taken to avoid work disputes and potential issues involving applicable union or labor councils.

Refer to risk: E-7

Risk If Standard Is Not Implemented

E-1 Individuals may be employed who do not meet the company's hiring criteria, resulting in an inadequate workforce in terms of numbers and/ or quality.

E-2 The company cannot accurately account for the applicants or reflect applicants against specific staffing requirements.

E-3 The company may be unaware of its future staffing needs and is unable to meet business objectives.

E-4 Outstanding advances or employee receivables may be uncollectible.

E-5 Unauthorized charges may be incurred subsequent to termination of employment for which the company may become liable.

E-6 Unnecessary computer or telephone charges may be incurred and access to company information by ex-employees may not be adequately restricted.

E-7 The company may not have the resources available to complete critical projects and meet deadlines.

5.6 EDUCATION, TRAINING, AND DEVELOPMENT

Introduction

HR management must establish and maintain policies and guidelines for developing employees to ensure job satisfaction, risk is mitigated, and value is provided to the company.

Standard of Internal Control

5.6.1 **Policies and Procedures.** It is the responsibility of Human Resources, the employee, and their management to adhere to the guidelines.
Refer to risk: F-1

5.6.2 **Monitoring.** Performance of development requirements and programs should be monitored and evaluated on a periodic basis. Findings that may indicate knowledge, skill, or capability deficiencies should be evaluated and addressed by HR management and the employee's organizational management.
Refer to risk: F-1

5.6.3 **Communication.** Development opportunities that are provided internally should be communicated to employees. Training/HR development professionals should gather input and ideas from management, supervisors, and employees to identify development needs.
Refer to risk: F-1

5.6.4 **Evaluations.** Annually, the completion of development plans with ongoing performance feedback needs to be created and communicated with the employee.
Refer to risk: F-1

Risk If Standard Is Not Implemented

F-1 Employees may not have adequate capabilities to perform their responsibilities.

 ## 5.7 CONTINGENT WORKFORCE

Introduction

HR must establish and maintain policies and guidelines for the hiring and tenure of temporary and contract workers, such as agency temporaries and contractors, consultants, individual contractors, and third-party service providers.

Standard of Internal Control

5.7.1 **Contingent Workforce Policies.** The policies and guidelines should be clearly defined by contingent workforce management in the form of specific criteria and procedures.
Refer to risk: G-1

5.7.2 **Contingent Workforce Policies and Guidelines Compliance.** Compliance with contingent workforce policies and guidelines is the responsibility of each business entity.
Refer to risks: G-1, G-2

5.7.3 **Contingent Workforce Program Management.** The contingent workforce organization must ensure that programs are established to meet the business requirements for contingent labor. Such programs should ensure that:
   a. The appropriate candidate identification and screening practices are maintained.
   b. Temporary labor is obtained only through the approved contingent workforce program.
   c. Standardized job profiles are established defining the roles and responsibilities of the position to identify appropriate billing rates and to determine if the work is exempt or nonexempt regarding payment of overtime.
Refer to risks: G-1, G-2, G-3

5.7.4 **Performance Management of Vendors.** The contingent workforce organization is responsible for insuring all performance measurements are established and monitored for all vendors used to acquire contingent workers. The measurements should include specific criteria, metrics, and service level agreement (SLA) criteria. The vendors should be monitored on a monthly basis to ensure compliance with contracts and performance agreements.
Refer to risks: G-1, G-2, G-3

5.7.5 **Authorized Transactions.** Hiring managers or business entities must maintain formal procedures, along with correctly authorized documentation, to ensure that only authorized payments are made for contingent workers.
Refer to risk: G-3

Risk If Standard Is Not Implemented

G-1 Laws and governmental regulations may be violated, resulting in fines, penalties, lawsuits, or contingent liabilities.

G-2 Individuals may be obtained who do not meet the company's pre-screening criteria, resulting in an inadequate workforce in terms of quality and risk to the company. Improper payments may not be detected and corrected.

G-3 Unauthorized transactions may be processed, resulting in improper payments and/or payments to fictitious workers.

CHAPTER SIX

The Supply Chain Process

 INTRODUCTION

The supply chain process includes the processes for planning, manufacturing, and warehousing product in anticipation of shipping it to a customer. This section covers functions traditionally performed by business units, manufacturing plants and distribution units (e.g. finished goods warehouses and international marketing houses). The process begins with the establishment of a sales and operations plan, includes the proper recording and understanding of manufacturing costs, and concludes with the management of finished goods inventory. Refer to the process flow included below.

The supply chain process can be complicated due to a combination of factors such as:

- Fluctuating demand requirements
- Vendor lead time and capacity constraints
- The need for flexibility while minimizing unit manufacturing costs and inventories

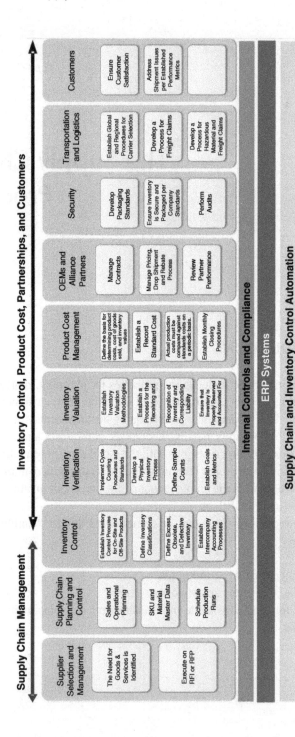

PROCESS OVERVIEW

The diagram below suggests that the foundational elements for the supply chain process are Internal Controls and Compliance, ERP Systems, and Supply Chain and Inventory Control Automation Solutions.

 ## METRICS

Table of Metrics

- **Perfect Order Measurement**—The percentage of orders that are error-free. Perfect Orders = ((Total Orders – Error Orders) / Total Orders) * 100.

- **Cash-to-Cash Cycle Time**—The number of days between paying for materials and getting paid for product. Cash-to-Cash Cycle Time = Materials Payment Date – Customer Order Payment Date.

- **Customer Order Cycle Time**—Measures how long it takes to deliver a customer order after the purchase order (PO) is received. Customer Order Cycle Time = Actual Delivery Date – Purchase Order Creation Date.

- **Fill Rate**—The percentage of a customer's order that is filled on the first shipment. This can be represented as the percentage of items, SKUs, or order value that is included with the first shipment.

- **Supply Chain Cycle Time**—Supply chain cycle time indicates the overall efficiency of the supply chain. Short cycles make for a more efficient and agile supply chain. Analysis of this critical metric can help recognize pain points or competitive advantages.

- **Inventory Days of Supply**—The number of days it would take to run out of supply if it was not replenished. Inventory Days of Supply = Inventory on Hand / Average Daily Usage.

- **Freight Bill Accuracy**—The percentage of freight bills that are error-free: (Error-Free Freight Bills / Total Freight Bills) * 100.

- **Freight Cost per Unit**—Usually measured as the cost of freight per item or SKU. Freight Cost per Unit = Total Freight Cost / Number of Items

- **Inventory Turnover**—The number of times that a company's inventory cycles per year. Inventory Turnover = Cost of Goods Sold / Average Inventory.

- **Average Payment Period for Production Materials**—The average time from receipt of materials and payment for those materials. Average Payment Period for Production Materials = (Materials Payables/Total Cost of Materials) * Days in Period

- **On-Time Shipping Rate**—The percentage of items, SKUs, or order value that arrives on or before the requested ship date. The on-time shipping metrics is used in determining customer satisfaction. A high rate indicates an efficient supply chain. On-Time Shipping Rate = (Number of On-Time Items / Total Items) * 100

Table of Metrics

- **Inventory Turnover Ratio (ITR)**—ITR helps us to measure the number of times we sell or turn our average inventory kept in the warehouse. It measures the number of opportunities to earn profit that we experience each year from our working capital invested in the inventory. It is calculated by dividing Cost of Goods Sold (COGS) by the average inventory investment.
- **Turn-Earn Index (TEI)**—TEI helps us to combine the gross margin and turnover.
- **Gross Margin Return on Investment (GMROI)**—GMROI represents the amount of gross profit earned for every AED (or $, £, €, £) of the average investment made in inventory. It is calculated by dividing gross profit by the average inventory investment.
- **Days of Supply (DoS)**—DoS is the most common KPI used by managers in measuring supply chain efficiency. It is calculated by dividing the average inventory on hand (as value) by the average monthly demand (as value) and then multiplying it by 30, when measuring on a monthly basis.
- **Inventory Velocity (IV)**—IV is the percentage of inventory we are projecting to be consumed within the next period. It helps managers to understand how well the inventory on hand matches demand. It is calculated by dividing the opening stock by the sales forecast of the following period.

 ## APPLICATION OF INTERNAL CONTROLS

In management's selection of procedures and techniques of control, the degree of control implemented is a matter of reasonable business judgment. The common guideline used in determining the degree of internal controls implementation is that the cost of a control should not exceed the benefit derived. However, there is a minimum set of controls that should exist in a normal business environment. The internal control standards listed here represent the minimum controls to be implemented within the supply chain process.

 ## SUB-PROCESSES

The specific functions or activities covered by the process include:

6.1 Planning and Control

6.2 Inventory Control

6.1 PLANNING AND CONTROL

Introduction

Effective planning and control enables all operating units within the supply chain to manage operational complexities and achieve the objective of delivering the right product at the right time and the right cost.

Standard of Internal Control

6.1.1 **Documented Policies and Procedures.** Documented policies and procedures defining the roles and responsibilities of all functions must exist and be reviewed at least annually. A formal process must be used to identify problems and improvement opportunities and to implement solutions and improvements.
Refer to risk: A-1

6.1.2 **Sales and Operations Planning.** Sales (or demand) forecasts must be prepared and approved through a formal sales and operations planning process. These forecasts must be at a meaningful level to allow for production and inventory planning, development of production schedules, detailed material and labor requirements, and financial planning in accordance with company requirements. Changes in the formal plan must be approved through the sales and operations planning process by the appropriate level of management.
Refer to risks: A-2, A-4

6.1.3 **Scheduled Orders and Production Runs.** Products must be manufactured or ordered according to a schedule (e.g., a master schedule) or a material requirements plan developed from the approved sales

(or demand) and operations plan. The schedule or material requirements plan must be achievable based on available labor, materials, and capacity.
Refer to risk: A-2

6.1.4 **Material Master Data.** Formal master data change control procedures must exist and be followed. All product and item or material master data must be reviewed at least annually and updated. Bills of material and routings must be established and updated to reflect current product specifications and manufacturing processes.
Refer to risks: A-2, A-3

6.1.5 **Scrap/Waste.** Operating and financial management must establish procedures and approval limits for the disposal of scrap/waste. Scrap/waste must be accumulated, safeguarded, monitored, and reported on a timely basis to the financial organization and operating management. Scrap/waste must be reprocessed or disposed of by persons independent of custodial responsibilities on a timely basis. Disposal of scrap/waste to non-company entities should be done through competitive bidding.
Refer to risks: A-3, A-4, A-5

6.1.6 **Allocation Model.** Profitability analysis, channel demand forecasting, and the global management of inventory must be integrated into the product allocation decisions of managers.
Refer to risks: A-1, A-4

Risk If Standard Is Not Implemented

A-1 Company resources may not be used efficiently or effectively, resulting in excessive cost and/or inability of the manufacturing unit to achieve its business objectives.

A-2 The ability to deliver against the agreed-upon production plan may be adversely impacted or achieved at excessive cost. Unauthorized products or quantities in excess of acceptable levels may be produced. Inadequate supply of components or parts inventories could result in interruption of production. The plant capacity may be underutilized or inadequate to meet specified customer requirements or service levels. Labor may be used in an inefficient manner impacting cost of goods sold.

A-3 Errors and omissions in transaction processing or poor physical safeguarding practices may result in inventory which is lost, stolen, destroyed, or temporarily diverted. Incorrect production may be reported which hides waste, shortages, or thefts.

A-4 Critical decisions may be based upon financial statements, records, or manufacturing reports which are inaccurate.

A-5 Scrap sales may be recorded incorrectly or not at all, sold at an inappropriate price, or sold to an unacceptable credit risk.

 ## 6.2 INVENTORY CONTROL

Introduction

Effective inventory controls within the supply chain are necessary to ensure (i) inventory levels are appropriate, (ii) inventory is safeguarded from theft and damage, and (iii) inventory is properly valued. The inventory control function must establish a formal plan to control all aspects of the inventory.

The receipt and transfer of inventory into, within, and out of a company facility must be made only upon the receipt of and in compliance with a properly authorized transaction (paper or electronic), which is used to update the inventory records in a timely manner.

Standard of Internal Control

6.2.1 **Segregation of Duties.** The inventory control process must have the following segregation of duties:
  a. Segregation of manufacturing and custodial responsibilities from accounting activities
  b. Segregation of the supervision and verification of the physical existence of inventory from the performance of the actual count
  Refer to risk: B-1

6.2.2 **Receipts and Issuing Inventory.** Monthly cutoff procedures must be established, documented, and coordinated with the financial organization to ensure all receipts and payments of inventory are properly recorded. Follow-up investigation and corrective action must be taken in a timely manner on any differences between reported deliveries and receipts.
  Refer to risks: B-1, B-2

6.2.3 **In-Transit Inventory.** Inventory in-transit between organizations must be reconciled (contents are known and status is current) and aged according to local written policies and procedures. Reconciling items and items in dispute must be resolved according to the guidelines

set by local written policies and procedures after expected delivery. It is assumed the unit sending the inventory will have the correct balance unless the receiving unit can demonstrate it was a shipping error.
Refer to risks: B-1, B-2

6.2.4 **Product Returns.** Returned product should be received against a notice of the return from a customer or distribution and must be entered into inventory records. Cost of goods manufactured (e.g., product bill) or inter-divisional billings must reflect adjustments for returned inventory. Returned product must be kept segregated from regular inventory unless returned to stock immediately. Disposition or restocking of all other returns (return to stock, remanufacture, or scrap) should be made within a reasonable amount of time.
Refer to risks: B-1, B-2, B-3

6.2.5 **Existence and Maintenance of Inventory Records.** Inventory records must be maintained to safeguard inventory and provide current information on inventory quantities available. On a periodic basis (at least annually), the quantities in the inventory records must be reconciled (contents are known and status is current) with the physical quantities through either cycle counting or physical inventories. Required adjustments must be made to the physical and financial inventory records on a timely basis to reflect actual quantities. Follow-up investigation and corrective action must be taken in a timely fashion on any differences.
Refer to risks: B-1, B-2

6.2.6 **Inventory Access Safeguards.** Inventory must be safeguarded from unauthorized access by the establishment of physical, system access or other compensating controls.
Refer to risks: B-1, B-2, B-4

6.2.7 **Protection of Inventory from Deterioration and Damage.** Inventory must be protected against physical deterioration and damage.
Refer to risks: B-1, B-4, B-5

6.2.8 **Off-site Inventory.** Company inventory stored or processed at offsite locations (e.g., non-company distribution, supplier, or vendor facilities or in the possession of sales, engineering, or other personnel, etc.) is subject to the same standards of internal control as any other inventory. Inventory quantities at offsite locations must be reconciled (contents are known and status is current) quarterly to statements provided by the custodian. All unexplained negative inventory variances must be

reported to company immediately. Follow-up investigation and corrective action must be taken in a timely fashion on any differences.
Refer to risks: B-1, B-2

6.2.9 **Supplier-Owned Consignment Inventory Located at the Company.** Supplier-owned inventory on consignment at company facilities is subject to the same standards of internal control as any other inventory. Inventory on consignment must be identified and reconciled (contents are known and status is current) with supplier records on a quarterly basis with follow-up investigation and corrective action taken in a timely fashion on any differences. Supplier-owned consignment inventory must be excluded from company's financial records and should *not* be reported to the corporate risk management/insurance department for inclusion in insurable asset calculations, as it is the owner's responsibility to insure the inventory.
Refer to risks: B-1, B-2, B-4

6.2.10 **Excess, Obsolete, and Defective Inventory.** On a periodic basis, management must review inventory. Inventory specifically identified as excess, obsolete, or defective must be disposed of by sale, scrap, returns to the vendor, or other suitable means in a prompt and timely manner. Inventory identified as potentially excess and obsolete must be reserved for in compliance with the company's inventory policy.
Refer to risks: B-2, B-3

6.2.11 **Information for the Elimination of Intercompany Profit in Inventory.** Inventory received from other company locations must be recorded by source and monitored to provide necessary support for the periodic elimination of intercompany profit.
Refer to risk: B-2

Risk If Standard Is Not Implemented

B-1 Errors and omissions in authorization and transaction processing or poor physical safeguarding practices may result in inventory which is lost, stolen, destroyed, or temporarily diverted. Theft of inventory may go undetected.

B-2 Critical decisions may be based upon financial statements, records, or manufacturing reports which are inaccurate. Inaccurate information may result in excessive inventory levels if unnecessary inventory is ordered or produced. Conversely, unexpected shortages could interrupt production and result in an inability to deliver products to customers.

B-3 Scrap or returns may be stolen. Scrap may be sold at an inappropriate price or to an unacceptable credit risk.

B-4 The company may be unnecessarily exposed to financial loss from damage to inventory and inability to meet future customer demand.

B-5 The quality of items transferred or shipped may be unacceptable, resulting in excessive returns or rework and customer dissatisfaction.

6.3 INVENTORY VERIFICATION

Introduction

Verification of inventories, whether accomplished through complete physical inventory verification procedures, process counting, or statistical sampling, is necessary to ensure accurate reporting of inventories for financial as well as operational purposes. Units are allowed to use cycle counting in place of annual physical inventories if they have documented and implemented process counting policies and procedures which meet the minimum corporate requirements. The following procedures must be adopted in performing, valuing, and reconciling the inventory counts with inventory records.

Standard of Internal Control

6.3.1 **Physical Inventory Procedures.** Where perpetual inventory records are not verified through cycle counting or statistical sampling procedures, the existence of inventory must be verified through an annual physical inventory conducted with appropriate procedures as stated in the authorized corporate policy to ensure the accuracy of the count.
Refer to risks: C-1, C-2, C-3, C-5

6.3.2 **Process Counting Procedures.** Where cycle counting is required, procedures must meet the minimum requirements specified in corporate policy.
Refer to risks: C-2, C-3, C-5

6.3.3 **Statistical Sampling Procedures.** Statistical sampling procedures must be approved by the company controller prior to implementation.
Refer to risks: C-2, C-3, C-5

6.3.4 **General Ledger Reconciliation.** Results from physical inventory verification procedures must be reconciled (contents are known and status is current) with the financial inventory records. The appropriate adjust-ments must be documented, approved, and made according to policies and procedures. In turn, these records must be reconciled to the gen-eral ledger.

Refer to risks: C-3, C-4, C-5

6.3.5 **Investigation, Reporting of Variances.** Significant inventory dis-crepancies must be investigated and reported to operating and financial management and corporate EHS&S. Corrective actions should be taken to eliminate the root causes of inventory discrepancies.

Refer to risks: C-4, C-5

Risk If Standard Is Not Implemented

C-1 Inventory may be improperly valued due to inadequate cutoffs or inaccu-rate compilations.

C-2 Inventory may be inaccurately counted. Counts may be improperly re-corded or omitted. Potential for errors and irregularities is substantially increased.

C-3 Incorrect toolkit-to-physical adjustments could result in inaccurate inventory valuations and misstatements in operating income.

C-4 If review procedures are inadequate, appropriate corrective actions for inventory management and recording may not be initiated in a timely manner.

C-5 Customer service may be negatively impacted if physical inventories do not match accounting and product handling records.

6.4 INVENTORY VALUATION

Introduction

Inventory must be valued using the company's valuation process consistently, for example, lower of cost (i.e. full acquisition cost plus any import, transporta-tion, etc., or manufactured cost) or market (i.e. net realizable value). Inventory reserves (e.g. shrinkage, excess, obsolete, write-down to net realizable value, etc.) must be established by operating and financial management in accor-dance with corporate policy.

Standard of Internal Control

6.4.1 **Receiving—Recognition of Inventory and Corresponding Liability.** Inventory and the corresponding liability must be recorded in the accounting records upon legal transfer of title. An estimate of known inventory in-transit for which title has legally transferred to company must be completed and required adjustments to inventory balances made monthly.
Refer to risk: D-1

6.4.2 **Inventory Valuation.** As an example, inventory must be valued at the lower of cost (i.e., full acquisition cost plus any import, transportation, etc., or manufactured cost) or market (i.e. net realizable value).
Refer to risk: D-1

6.4.3 **Inventory Reserves.** The reserves must be reviewed for adequacy and reasonableness according to corporate policy and adjusted accordingly.
Refer to risk: D-1

Risk If Standard Is Not Implemented

D-1 Individual product costs, total cost of goods manufactured (e.g., product bill), and inventories may be misstated in financial statements, records, and manufacturing reports. Critical decisions on product pricing, product line investment or discontinuance, and factory sourcing and loading may be based upon inaccurate information.

 6.5 PRODUCT COST MANAGEMENT

Introduction

The cost accounting function provides the basis for determining product costs, cost of goods sold, and inventory values in financial statements and other management reports. When functioning properly, it aids management in making decisions and developing plans and strategies for manufacturing and service delivery.

All ledger accounts, which are used in the manufacturing unit's cost accounting function, must be identified, and the basis for making entries into and between ledger accounts, including system feeds and manual transactions, should be clearly described.

Standard of Internal Control

6.5.1 **Documented Cost Accounting Procedures.** Documented cost accounting procedures must exist and describe, at a minimum, the methodologies used to determine product costs, total cost of goods manufactured (e.g., product bill), and inventory values.
Refer to risks: E-1, E-2

6.5.2 **Cost Accounting System.** A cost accounting system must be maintained which accurately accumulates and identifies manufacturing costs in an appropriate manner (e.g. by cost center or product) and provides adequate information to analyze standard and actual manufacturing costs and variances.
Refer to risk: E-1

6.5.3 **Annual Establishment of Item-Level Standard Costs.** Accurate item-level standard costs must be established or revised in accordance with established policies and procedures through the joint efforts of supply chain. Manufacturing management is responsible for the accuracy and approval of standard costs and must ensure standard costs are developed for all items in the item master or planned for production and is based on information in the relevant company database.
Refer to risk: E-1

6.5.4 **Bills of Material (BOM).** A single identifiable bill of material used for manufacturing, planning, purchasing, and costing must exist for each manufactured product or subassembly. Site BOMs are extensions from corporate and engineering BOMs and can be different from site to site. It is Engineering's responsibility to make changes with input from the operating unit and site product cost analysts.
Refer to risks: E-1, E-3, E-4

6.5.5 **Material and Labor Transactions.** Issues of material and labor into production and receipts of items out of production must be controlled by appropriate transaction accountability. Monthly cutoff procedures must be coordinated with the financial organization.
Refer to risks: E-1, E-2, E-4

6.5.6 **Labor and Overhead Distribution.** Labor and overhead costs must be completely distributed to products on a rational and consistent basis. Such activity drivers as current operational conditions, production rates, and capacity utilization must support cost distributions. Significant changes in allocation methodologies must be reviewed and approved by the appropriate level of operating and financial management.
Refer to risks: E-1, E-3

6.5.7 **Variance Analysis and Disposition.** Actual production costs must be compared against standard costs on a periodic basis. All variances must be reported to management and significant variances must be investigated with appropriate action taken in a timely manner. Variances must be allocated to cost of goods sold and inventory in a way that reflects the proportion of sales quantities to inventory levels.
Refer to risks: E-1, E-3

6.5.8 **Receipts and Issues of Inventory.** Receipts and inventory issued must be identified, accurately costed, and accounted for in a timely manner.
Refer to risks: E-1, E-2, E-4

6.5.9 **Monthly Closing Procedures.** Costs incurred by the manufacturing unit must be fully and accurately distributed to inventory, cost of goods sold, or approved special accounts (special items of cost, research & development, etc.) on a regular (monthly) basis. To facilitate this, consistent, documented monthly closing procedures must be developed in conjunction with operational and financial management to ensure proper cutoffs in manufacturing, systems, and financial processes. General ledger account balances must be reconciled (contents are known and status is current) monthly to support item-level detail; significant adjustments must be approved by the appropriate level of financial and operational management.
Refer to risk: E-1

Risk If Standard Is Not Implemented

E-1 Individual product costs, total cost of goods manufactured (e.g., product bill), and inventories may be misstated in financial statements, records, and manufacturing reports. Critical decisions on product pricing, product line investment or discontinuance, and factory sourcing and loading may be based upon inaccurate information.

E-2 Potential for errors and irregularities is substantially increased. Inventory may also be lost, stolen, destroyed, or temporarily diverted.

E-3 If review procedures are inadequate, appropriate corrective actions to production plans and strategies may not be initiated in a timely manner.

E-4 Operations may be adversely impacted. Incorrect amounts of materials and supplies may be issued to production or unauthorized quantities of products may be produced.

6.6 ORIGINAL EQUIPMENT MANUFACTURERS (OEMs)/ALLIANCE PARTNERS

Introduction

All appropriate personnel must review OEM/Alliance Partner contracts to ensure there are no unfavorable terms and conditions, all aspects affecting processes are understood, and payment terms do not include items outside the contract.

Standard of Internal Control

6.6.1 **Contract Administration.** The following standards of internal control should be in place:
  a. OEM/Alliance Contracts must be approved by a person with proper Delegation of Authority (DoA). Contract total value should be calculated by multiplying the annual value of contract times the duration of contract.
  b. Legal should review and approve all contracts with OEM/Alliance Partners.
  c. The right to audit clauses should be included in the contracts; Internal Audit department should review and approve the audit clause.
  d. All changes to the original contract (e.g. pricing, delivery, etc.) should have a sequentially numbered corresponding addendum. All changes should be communicated to appropriate personnel.
  e. Metrics detailing delivery, quality, pricing and financial performance measurements should be developed, monitored, and discussed with the alliance partner periodically (e.g. percentage of on-time deliveries). Contract compliance with metrics and terms and conditions should be validated periodically.
  Refer to risks: F-1, F-2, F-3, and F-4

6.6.2 **Pricing.** The OEM/Alliance Partner and company must agree on pricing prior to the completion and shipment of goods. To ensure correct pricing is always used:
  a. Current price records must be stored and maintained.
  b. Prior to payment for goods, the company must match the OEM's invoice price against the contract price.
  c. PO audits which determine the final price paid to OEMs shall be finalized in a timely manner according to written policies and procedures.
  Refer to Risks: F-3, F-4, F-5

6.6.3 **Non-price impacts.** Warranties, rework, freight, expediting costs, tooling, etc. that do not directly adjust the list price must be approved by personnel with appropriate DOA prior to remitting payment.
Refer to risks: F-3, F-4

6.6.4 **Rebates.** A rebate process should be implemented and followed that allows all rebates to be identified and collected on a timely basis. The process should include metrics and ownership of specific processes.
Refer to risk: F-4

6.6.5 **Drop Shipments.** All drop shipments related to critical components should be properly accounted for, such as:
a. Drop shipments (from external suppliers and from the company) should be recorded, with appropriate quantity and line item information.
b. The company should create a debit memo for the appropriate price and quantity to OEM for each drop shipment. The debit memos should be applied to the OEM's accounts payable within the contract period.
c. Drop shipments must be reconciled (contents are known and status is current) on a periodic basis according to policies and procedures.
Refer to risks: F-3, F-4

6.6.6 **Reconciliations.** The following reconciliations should be performed on a periodic basis:
a. The company accounts payable to the OEM accounts receivable; any variances should be resolved according to applicable policies and procedures.
b. All OEM business transactions should be reconciled according to policies and procedures.
Refer to risks: F-3, F-4, F-5

Risk If Standard Is Not Implemented

F-1 The company could enter into a contract that is not in the best interest of the corporation. Unfavorable terms or conditions could exist.

F-2 Appropriate personnel may not understand all aspects of the current contract that affect their processes.

F-3 Financial disadvantages could be incurred by the company.

F-4 The company could overpay or underpay for goods and services. The company could pay for items outside the contract terms.

F-5 Financial statements could be misstated.

6.7 SUPPLY CHAIN SECURITY

Introduction

All transportation and logistics supplier facilities and operations must be in compliance with the company's freight or logistics supplier's minimum security requirements. All company raw materials and finished products need to be packaged and palletized so as to deter theft. Product packaging should be sturdy and not identify the part/product in any way.

Standard of Internal Control

6.7.1 **Contracts.** All contracts with transportation and logistics suppliers should include the company's freight or logistics supplier's minimum security requirements. Exceptions to the security requirements can only be granted by corporate security.
Refer to risks: G-1, G-2, G-3, G-4, G-5

6.7.2 **Supplier Operations.** All transportation and logistics supplier facilities and operations must be in compliance with the company's freight or logistics supplier's minimum security requirements. Exceptions to the security requirements can only be granted by corporate security.
Refer to risks: G-2, G-3, G-4

6.7.3 **Packaging and Palletization.** Transportation suppliers are not allowed to remove parts/product from packaging. Palletization should not allow the easy removal of items but easily identify tampering.
Refer to risks: G-2, G-3

6.7.4 **Audits.** All transportation and logistics suppliers are subject to being audited for compliance to the company's minimum security requirements on an annual basis using applicable audit guidelines. Company management is responsible for ensuring that corrective actions are implemented within the agreed-upon timeframes.
Refer to risks: G-2, G-3, G-4

Risk If Standard Is Not Implemented

G-1 Suppliers may be unaware of the company's security requirements.

G-2 The company's assets may be stolen.

G-3 Customer satisfaction may suffer because product cannot be delivered due to theft.

G-4 Suppliers' security performance may decrease and theft may increase.

G-5 The company is unable to contractually hold supplier accountable for security performance and the expected level of service level agreement (SLA) metrics.

 ## 6.8 TRANSPORTATION AND LOGISTICS

Introduction

Policies and procedures exist to provide guidance on business practices, promote corporate consistency, and clarify roles, responsibility, and accountability within transportation and logistics. The company has contracts established with transportation carriers and those contracts are current, complete, and contain adequate protection clauses if corporate fleet resources are not in place or used.

Standard of Internal Control

6.8.1 **Corporate Policies and Procedures.** Policies and procedures exist to provide guidance on business practices, promote corporate consistency, and clarify roles, responsibility, and accountability within transportation and logistics.
Refer to risk: H-1

6.8.2 **Contract Administration.** The company has contracts established with transportation carriers and those contracts are current, complete, and contain adequate protection clauses.
Refer to risks: H-2, H-3, H-4

6.8.3 **Freight Claims.** All eligible freight claims are filed, processed on time, communicated to appropriate support and control groups, and paid timely. The corporate transportation department monitors regional compliance with related procedures and works with the regions to establish action.
Refer to risk: H-5

6.8.4 **Hazardous Materials Management.** The corporate transportation department has an adequate program for hazardous materials awareness, training, and enforcement.
Refer to risk: H-6

6.8.5 **Logistics Providers Contracts.** All third-party logistics providers understand and follow the standards for damaged goods. Compliance with these standards are included as part of the company's audit of logistics providers.
Refer to risks: H-8, H-9, H-10

6.8.6 **Selection of Transportation Carriers.** All third-party logistics providers and carriers have been selected in accordance with the respective regional carrier selection process and procedures.
Refer to risks: H-4, H-9, H-10

6.8.7 **Policies and Procedures for Damaged Product.** Policies and procedures have been developed and implemented to resolve products damaged at a third-party logistics provider's site.
Refer to risks: H-3, H-9, H-10

6.8.8 **Monitoring Logistics Providers.** Third-party logistics providers understand and comply with the company's inventory classification process and procedures.
Refer to risks: H-2, H-7

6.8.9 **Regional Policies and Procedures.** Regional policies and procedures have been developed, documented, and implemented related to transportation and logistics.
Refer to risks: H-1, H-10

6.8.10 **Damaged Goods.** Damaged goods process includes criteria to determine cost benefit analysis to retest and/or repackage damaged goods and timelines to redirect damaged goods to alternate flows.
Refer to risk: H-1

6.8.11 **Regional Contract Administration.** Agreements with third-party providers include metrics and recourse, including financial liability, for goods damaged while in their possession.
Refer to risks: H-3, H-8, H-9, H-10

6.8.12 **Regional Location Management.** A process for location management has been developed and implemented in accordance with corporate operating procedures.
Refer to risk: H-1

Risk If Standard Is Not Implemented

H-1 Company resources may not be used efficiently or effectively, resulting in excessive cost and/or inability of the manufacturing unit to achieve its business objectives.

H-2 Suppliers may be unaware of the company's standards for performance.

H-3 Suppliers' performance may decrease and damages and delays in delivery may increase.

H-4 The company may be unable to contractually hold supplier accountable for performance.

H-5 Payments may be made on claims for services that have not been rendered, or duplicate or fraudulent freight claims.

H-6 Fines and penalties may be assessed increasing costs for noncompliance with hazardous materials laws and regulations.

H-7 Suppliers may improperly classify inventory, which may reduce efficiencies in the inventory process.

H-8 Suppliers may be unaware of the company's standards for damaged goods.

H-9 Company's assets may be damaged.

H-10 Customer satisfaction may suffer because product cannot be delivered due to damage or other delays in delivery.

CHAPTER SEVEN

Record to Report (R2R)

INTRODUCTION

The R2R process encompasses the finance and transactional functions involved in ensuring that IFRS requirements are followed by the company; preparing journal entries and posting to the general ledger; gathering and consolidating the information required for the preparation of financial statements and other external financial reports; and preparing and reviewing the financial statements and other external reports.

Many factors place the spotlight on the fiscal closing process, which is usually led by a team of individuals in the corporate finance and accounting department and managed by the corporate controller. The complexity of the process is driven by the nature of the company (private, public, nonprofit [tax-exempt or mission-based], or government) and the type of industry or industries for which the company is responsible.

A recent survey conducted by the <u>Institute of Finance & Management (IOFM)</u> with approximately 100 controllers revealed the resources that the finance and accounting team typically uses to execute this critical process is less than strategic; primarily, they tend to focus on enhancing technology and process gaps that include the following:

- Multiple general ledgers and disparate transactional systems with inconsistent data structures that must be mapped to a consistent reporting format

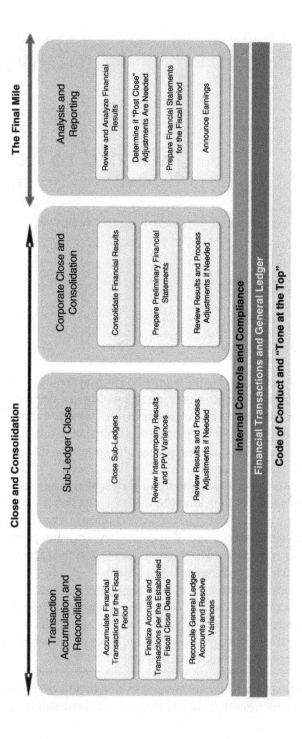

- A lack of visibility to the status and execution of the closing process, and the related tasks and evidence-gathering performed by finance, with the knowledge of these processes in the heads of just a few employees
- Limited reporting capabilities that result in spreadsheet-based reports full of critical financial data, which are the company's "corporate records"
- Spreadsheets used to support multiple manipulations of the same data over and over to meet various reporting requirements
- A lack of focus on the process basics, such as closing process checklists, reporting templates, standard operating procedures, and business continuity plans
- An absence of staffing and training plans, creating a resource gap during each closing cycle

PROCESS OVERVIEW

The diagram below suggests that the foundational elements for the R2R process are Internal Controls and Compliance, Financial Transactions and General Ledger, and Code of Conduct and "Tone at the Top."

METRICS

Table of Metrics

---

1. **Gross Number of Adjusting Entries**—Transaction errors can significantly delay the fiscal closing process. Investigating the gross number of adjusting entries can be used to identify the root cause of a potential process or system issue.

2. **Review Error**—Focus on the types of errors found during the initial review of the financial statements. This information can be used to identify and correct underlying problems that can be prevented during future closing processes. These errors should be documented and discussed during post-close reviews.

3. **Completion Times**—Further refine the duration of the fiscal closing process to focus on each category of activities that must be completed to understand not only how long they take, but also how they are impacted by other steps in the closing process. Some of these measurements by activity type are:

   - Time for subsidiaries to forward their results to corporate headquarters
   - Time to close the processing of period-end cash
   - Time to finish processing accounts payable

Table of Metrics
■ Time to issue billings to customers
■ Time to close payroll and record accrued wages
■ Time to count and value ending inventory
■ Time to issue related management reports

DIFFERENCES BETWEEN IFRS AND U.S. GAAP THAT IMPACT THE R2R PROCESS

While this is not a comprehensive list of differences that exist, these examples provide a flavor of impacts on the financial statements and therefore on the conduct of businesses:

- **Consolidation**—IFRS favors a control model, whereas U.S. GAAP prefers a risks-and-rewards model. Some entities consolidated in accordance with FIN 46(R) may have to be shown separately under IFRS.
- **Statement of Income**—Under IFRS, extraordinary items are not segregated in the income statement, whereas under U.S. GAAP they are shown below the net income.
- **Inventory**—Under IFRS, LIFO (a historical method of recording the value of inventory wherein a firm records the last units purchased as the first units sold) cannot be used, whereas under U.S. GAAP companies have the choice between LIFO and FIFO (a common method for recording the value of inventory).
- **Earning-per-Share**—Under IFRS, the earning-per-share calculation does not average the individual interim period calculations, whereas under U.S. GAAP the computation averages the individual interim period incremental shares.
- **Development Costs**—These costs can be capitalized under IFRS if certain criteria are met, whereas it is considered as "expenses" under U.S. GAAP.[1]

[1]The American Institute of CPAs (AICPA), "Is IFRS That Different from U.S. GAAP?," accessed January 17, 2019, https://www.ifrs.com/overview/General/differences.html.

APPLICATION OF INTERNAL CONTROLS

In management's selection of procedures and techniques of control, the degree of control implemented is a matter of reasonable business judgment. The common guideline that should be used in determining the degree of internal controls implementation is that the cost of a control should not exceed the benefit derived. There is a minimum set of controls that should exist in a normal business environment. The internal control standards listed here represent the minimum controls to be implemented for the financial reporting process.

 ## SUB-PROCESSES

The specific functions or activities included in the Financial Reporting process are:

7.1 International Transfer Pricing

7.2 Intercompany Transactions

7.3 Accumulation of Financial Information

7.4 Processing and Reporting of Financial Information (The Final Mile)

7.5 Fixed Assets

 ## 7.1 INTERNATIONAL TRANSFER PRICING

Introduction

International transfer pricing relates to the cross-border transfer of goods, services, or technology between legal entities of the company. It is the company's policy to establish transfer prices, which fairly apportion profits earned from the sale of its products and services to the subsidiaries involved in generating those profits.

The company follows the arm's-length principle as defined by the Organization for Economic Cooperation and Development (OECD) Transfer Pricing Guidelines for Multinational Enterprises and Tax Administration.

The OECD provides a forum in which governments can work together to share experiences and seek solutions to common problems and works with governments to understand what drives economic, social, and environmental change. The OECD measures productivity and global flows of trade and investments and analyses and compares data to predict future trends.[2]

Standard of Internal Control

7.1.1 **Pricing Method.** The company uses the specified pricing method which best fits the circumstances of each category of transactions, according to the OECD guidelines and the laws and regulations of the United States and other jurisdictions in which the company operates. When no specified method is applicable, another method is used which best approximates arm's-length conditions.
Refer to risks: A-1, A-2

7.1.2 **Responsibilities.** The standard transfer pricing method for each category of international transactions must be reviewed by the corporate tax department and approved by the company's treasurer and controller. Implementation of the approved methods is the responsibility of the regional finance directors and the corporate finance manager of transfer pricing.
Refer to risks: A-1, A-2

Risk If Standard Is Not Implemented

A-1 The company may be subjected to double taxation due to adjustments made by the taxing authorities.

A-2 The company may be subjected to penalties or fines by the taxing authorities.

 ## 7.2 INTERCOMPANY TRANSACTIONS

Introduction

The scope of this section includes all intercompany and interdivisional transactions involving products and/or services. Intercompany transactions are defined as those between two company legal entities. Interdivisional transactions are defined as those within the same legal entity and between two company divisions.

---

[2]The Organization for Economic Co-operation and Development (OECD), "About the OECD," accessed January 16, 2019, http://www.oecd.org/about/.

Standard of Internal Control

7.2.1 **Transaction Processing.** All intercompany transactions must be processed in accordance with written corporate policy.
Refer to risks: B-1, B-2, B-3, B-4

7.2.2 **Required Information.** Intercompany suppliers must provide to their trading partners appropriate, relevant, and accurate information on all products or service billing transactions. At a minimum, valid charge numbers, descriptions, receiving party information, supplier contact information, and billed value should be provided on all non-finished product or service billing transactions. The information supplied must be sufficient to allow account reconciliations to be performed.
Refer to risks: B-1, B-2, B-3, B-4

7.2.3 **Transaction Recording.** All intercompany transactions must be recorded in the same accounting period by both parties.
Refer to risks: B-1, B-2, B-3

7.2.4 **On-Time Payments.** All intercompany receivables/payables must be paid at specified terms and conditions.
Refer to risks: B-1, B-3

7.2.5 **Management Reviews.** Intercompany account imbalances must be reported to corporate and local management monthly for review and resolution.
Refer to risks: B-2, B-3

7.2.6 **Account Reconciliations.** Intercompany imbalances must be reconciled (contents are known and status is current) and aged monthly. Reconciling items and items in dispute must be resolved within 60 days. The operating unit with the receivable balance is assumed to have the correct balance unless the operating unit with the payable balance can demonstrate proof of delivery.
Refer to risks: B-1, B-2, B-3, B-4

7.2.7 **General Ledger Reconciliations.** Subsidiary (detail) ledgers supporting related-party accounts should be reconciled (contents are known and status is current) to the corresponding general ledger control accounts monthly.
Refer to risks: B-1, B-2, B-3

7.2.8 **Minimum Billing Amount.** Intercompany transactions must be above the minimum amount defined in corporate policy (e.g. $50,000 unless it affects cost of sales or is legally required) to be billed.
Refer to risks: B-3, B-4

Risk If Standard Is Not Implemented

B-1 Cash flows may not be maximized as projected receipts may not be accurate. Unanticipated currency purchases may be required or excess financing incurred.

B-2 The financial records and financial statements may be misstated.

B-3 Transactions may result in inefficient use of company resources.

B-4 Transactions may result in undesirable legal and/or tax implications.

7.3 ACCUMULATION OF FINANCIAL INFORMATION

Introduction

To support the R2R process, accounting policies and procedures must be developed and documented in accordance with IFRS requirements. New accounting policies or changes to existing policies should be properly researched, reviewed, documented, and communicated on a timely basis. The corporate controller must authorize all changes in accounting policies. Local finance management may also develop applicable policies and procedures for the accumulation of financial information to ensure compliance.

Standard of Internal Control

7.3.1 **Policy and Procedures.** These policies and procedures must be followed regardless of "materiality." A current version of the above mentioned policies and procedures should be readily available in all company locations.
Refer to risks: C-1, C-2, C-3, C-4

7.3.2 **Policy Changes.** Policies conflicting with corporate policy must be approved in writing by corporate controller.
Refer to risks: C-1, C-2, C-3, C-4

7.3.3 **Journal Entries.** Journal entries must be accurately input to the general ledger in the correct accounting period. Processes should be in place to ensure journal entry postings to the general ledger are accurate and timely.
Refer to risks: C-1, C-2, C-4, C-5

7.3.4 **Documented Journal Entries.** All manual general ledger journal entries must be documented, reviewed, and approved by finance management. A process should also be in place to identify manual journal entries so that it may be determined if any were omitted or duplicated.

Refer to risks: C-1, C-2, C-4, C-5

7.3.5 **Standardized Journal Entries.** Standardized (i.e. system calculated and posted) general ledger journal entries must be utilized whenever possible. When the journal entry is established, the process for calculation must be reviewed, approved, and documented by local financial management. A process should also be in place to identify standardized journal entries so that it may be determined if any were omitted, duplicated, or have unreasonable values.

Refer to risks: C-1, C-2, C-4, C-5

7.3.6 **Non-standard Transactions.** Policies must be established to review and approve the accounting treatment of general ledger journal entries that do not occur on a regular basis.

Refer to risks: C-1, C-2, C-4, C-5

7.3.7 **Contra Asset Accounts.** Contra asset accounts should be utilized where necessary to maintain both proper asset valuation and detailed accounting records (e.g. receivables, inventory, and property).

Refer to risks: C-1, C-2, C-4, C-6

7.3.8 **Monthly Accruals.** On a monthly basis, an accrual must be made of all known liabilities that have not been processed for payment or recorded in the accounting records, as determined by corporate policy. A quarterly review and evaluation should be conducted at the operating unit reporting level to determine if any existing contingent liabilities should be recorded in accordance with U.S. GAAP requirements.

Refer to risks: C-1, C-2, C-4, C-7

7.3.9 **Asset Account Reviews.** All non-current asset accounts should be reviewed at least annually to ensure values do not exceed the lower of cost or market value. All current asset accounts should be reviewed at least quarterly to ensure that values do not exceed the lower of cost or market value.

Refer to risks: C-1, C-4

Risk If Standard Is Not Implemented

C-1 The financial statements issued to the public may not be prepared in accordance with GAAP.

C-2 Reports may not be accurate, and critical decisions may be based upon erroneous information.

C-3 Cash or securities may be stolen, lost, destroyed, or temporarily diverted.

C-4 SEC, IFRS, and other governmental reporting requirements and/or loan restrictions may be violated. Exposure to shareholder litigation increases substantially due to improper reporting.

C-5 Journal entries may be incorrectly prepared, duplicated, omitted, or made for the purposes of misstating account balances to conceal irregularities or shortages.

C-6 Accountability over recorded transactions may not be maintained.

C-7 Amounts could be accrued for expenses that are not likely to occur in order to generate "funding" sources for future periods.

7.4 PROCESSING AND REPORTING OF FINANCIAL INFORMATION (THE FINAL MILE)

Introduction

As part of the "final mile of the R2R process, "financial information and general ledger balances must be formally reconciled (contents are known and status is current) to the subsidiary ledgers or other supporting records on a timely basis. Contents and aging of the subsidiary ledger are provided in the reconciliation process along with a concise definition of the account. Additionally, significant fluctuations in general ledger account balances are explained as part of the reconciliation process. Any differences must be promptly resolved and recorded, generally by the next monthly reporting interval. The aging of all differences is provided with action plans for resolution and/or the date of resolution if already corrected.

Standard of Internal Control

7.4.1 **Journal Entry Processing.** Controls must be established to ensure all journal entries have been processed and posted once they have been input into the system. Transaction error registers should be generated and significant discrepancies resolved prior to the period close.
Refer to risks: D-1, D-2, D-3, D-4, D-5

7.4.2 **Reporting Schedules and Cutoffs.** Monthly, quarterly, annual closing reporting schedules and cutoffs must be adhered to and consistently applied in the financial operations processes across the company.
Refer to risks: D-1, D-2, D-3, D-5, D-9

7.4.3 **General Ledger Reconciliations.** All unexplained differences must be reported to appropriate financial management as soon as discovered even if not yet resolved. It is management's responsibility to follow up on all unexplained differences on a monthly basis that reconciliation standards are in place.
Refer to risks: D-1, D-2, D-3, D-4, D-5

7.4.4 **Suspense Account Transactions.** Clearing and suspense account transactions, including the transfer of expense, income, or capital, must be resolved on a timely basis. Proper recognition of income or expense for these accounts must be made on at least a quarterly basis and on a monthly basis where possible.
Refer to risks: D-1, D-2, D-3, D-4, D-5

7.4.5 **General Ledger Adjustments.** Consolidation, reclassification, and other adjustments to the general ledger balances must be adequately explained and documented. Such adjustments must be approved by the appropriate Controller/Manager or authorized designee.
Refer to risks: D-1, D-2, D-3, D-4, D-5

7.4.6 **Financial Report Preparation.** Procedures and responsibilities must be established and maintained to ensure timely and accurate preparation, review, and approval of external financial reports, including reports to governmental and regulatory bodies. These procedures must also ensure that such reports comply with the established requirements for financial information and related disclosures.
Refer to risks: D-1, D-2, D-5, D-8, D-9

7.4.7 **Access to Records.** Access to accounting and finance records, documents, and information systems must be safeguarded and access granted only on the principle of the "need to know" basis based on the company's system access policy.
Refer to risks: D-6, D-7, D-8, D-11

7.4.8 **Records Management.** Accounting and financial records must be complete, well organized, and retained in accordance with corporate policy on records management and tax requirements. Sufficient records must be kept in a secure but accessible environment to accurately and completely support all non-fixed assets and all liabilities.
Refer to risks: D-5, D-7, D-8, D-10, D-11

7.4.9 **Financial Results.** Only authorized individuals must be given the responsibility to discuss financial results with individuals outside of the company.
Refer to risk: D-6

7.4.10 **Financial Reporting Requirements.** All company operating units must comply with the current financial reporting requirements established by the controller.
Refer to risks: D-1, D-2, D-5, D-9, D-10

7.4.11 **Legal Financial Reporting Requirements.** All legal reporting requirements (e.g. tax returns, statutory audits, etc.) must be adhered to and consistently applied.
Refer to risks: D-1, D-5

7.4.12 **Financial Statement Translation.** Foreign financial statements must be translated in accordance with U.S. GAAP and corporate policy.
Refer to risks: D-1, D-2, D-5, D-9

7.4.13 **General Ledger Accounts Definitions.** Current definitions must be documented and maintained for all ledger accounts.
Refer to risks: D-2, D-9, D-10

7.4.14 **General Ledger Account Owners.** Lists of general ledger account owners must be kept current and cost center managers shall have responsibility for the accuracy of account balances.
Refer to risks: D-2, D-10

7.4.15 **Actual to Forecast Comparisons.** Comparisons and explanations of actual financial information to forecast information must be routinely completed according to established policies and procedures; all significant variances must be researched and reflected in revised estimates/plans as appropriate in a timely manner. Uniformly defined (same methodology) balance sheet performance measures must be established and actual performance measured against forecast on a monthly basis.
Refer to risks: D-1, D-2, D-4, D-5, D-8, D-9

7.4.16 **Related-Party Transactions.** Related-party transactions should be defined and reported. Examples of related-party transactions are the transactions between:
a. A parent entity and its subsidiaries
b. Subsidiaries of a common parent

      c. An entity and trusts for the benefit of employees, such as pension and profit-sharing trusts that are managed by or under the trusteeship of the entity's management

      d. An entity and its principal owners, management, or members of their immediate families

      e. Affiliates

      Refer to risk: D-5

Risk If Standard Is Not Implemented

D-1 The financial statements issued to the public may not be prepared in accordance with GAAP applied on a consistent basis.

D-2 Reports may not be accurate, and critical decisions may then be based upon erroneous information.

D-3 Financial statements may be misstated as journal entries may be omitted, recorded in the wrong period, duplicated, and/or incorrectly made.

D-4 Errors and omissions in physical safeguarding, authorization, and transaction processing may go undetected and uncorrected. Financial statements and records may be prepared inaccurately or untimely.

D-5 SEC and other governmental reporting requirements and/or loan restrictions may be violated. Exposure to litigation increases substantially due to improper financial reporting.

D-6 Confidential and proprietary information may be reviewed and disclosed by unauthorized individuals. The company's competitive position and reputation may be adversely affected.

D-7 Records may be destroyed or altered. This may result in the inability to prepare accurate and reliable financial statements.

D-8 Financial information required for budgeting, forecasting, or analysis may not be available.

D-9 Policies and procedures may not be properly or consistently applied by or between company operating units. Financial statements may be prepared inaccurately or untimely.

D-10 The risk of error in the accumulation and reporting of financial information is increased.

D-11 The company may be exposed to litigation due to inadequate record maintenance.

7.5 FIXED ASSETS

Introduction

For the purposes of this toolkit, fixed assets include land, buildings, capital projects, machinery and equipment, furniture, fixtures, tools, and similar assets used in the business, as well as all categories of leased equipment (rented assets, capital leases, direct financing leases, and operating leases). Revenue is derived from the use of these assets, rather than from their sales. Generally, an item must have an estimated useful life of at least two years to be classified as a fixed asset.

Fixed assets are generally high-value assets that companies make use of over the course of several to many years. For this reason, it may seem as though fixed asset management is less critical than tracking moveable assets. There's little or no risk of loss, theft, and unauthorized transfer with fixed assets, but tracking these assets is an important business function.[3]

Standard of Internal Control

7.5.1 **Record Keeping.** Detailed records of fixed assets must be maintained and must include the cost and accumulated depreciation of individual assets. These records should also include information regarding serial number, asset description, location, asset number, lease data, tax data, operating unit data, etc., where appropriate.
Refer to risks: E-1, E-2, E-5

7.5.2 **Capital Projects.** Detailed records must be maintained for capital projects such as construction-in-progress to facilitate accurate and timely classification of assets when work is completed.
Refer to risks: E-1, E-3, E-5, E-7

7.5.3 **Safeguarded Records.** Detailed fixed asset and construction-in-progress records must be safeguarded, including system access security.
Refer to risks: E-5, E-6

7.5.4 **General Ledger Reconciliations.** Detailed fixed asset records must be reconciled (contents are known and status is current) to the general ledger and all differences researched and resolved in a timely manner. General ledger records must balance with consolidated financial statements.
Refer to risks: E-1, E-3, E-5

---

[3] Camcode Durable Barcode Solutions, "What Are Fixed Assets?," posted by Nicole Pontius in *Asset Management Resources*, updated June 28, 2018, accessed January 1, 2019, https://www.camcode.com/asset-tags/what-are-fixed-assets/.

7.5.5 **Accounting Procedures.** Accounting procedures for fixed assets should follow corporate policy and local statutory requirements. Examples include:

a. Operating vs. capital leases

b. Capitalization vs. expensing for improvements, repairs, refurbishments

c. Depreciation method and useful life

d. Additions, transfers, and dispositions.

Refer to risks: E-1, E-2, E-5

7.5.6 **Approval Process.** A formal approval process for all capital expenditures should be established and include obtaining additional approval when individual expenditures exceed original approved amounts.

Refer to risk: E-9

7.5.7 **Asset Verification.** Physical verification of fixed assets must be completed at least every two years. Physical counts must be compared to detailed records and the general ledger with any differences investigated and recorded in a timely manner.

Refer to risks: E-1, E-3, E-4, E-5

7.5.8 **Safeguarded Assets.** Policies must be developed and documented to establish accountability for safeguarding assets. All fixed assets must be adequately safeguarded. Highly portable assets (e.g. laptop PCs) should be physically secured to the extent possible.

Refer to risks: E-1, E-3

7.5.9 **Surplus Assets.** Any significant accumulation of underutilized (i.e., idle or surplus) fixed assets must be reported to local management. Such assets should be reviewed for disposition opportunities and proper valuation on the balance sheet; impairment of the assets should be recognized appropriately in the financial statements.

Refer to risks: E-1, E-2, E-4

7.5.10 **Asset Disposal Process.** A formal approval process is required for any sale, disposal, abandonment, loss, or transfer of fixed assets. Sales will be made, invoiced, and recorded in the same accounting year as the disposition, after an appropriate credit review is performed.

Refer to risks: E-3, E-5, E-8

7.5.11 **Tax Calculations.** Procedures must be maintained to support the calculation of tax (associated with fixed assets, for example, property tax, use tax, etc.) in accordance with local country and/or U.S. tax laws.

Refer to risks: E-1, E-5

7.5.12 **Segregation of Duties.** All fixed asset functions must have the following segregation of duties controls in place:
  a. Initiating, evaluating, and approving fixed asset expenditures from property records and general ledger functions
  b. Property record and general ledger functions from fixed asset custody
  c. Fixed asset accounting, procurement, and custodial functions from performing physical inventories
  Refer to risks: E-1, E-3, E-10

7.5.13 **Capitalization.** Fixed assets must be capitalized on a timely basis in accordance with tax regulations and GAAP.
  Refer to risks: E-1, E-2, E-3

Risk If Standard Is Not Implemented

E-1 Financial statements could be misstated.

E-2 Financial/tax information could be misstated, resulting in inaccurate business valuations or inappropriate decisions.

E-3 Assets could be misappropriated/stolen from the company.

E-4 Assets could be underutilized.

E-5 Without adequate supporting documentation, there is a potential to violate local country and U.S. tax laws.

E-6 Destruction or loss of records could lead to business interruption and unnecessary expense.

E-7 In the event of loss of or damage to assets, insurance recovery may not be sufficient to fund repair or replacement of like-kind/similar quality fixed assets.

E-8 If the calculation of replacement value is not accurate, insurance premiums will be overstated/understated.

E-9 Capital spending could be excessive, negatively impacting the company's cash flow.

E-10 Errors and omissions in authorization and transaction processing or poor physical safeguarding practices may result in assets which are lost, stolen, destroyed, or temporarily diverted. Asset thefts may go undetected.

CHAPTER EIGHT

Government Contracts

 ## INTRODUCTION

The government contracts process includes an overview of those controls necessary for compliance with governmental requirements and provides an indication of where they may be applicable to the company.

 ## APPLICATION OF INTERNAL CONTROLS

In management's selection of procedures and techniques of control, the degree of control implemented is a matter of reasonable business judgment. The common guideline used in determining the degree of internal controls implementation is that the cost of a control should not exceed the benefit derived. However, there is a minimum set of controls that should exist in a normal business environment. The internal control standards listed here represent the minimum controls to be implemented for the government contracts process.

 ## PROCESS OVERVIEW

The diagram below suggests that the foundational elements for the government contract process are Internal Controls and Compliance, Government Contract Controls, and Code of Conduct and "Tone at the Top."

Government Contracts

Contract Compliance for Commercial and Non-Commercial Projects

Ensure that new contracts are compliant with state and federal regulatory requirements

Ensure that those responsible for contracts adhere to the company's "Tone at the Top" and business conduct requirements

Classify the Sale

Order Management and Fulfillment

Establish Pricing

Adhere to Delivery Requirements

Create the Customer Invoice

Cost Accounting Processess

Establish Cost Accounting Standards

Monies collected from contract users are accurately identified, segregated, accounted for and paid over to the government in accordance with the contract.

Follow Revenue Recognition Rules

Internal Controls and Compliance

Government Contracts Controls

Code of Conduct and "Tone at the Top"

METRICS

Table of Metrics

- Cycle Time for Contract Approvals
- Number and Percentage of Contract Defects
- Number, Percentage, and Value of Contract Compliance Issues
- Number of Contracts Produced per Fiscal Period
- Cost to Produce a Contract

 SUB-PROCESSES

The specific sub-processes included are:

8.1 U.S. Government Contracts—General

8.2 U.S. Government Contracts—Non-Commercial Products

8.3 U.S. Government Contracts—Commercial Products

8.4 Contracts with State and Local Governments and Educational Institutions Within the United States

8.5 Contracts with Governments Outside the United States

 8.1 U.S. GOVERNMENT CONTRACTS—GENERAL

Introduction

If a subsidiary does business with a government entity either as a prime contractor or subcontractor, the subsidiary, in its entirety, must comply with certain government statutory and regulatory requirements. However, subsidiaries, as distinct legal entities, are not required to comply with contractually imposed government statutory and regulatory requirements by virtue of the company, the parent corporation, being a government contractor. Likewise, the parent corporation is not necessarily bound by specific terms and conditions of government contracts of the subsidiaries.

In addition to the general requirements applicable company-wide, the corporation or subsidiary holding the government prime contract or subcontract must comply with additional contract-specific requirements. The type of contract or arrangement company or a subsidiary has with government entities or a government prime contractor usually determines the specific responsibilities of the company or its subsidiary with respect to government regulations and laws.

The entire corporation may be held responsible for the failure of any single operating unit to comply with the laws and regulations imposed by government entities accepted by the company as a result of doing business with government entities, especially ethics and integrity requirements. This exposes the entire company to adverse actions, such as civil and criminal fines and penalties, debarment from future government business, and/or damage to the corporate image. In some instances, this could also create personal liability as a result of the action of an individual.

The corporation and its subsidiaries must establish and document policies and procedures to ensure compliance with the government core compliance elements, and flow them down, as applicable, to subcontractors and suppliers. These include:

a. Procurement Integrity Act
b. Clean Air and Water Acts
c. Employment of former government officials and other Department of Defense hiring restrictions
d. Affirmative Action and Equal Employment Opportunity compliance
e. Socioeconomic regulations (e.g. small business/minority business enterprises)
f. State and local ethics provisions
g. Federal Acquisition Regulations (FAR)
h. Trade regulations
i. Contract-specific requirements

This section applies to all company operating units (Sales, Global Services, certain affected functional departments such as Human Resources, EHS&S, Supply Chain, and Accounting) and to those subsidiaries which, directly or indirectly, provide products or services to the U.S. government. The company and its subsidiaries will operate in full compliance with all statutory and regulatory requirements applicable to government contractors as well as specific contract requirements.

Standard of Internal Control

8.1.1 **Compliance.** Overall responsibility for compliance with government entities in North America rests jointly between the Director, Contracts and Bids North America (DCBNA), and the applicable General Manager, with support from Corporate Legal. The DCBNA shall coordinate all communication and activities with regard to compliance for all government contracts for the company in North America. Each operating unit (as stated above) and subsidiary must designate a Government Compliance Coordinator. This person shall coordinate activities and communications with regard to compliance with government contract requirements for that operating unit or subsidiary. Each operating unit and subsidiary must have a Government Contract Compliance Plan (GCCP). This must be approved by the operating unit's or subsidiary's vice president or general manager and forwarded to the DCBNA. The plan shall be updated annually, or more frequently, if required. In addition to the Government's Core Compliance elements applicable to the company as a whole, the operating units and subsidiaries must establish and document policies and procedures to ensure compliance with the following federal and/or state statutes:

a. False Claims and Statements Statutes

b. Anti-Kickback Statutes

c. Bribery and Gratuities Statutes

d. Competition in Contracting Act

e. Buy America and Trade Agreements Acts

Adequate systems, resources, and controls must be established to implement the policies and procedures outlined in the GCCP. The written policies and procedures must document the process for preparing bids, proposals, and claims. The submission of contracts and bids must be current, accurate, complete, properly certified, and support any certifications made. Only personnel designated by the appropriate operating unit or subsidiary are allowed to commit the Corporation to government contracts. Operating units or subsidiaries shall establish and enforce procedures that control the negotiation and execution of contracts.

Refer to risks: A-1, A-2, A-3, A-4, A-5, A-6, A-7, A-8, A-9, A-10, A-11

8.1.2 **Business Conduct.** Each operating unit and subsidiary must be able to demonstrate that employees having responsibilities related to government contracting have participated in all training required by law, regulation, or contractual obligation; have read and understood applicable code of conduct guides and any supplemental guidelines pertaining to government contracting; and where appropriate, have signed a certification. In particular, employees must adhere to the highest standards of ethical conduct in all relationships with government employees and must not attempt to improperly influence the actions of any public official.
Refer to risks: A-1, A-2, A-3, A-4, A-5, A-6, A-7, A-8, A-9, A-10, A-11

8.1.3 **Training.** Each operating unit and subsidiary must ensure all personnel performing functions requiring compliance with U.S. government regulations receive adequate training. Training requirements, including frequency, must be included in the operating unit's or subsidiary's FGCCP. Procedures must be implemented to effectively monitor and document fulfillment of those requirements.
Refer to risks: A-l, A-2, A-4, A-7

8.1.4 **Joint Ventures.** Company operating units and subsidiaries participating in joint ventures seeking government business must:
   a. Ensure that each joint venture has a policy for doing business with government entities.
   b. Identify an individual, by name or position, within the operating unit or subsidiary who will fulfill the operating unit's or subsidiary's responsibility for contract compliance in each joint venture.
Refer to risks: A-1, A-2, A-3, A-4, A-5, A-6, A-10

8.1.5 **Memorandums of Understanding.** Memorandums of Understanding (MOUs) must be established between all operating units or subsidiaries having intercompany transfers related to U.S. government contracts. All MOUs must specify the compliance responsibility for both the receiving and the transferring operating units or subsidiaries and they must be approved by either the operating units or subsidiary's general manager. All MOUs must be on file with the DCBNA. Additional requirements that are contract specific should be captured under an Interdivisional Work Order (IWO).
Refer to risks: A-1, A-2, A-3, A-7

8.1.6 **Records Management.** Operating units and subsidiaries performing government contracts must establish and maintain adequate record management systems. Controls must ensure contract files are adequately maintained during the contract performance period and after the contract is closed. A contract file should include documentation pertinent to the contract, including at least the following: solicitation, proposal, cost and pricing data, contract document, change orders, if any, and negotiation memoranda.
Refer to risks: A-1, A-2, A-3, A-5, A-6, A-7, A-8, A-9, A-10, A-11

8.1.7 **Order Processing.** Order processing controls must include procedures for identifying government orders and orders containing government terms and conditions. Procedures must be established to ensure:
a. All such orders are reviewed and approved prior to acceptance.
b. The operating unit or subsidiary can fulfill the requirements of the order.
c. The contract terms and conditions are communicated to the appropriate functions responsible for compliance.
Controls must exist to:
a. Ensure compliance with contract terms.
b. Identify, negotiate, and process any change orders and potential claims.
Refer to risks: A-1, A-2, A-3, A-6, A-7, A-9, A-10, A-11

8.1.8 **Delivery Requirements.** Each operating unit and subsidiary must have established controls, to identify orders with specific delivery requirements, including defense priority rated orders, and to ensure compliance with all notification and shipment requirements.
Refer to risks: A-1, A-6, A-10

8.1.9 **Revenue Recognition.** Revenue recognition is an accounting principle that outlines the specific conditions under which revenue is recognized. According to the IFRS criteria, for revenue to be recognized, the following conditions must be satisfied:
a. Risks and rewards have been transferred from the seller to the buyer.
b. The seller does not have control over the goods sold.
c. The collection of payment from goods or services is reasonably assured.
d. The amount of revenue can be reasonably measured.
e. Costs of revenue can be reasonably measured.
Refer to risks: A-1, A-2, A-4, A-6

8.1.10 **Invoicing.** Controls must be established by each operating unit and subsidiary to ensure that invoices to the government are prepared correctly, in accordance with contract terms, and are based on accurate and timely information.
Refer to risks: A-1, A-2, A-3, A-4, A-5, A-6, A-8, A-10, A-11

8.1.11 **Content.** Each operating unit and subsidiary must have procedures and controls to properly classify and report end products sold to the federal government as either domestic or foreign as specified in the Buy American Act, Balance of Payments Programs, the Trade Agreements Act of 1979, or other similar regulations. Additionally, these controls must ensure fulfillment of all quality assurance, new material, and product substitution requirements of its U.S. government contracts.
Refer to risks: A-1, A-2, A-3, A-5, A-6, A-7, A-8, A-9, A-10, A-11

8.1.12 **Government Entities Outside the United States.** Government units outside the United States are subject to the same policies and procedures relative to sales within the United States.
Refer to risks: A-1, A-2, A-3, A-5, A-6, A-7, A-8, A-9, A-10, A-11

8.1.13 **Non-Commercial Products U.S. Government Contracts.** Operating units or subsidiaries must seek approval from the CFO prior to entering into a Non-Commercial Products U.S. government contract. These types of contracts require specific accounting policies and procedures that may be in conflict with existing accounting policies and procedures.
Refer to risk: A-11

Risk If Standard Is Not Implemented

A-1 U.S. government and SEC reporting regulations may be violated.

A-2 Civil and criminal fines and penalties against the company and/or individual employees may occur.

A-3 Contract prices may be reduced and/or costs disallowed due to noncompliance, defective pricing, and/or inadequate supporting documentation for reported costs.

A-4 Financial statements and records may be misstated. Critical decisions may be based upon erroneous information.

A-5 Debarment or suspension from receiving U.S. government contracts may occur.

A-6 If review procedures are inadequate, appropriate corrective actions may not be initiated in a timely manner.

A-7 Contractual obligations may be accepted which are not within the company's compliance capabilities.

A-8 Costs incurred in excess of funding limitations may not be reimbursed if improper or untimely notice is given to the U.S. government.

A-9 The contract may be terminated for default, and damages sought by the U.S. government.

A-10 Public embarrassment and damage to the company's reputation could result from failure, alleged or actual, to comply fully with all contract terms.

A-11 Extensive legal and other costs may be incurred.

8.2 U.S. GOVERNMENT CONTRACTS— NON-COMMERCIAL PRODUCTS

Introduction

This section applies to all company operating units and to those subsidiaries which, directly or indirectly, provide non-commercial products or services to the U.S. government. Non-commercial products or services are developed based on specifications and are not generally items sold to other customers in the normal course of business. They are sold based on either fixed price or cost reimbursement contracts. These types of contracts should not be entered into without the specific approval of the chief financial officer.

Standard of Internal Control

8.2.1 **Government Property.** Operating units possessing property furnished by the U.S. government shall use applicable company policies to establish and maintain adequate controls over such property's accountability, use, and disposition as required by the Federal Acquisition Regulation (FAR) and contract terms. Subsidiaries must establish their own government property control policies and systems that are consistent with corporate requirements.

Refer to risks: B-1, B-2, B-4, B-6

8.2.2 **Flow-Down Clauses.** Operating units and subsidiaries must have established controls to ensure that agreements with subcontractors include all required flow-down clauses.
Refer to risks: B-2, B-3, B-5, B-6

8.2.3 **Indirect Rates.** For cost reimbursement/progress billings, actual indirect rates should be monitored and compared to billing rates. Billing rates should be renegotiated with the U.S. government when differences are significant. Indirect rate submissions must be prepared timely and submitted and certified in accordance with FAR requirements.
Refer to risks: B-1, B-2, B-3, B-4, B-5, B-6, B-7, B-8, B-9

8.2.4 **Subcontracts.** Operating units and subsidiaries incurring significant subcontract costs shall establish procedures to periodically review the progress of work performed by major subcontractors to ensure that:
   a. Payments to subcontractors are made only on the basis of work performed and in accordance with contract terms.
   b. Withholdings of payments from the subcontractor are made where appropriate (e.g. lack of progress or noncompliance with specifications) and are recorded and accounted for properly.
Refer to risks: B-1, B-4, B-5, B-7

8.2.5 **Cost Accounting Standards.** Cost accounting standards (CASs) must be documented and must provide for the accurate determination, classification, and accumulation of cost information in accordance with federal CAS and other U.S. government requirements.
Refer to risks: B-1, B-2, B-3, B-4, B-5, B-7, B-8, B-9

8.2.6 **Disclosure Statement.** Each operating unit and subsidiary submitting must establish internal controls to detect the need for developing and submitting revisions to the disclosure statement (including any necessary cost impact statements) whenever changes occur in the operating unit's or subsidiary's accounting practices. These controls should include notification by the controller for each operating unit or subsidiary of any changes to corporate allocations for such costs as pension or administrative support, which may require disclosure of a change in accounting practice to the U.S. government.
Refer to risks: B-1, B-2, B-3, B-4, B-6, B-8, B-9

Risk If Standard Is Not Implemented

B-1   U.S. government and SEC reporting regulations may be violated.

B-2 Civil and criminal fines and penalties against the company and/or individual employees may occur.

B-3 Contract prices may be reduced and/or costs disallowed due to noncompliance, defective pricing, and/or inadequate supporting documentation for reported costs.

B-4 Financial statements and records may be misstated. Critical decisions may be based upon erroneous information.

B-5 Debarment or suspension from receiving U.S. government contracts may occur.

B-6 If review procedures are inadequate, appropriate corrective actions may not be initiated in a timely manner.

B-7 Costs incurred in excess of funding limitations may not be reimbursed if improper or untimely notice is given to the U.S. government.

B-8 Public embarrassment and damage to the company's reputation could result from failure, alleged or actual, to comply fully with all contract terms.

B-9 Extensive legal and other costs may be incurred.

8.3 U.S. GOVERNMENT CONTRACTS— COMMERCIAL PRODUCTS

Introduction

This section applies to all company operating units (business units, manufacturing divisions, and service and support organizations) and to those subsidiaries which, directly or indirectly, provide commercial products or services to the U.S. government. Commercial products are considered "off-the-shelf" items which are sold to other customers in the normal course of business. The prices of such products generally are negotiated and agreed to be based on certified commercial transaction data.

Standard of Internal Control

8.3.1 **Pricing Policy.** Each operating unit or subsidiary must develop and maintain, on file, commercial pricing policies and procedures that define how prices are established and authorized. The policy should address customer classifications, discounts and terms, variances from discounts and terms, non-invoice transactions, and business to customers of particular interest to the U.S. government (i.e. most favored customers and basis of contract award customers).

Refer to risks: C-1, C-2, C-3, C-5, C-6, C-7, C-8, C-9, C-10, C-11

8.3.2 **Records Management.** If commercial transaction data is submitted to the U.S. government during contract negotiation or performance, the operating unit's or subsidiary's records management system shall ensure that data concerning all commercial transactions during the relevant time period(s) are preserved for a period of three years, according to the federal regulations.

Refer to risks: C-1, C-2, C-3, C-5, C-6, C-7, C-8, C-9, C-10, C-11

8.3.3 **Invoicing.** Operating units and subsidiaries must establish adequate controls over invoice compliance in order to adhere to the established pricing policy and contract requirements.

Refer to risks: C-1, C-2, C-3, C-5, C-6, C-7, C-8, C-9, C-10, C-11

8.3.4 **Pricing Policy Changes.** The compliance plan developed and implemented by the operating unit or subsidiary should include a process that will ensure the government receives proper notification of changes in the pricing policy.

Refer to risks: C-1, C-2, C-3, C-5, C-8, C-10, C-11

8.3.5 **Exemptions.** Operating units and subsidiaries claiming exemptions from submission of certified cost or pricing data must have controls in place to ensure they meet the FAR requirements for the exemption claimed and must maintain adequate documentation to support the basis for seeking the exemption.

Refer to risks: C-1, C-2, C-3, C-4, C-5, C-8, C-10, C-11

8.3.6 **Sales Classification.** Operating units and subsidiaries selling commercial products to the U.S. government must maintain adequate data processing systems to provide accurate and complete information concerning all commercial and U.S. government sales. These systems must be capable of:

a. Distinguishing between federal government, state government, local government, and commercial sales and transactions and identifying sales under GSA (General Services Administration) contracts

b. Properly classifying and identifying each aspect of any sale or transaction (e.g. rebates, credits, trade-ins, free goods)

c. Properly and accurately reporting sales volume by product, customer, category, etc.

Refer to risks: C-1, C-2, C-3, C-4, C-5, C-6, C-7, C-9, C-10, C-11

8.3.7 **Accounting.** Operating units and subsidiaries holding contracts which require industrial funding fees, rebates, or other remuneration must make certain their accounting systems are sufficient to ensure that monies collected from contract users are accurately identified, segregated, accounted for, and paid to the government in accordance with the contract.
Refer to risks: C-2, C-5, C-10, C-11

Risk If Standard Is Not Implemented

C-1 U.S. government and SEC reporting regulations may be violated.

C-2 Civil and criminal fines and penalties against the company and/or individual employees may occur.

C-3 Contract prices may be reduced and/or costs disallowed due to noncompliance, defective pricing, and/or inadequate supporting documentation for reported costs.

C-4 Financial statements and records may be misstated. Critical decisions may be based upon erroneous information.

C-5 Debarment or suspension from receiving U.S. government contracts may occur.

C-6 If review procedures are inadequate, appropriate corrective actions may not be initiated in a timely manner.

C-7 Contractual obligations may be accepted which are not within the company's compliance capabilities.

C-8 Costs incurred in excess of funding limitations may not be reimbursed if improper or untimely notice is given to the U.S. government.

C-9 The contract may be terminated for default, and damages sought by the government.

C-10 Public embarrassment and damage to the company's reputation could result from failure, alleged or actual, to comply fully with all contract terms.

C-11 Extensive legal and other costs may be incurred.

8.4 CONTRACTS WITH STATE AND LOCAL GOVERNMENTS AND EDUCATIONAL INSTITUTIONS WITHIN THE UNITED STATES

Introduction

The company and its subsidiaries are suppliers to both state and local governments. Doing business with these entities poses unique requirements, remedies, and penalties not encountered in normal commercial business.

Standard of Internal Control

8.4.1 **General.** Standards of Internal Control 8.1.1 through 8.1.11 relative to government contracts are applicable to contracts with U.S. state and local governments.
Refer to risks: D-1, D-2, D-3, D-4, D-5, D-6, D-7, D-8, D-9, D-10

8.4.2 **Applicable Laws and Regulations.** Each operating unit and subsidiary must establish appropriate responsibilities, plans, policies, and procedures in order to propose, negotiate, and contract with U.S. state and local governments. The statutory and regulatory requirements of each state and local governmental agency must be researched and understood in order to ensure compliance prior to the commitment of the company to such contracts.
Refer to risks: D-1, D-2, D-3, D-4, D-5, D-6, D-7, D-8, D-9, D-10

8.4.3 **Accounting.** Operating units and subsidiaries holding contracts which require industrial funding fees, rebates, or other remuneration must make certain their accounting systems are sufficient to ensure that monies collected from contract users are accurately identified, segregated, accounted for, and paid over to the government in accordance with the contract.
Refer to risks: D-2, D-5, D-10

Risk If Standard Is Not Implemented

D-1 State and local government reporting regulations may be violated.

D-2 Civil and criminal fine and penalties against the company and/or individual employees may occur.

D-3 Contract prices may subsequently be reduced due to noncompliance and/or inadequate supporting documentation for reported costs.

D-4 Financial statements and records may be based upon erroneous information.

D-5 Debarment or suspension from receiving state or local government contracts may occur.

D-6 If review of procedures is inadequate, appropriate corrective actions may not be initiated in a timely manner.

D-7 Contractual obligations may be accepted which are not within the operating unit's or subsidiary's compliance capabilities.

D-8 The contract may be terminated for default, and damages sought by the state or local government.

D-9 Public embarrassment and damage to the company's reputation could result from failure, alleged or actual, to comply fully with all terms of a state or local government contract.

D-10 Extensive legal and other costs may be incurred.

8.5 CONTRACTS WITH GOVERNMENTS OUTSIDE THE UNITED STATES

Introduction

The company and its subsidiaries contract with non-U.S. government entities, including quasi-governmental customers (i.e. government owned industry or multi-government sponsored agencies), all over the world.

Standard of Internal Control

8.5.1 **Responsibility.** Overall responsibility for compliance to contracts with governments outside the United States rests with the Country General Manager with support from the appropriate legal department. These individuals shall coordinate all communication and activities with regard to compliance with all government contracts within that country for the company.
Refer to risks: E-1, E-2, E-3

8.5.2 **Contracting Authorization.** Only specific personnel, identified within authorizing resolutions approved by the appropriate board of directors, are allowed to commit the company or any of its subsidiaries to contracts with governments outside the United States.
Refer to risks: E-1, E-2, E-3

8.5.3 **Contracting Entity.** As a general matter, contracts with governments outside the United States must be entered into by the company subsidiary located in that country. Approval of the Tax and Legal departments must be obtained prior to the company entering into any contract not to be performed entirely within the United States.
Refer to risks: E-1, E-2, E-3

8.5.4 **Contracting Capabilities.** Each operating unit or subsidiary that initiates contracts with governments outside the United States must have a program for identifying and fulfilling such contracts and orders and ensuring such orders are performed by the appropriate operating unit or subsidiary in accordance with contractual requirements. Terms and conditions must be reviewed by trained specialists during contract formation.
Refer to risks: E-1, E-2, E-3

8.5.5 **Risk Mitigation.** An operating unit or subsidiary doing business with governments outside its own country must fully investigate, with the assistance of specialists, that location's business environment in an effort to mitigate any risks associated with doing business in that country (e.g. political instability, distribution channels) and ensure all obligations and regulations are met.
Refer to risks: E-1, E-2, E-3

8.5.6 **Business Conduct.** Operating units and subsidiaries must be able to demonstrate employees having responsibilities related to government contracting have read and understood the company's code of conduct and any supplemental guidelines pertaining to government relations, and where appropriate, have signed an affidavit. In particular, employees must adhere to the highest standards of ethical conduct in all relationships with government employees and must not improperly attempt to influence the actions of any public official. Also, payments of gifts shall not be made directly or indirectly to any government official or employee if the gift is illegal under the laws of that country or the United States (Foreign Corrupt Practices Act).
Refer to risks: E-1, E-2, E-3

8.5.7 **Training.** Each operating unit and subsidiary performing business with governments outside the United States must ensure all personnel involved in this business are appropriately trained. A training plan is advisable, along with documentation that training was accomplished.
Refer to risks: E-1, E-2, E-3

8.5.8 **Self-Audits.** Operating units and subsidiaries performing business with governments outside the United States will conduct periodic self-audits of this business.
Refer to risks: E-1, E-2, E-3

8.5.9 **Import/Export Regulations.** Operating units and subsidiaries performing business with governments outside the United States must fully understand and comply with all applicable import and export laws. Refer to Section 2.2, Export Controls, and Section 4.3, Import Controls.
Refer to risks: E-1, E-2, E-3

Risk If Standard Is Not Implemented

E-1 U.S. and/or non-U.S. government laws or regulations may be violated.

E-2 Legal action against the company and/or individual employees may be initiated resulting in fines which must be paid by the company.

E-3 Public embarrassment and damage to the company's reputation could result from failure, alleged or actual, to comply fully with all terms of a non-U.S. government contract.

CHAPTER NINE

Records and Information Management

 INTRODUCTION

Records and information management includes an overview of those controls necessary to adequately protect the company's information and for maintaining its critical business records. It is corporate policy that only those records required for the operation of the company's business will be generated, and that such records shall be held only as long as there is a recognized business need or legal requirement for their retention. When the business need or legal requirement no longer exists, the records will be retained as specified by company's global records retention schedules and will adhere to General Data Protection Regulations (GPDR) and the HIPAA security rule.

 PROCESS OVERVIEW

The diagram below suggests that the foundational elements that support the records and information management process are Internal Controls and Compliance, Records Management and Classification Standards, and Code of Conduct and "Tone at the Top."

Records Management

Define Records Management Program Roles and Responsibilities

- Define Responsibilities for Program Management, Supporting Committees, Company Management and Employees
- Define Responsibilities for Program Reviews and Assessments

Standards of Records Management and Classification

- Define Records Classification Criteria
- Implement Business Unit Information Profiles
- Define Records Requiring Additional Clearance
- Add Controls for Terminated Employees
- Communicate the Standards

Non-Compliance and Remediation

- Report Non-Compliance Issues by Business Unit
- Implement Remediation Plans
- Update Records Management Standards and Classification As Needed

Internal Controls and Compliance

Records Management and Classification Standards

Code of Conduct and "Tone at the Top"

METRICS

Table of Metrics
■ Percentage Adherence to Policies and Procedures
■ Number of Training Courses Offered
■ Percentage of Employees Attending Training Courses
■ Number of Compliance Reviews Conducted Annually
■ Number of Issues Found in Self-Audit Programs
■ Number of Process Improvements Identified per Fiscal Period
■ Value of Compliance Issues Identified per Fiscal Period
■ Value of Noncompliance Fines Paid per Fiscal Period

 APPLICATION OF INTERNAL CONTROL AND DEFINITIONS

- **Company Confidential (CC)**—This classification applies to information intended for use within the company or to further its business endeavors. Material requires protection because of its personnel, technical, or business sensitivity. Unauthorized release or loss of this information can reasonably be expected to harm the company's business or internal operations.
- **Company Restricted**—This classification applies to strategic, corporate-level information providing the company significant future competitive advantage or causing serious harm to the company's image, stock price, or market share if disclosed.
- **Copy**—Any information that is duplicated and is used for reference purposes only. Copies are normally kept for a short period of time and are never sent to offsite storage. Each employee/contractor and business unit is responsible for disposing of their copies within the time frame specified under the column "Copy Retention Maximum" as specified on a records retention schedule.
- **Non-Records**—Any tangible information that does not typically contain data pertaining to or originated by the company. Materials are typically used as reference or research tools by the staff and include such items as newspapers, periodicals, brochures, public and Internet information, and toolkits.
- **Office of Record**—Any business unit that is assigned responsibility for maintaining "official" company records.

- **Official Records**—These records are those which are required to be kept to meet statutory, regulatory, or contractual requirements, and those kept pursuant to good business practice for periods of time as specified in the global records retention schedule.
- **Owner**—The term *owner* is used in this document as a convention to identify an individual or business unit who has approved management responsibility for acquiring, maintaining, and controlling "official" company records. All company records must have a defined "owner" or "Office of Record."
- **Ownership**—Records are the property of the company and not the property of the individual who creates generates or receives them.
- **Records**—In the context of this document, the term *record* includes all information concerning the company's business whether such information is in paper, photographic, electronic (including an individual's PC, network files, and legacy systems), video, or audio form. Such information may be used or stored on or off the premises.

GENERAL DATA PROTECTION REGULATION (GDPR)

The GDPR was approved and adopted by the European Union (EU) Parliament in April 2016. The regulation took effect after a two-year transition period and, unlike a directive, did not require any legislation to be passed by government. GDPR came into force on May 25, 2018. The GDPR not only applies to organizations located within the EU but also applies to organizations located outside of the EU if they offer goods or services to, or monitor the behavior of, EU data subjects. It applies to all companies processing and holding the personal data of data subjects residing in the EU, regardless of the company's location.

The GDPR applies to *personal data*, meaning any information relating to an identifiable person who can be directly or indirectly identified in particular by reference to an identifier. This definition provides for a wide range of personal identifiers to constitute personal data, including name, identification number, location data, or online identifier, reflecting changes in technology and the way organizations collect information about people.[1]

---

[1] European Union (EU) General Data Protection Regulation (GDPR), "GDPR FAQs," accessed January 4, 2019, https://eugdpr.org/the-regulation/gdpr-faqs/.

THE HEALTH INSURANCE PORTABILITY AND ACCOUNTABILITY ACT (HIPAA)

The Health Insurance Portability and Accountability Act of 1996 (HIPAA) required the Secretary of the U.S. Department of Health and Human Services (HHS) to develop regulations protecting the privacy and security of certain health information. To fulfill this requirement, HHS published what are commonly known as the HIPAA Privacy Rule and the HIPAA Security Rule. The Privacy Rule, or Standards for Privacy of Individually Identifiable Health Information, establishes national standards for the protection of certain health information. The Security Standards for the Protection of Electronic Protected Health Information (the Security Rule) establish a national set of security standards for protecting certain health information that is held or transferred in electronic form. The Security Rule operationalizes the protections contained in the Privacy Rule by addressing the technical and nontechnical safeguards that organizations called "covered entities" must put in place to secure individuals' "electronic protected health information" (e-PHI). Within HHS, the Office for Civil Rights (OCR) has responsibility for enforcing the Privacy and Security Rules with voluntary compliance activities and civil money penalties.[2]

SUB-PROCESSES

The specific sub-processes included in the records and information management process are:

9.1 Standards of Internal Control Responsibilities

9.2 Standards of Internal Record-Keeping Requirements

9.1 STANDARDS OF INTERNAL CONTROL RESPONSIBILITIES

Standard of Internal Control

9.1.1 **Responsibilities of Global Records Management.** Responsibilities for the global records management process include:

---

[2]U.S. Department of Health & Human Services, HIPAA Health Information Privacy, "Summary of the HIPAA Security Rule," accessed January 13, 2019, https://www.hhs.gov/hipaa/for-professionals/security/laws-regulations/index.html.

    a. Developing and maintaining global records retention schedules for managing records retention and disposition in accordance with GPDR requirements

    b. Communicating these retention requirements to operating units and offering training to effectively implement the retention program

    c. Establishing and maintaining worldwide policies, standards, and quality processes to ensure authenticity, integrity, and accessibility of all records and information management systems

    d. Maintaining a vital records and disaster recovery records program to protect valuable records and, in the event of a disaster, ensure the availability of business critical records

    e. Conducting annual compliance reviews to encourage good record management practices

    Refer to risks: A-1, A-2, A-3, A-4, A-5, A-6

9.1.2 **Responsibilities of the Global Records Retention Review Committee.** The Global Records Retention Review Committee (GRRRC) is comprised of a cross-section of representatives within the company, including at least one representative from the legal and finance organizations. Responsibilities of GRRRC members include:

    a. Reviewing proposed changes or additions to all global records retention schedules to ensure all operating, business, and reporting requirements of their organizations are accurately reflected in the proposed retention time

    b. Approving proposed changes or additions to all global records retention schedules as submitted by the manager of global records management

    Refer to risks: A-1, A-2, A-5

9.1.3 **Responsibilities of Global Records Management Coordinators.** Global Records Management Coordinators (GEO-RMC) are those individuals designated at the GEO level to be focal points for certain global records management activity. Responsibilities of the GEO-RMCs include:

    a. Identifying storage facilities utilized by company sites for the storage of records

    b. Maintaining a GEO repository of offsite storage inventory sheets

    c. Initiating records dispensation activities in accordance with approved Global Records Management procedures

    Refer to risks: A-1, A-2, A-3, A-4, A-6

9.1.4 **Responsibilities of Operating Units.** Each operating unit is responsible for:

    a. Providing appropriate protection for those records identified as vital records

    b. Conducting annual compliance audits of its record-keeping practices

    Refer to risks: A-1, A-3, A-4, A-6

9.1.5 **Responsibilities of Cost Center Managers.** Cost center managers have responsibility to:

    a. Ensure that their departments comply with company's records management policy.

    b. Follow established standards and guidelines.

    c. Inform employees about the policy.

    Refer to risks: A-1, A-2, A-3, A-4, A-5, A-6

9.1.6 **Responsibilities of Employees.** Each employee is responsible for complying with the company's records management policy and following established standards and guidelines.

    Refer to risks: A-1, A-2, A-3, A-4, A-5, A-6

9.1.7 **Responsibilities of Internal Audit.** Internal Audit is responsible for reviewing departmental compliance with approved global records retention schedules as part of departmental audit findings.

    Refer to risks: A-3, A-4, A-6

Risk If Standard Is Not Implemented

A-1 Noncompliance with government regulation may result in substantial fines, penalties, and/or loss of business.

A-2 The company could be held responsible for negligence, errors, or omissions resulting in financial loss to its shareholders.

A-3 Intentional errors or misappropriation of assets could go undetected.

A-4 The company's competitive position or reputation could be adversely affected.

A-5 Legal restrictions and covenants may be violated.

A-6 Operational efficiency and reliability may be impaired and significantly disrupt the manufacturing/business process.

9.2 STANDARDS OF INTERNAL RECORD-KEEPING REQUIREMENTS

Introduction

This section recommends the internal record-keeping requirements and classifications that a company should consider for the data and records management process.

Standard of Internal Control

9.2.1 **Information Profile.** Each business unit must maintain records profile details for records retained within the department. The profile should include the following information:
   a. File name
   b. Record type (official, vital, historical)
   c. Record description/title
   d. Format (paper, electronic, etc.)
   e. Record series code (the alphanumeric code used to designate the appropriate record series that a record falls under per the established schedule)
   f. Security classification
   g. Location/site
   Refer to risks: B-1, B-2, B-3, B-4, B-5, B-6

9.2.2 **Classification.** Records are to be filed and indexed in such a way as to maximize their usefulness to the company and its employees and to prevent loss or inappropriate disclosure. Information should be classified: (i) as either official record or copy and (ii) with an appropriate security classification.
   Refer to risks: B-1, B-2, B-3, B-4, B-5, B-6

9.2.3 **Exemptions.** Exemptions from normal retention policies can be granted through request and approval.
   Refer to risks: B-1, B-2, B-3, B-5, B-6

9.2.4 **Compliance Reviews.** Each operating unit should perform an annual compliance review to:
   a. Determine the level of employee understanding of records management policy and practices.
   b. Ensure appropriate classification and handling of information.
   c. Identify any problems that exist with respect to its overall operations.
   Refer to risks: B-1, B-2, B-3, B-5, B-6

9.2.5 **Reclassification.** "Company Confidential" and "Company Restricted" information may also be marked with a reclassification date. When a reclassify date is specified, information will be reclassified on that date to Unrestricted Internal Use. If no reclassification date is specified, the information retains its classification as marked unless changed by the owner.
Refer to risk: B-6

9.2.6 **Corporate Clearance Materials.** Corporate clearance materials (e.g., speeches, papers, publications, presentations) that are to be released externally must be reviewed relative to:
a. The material's proprietary value to the company,
b. Its potential use by competitors,
c. The timing of the release,
d. The currency of the information, and
e. The consistency of the information with company announcements.
   This review and approval process is coordinated by the corporate communications department.
Refer to risks: B-2, B-3, B-4, B-5, B-6

9.2.7 **Information Protection.** Users of information must ensure they are protecting information in accordance with all applicable internal control standards and with all relevant company practices. Appropriate measures should be taken to ensure that any information designated as vital is protected from loss and damage to the company.
Refer to risks: B-1, B-2, B-3, B-4, B-5, B-6

9.2.8 **Terminated Employees.** Managers of individuals no longer employed by the company should take the necessary steps to ensure that any records generated, maintained, or utilized by that employee are handled in an appropriate and timely manner.
Refer to risks: B-3, B-4, B-6

9.2.9 **Alternative Media Usage.** Use of alternative media for the storage of official records must be approved prior to implementation.
Refer to risks: B-1, B-2, B-5, and B-6

Risk If Standard Is Not Implemented

B-1 Noncompliance with government regulation may result in substantial fines, penalties, and/or loss of business.

B-2 The company could be held responsible for negligence, errors or omissions resulting in financial loss to its shareholders.

B-3 Intentional errors or misappropriation of assets could go undetected.

B-4 The company's competitive position or reputation could be adversely affected.

B-5 Legal restrictions and covenants may be violated.

B-6 Operational efficiency and reliability may be impaired and significantly disrupt the manufacturing/business process.

See Table 9.1 for examples of classification by type of information and Table 9.2 for protection requirements of physical and electronic records.

TABLE 9.1 Examples of Classification Category by Information Type

Company Restricted	Company Confidential
Product roadmaps	Employee information: performance appraisals, salary data, specific personnel case files and data, phone lists, employee rosters
Strategic plans or forecasts	Internal policies
Corporate-/group-level business plans	Unique manufacturing processes, manufacturing specifications, pricing/data methods
Data on mergers and potential acquisitions	Financial data prior to public disclosure
Reorganizations	Customer lists, sales reports, major prospective reports, product reports
Changes in business objectives	Trade secrets, division-level roadmaps
	Key manufacturing drawings or other critical technical/design data
	Competitive intelligence reports

The examples are intended to aid in the selection of a classification category that most closely approximates the information protection needs. The examples are not intended to be all-inclusive or definitive. Choice of the appropriate classification is always based on how the records disclose the information and impact the company. This evaluation may suggest a different category than that illustrated below.

TABLE 9.2 Protection Requirements for Physical and Electronic Records

	Classification Category	
Action to Be Taken or Controlled	**Company Restricted**	**Company Confidential**
Identifying Record	Classification identified on cover sheet. Reclassification date noted as appropriate.	Classification identified on all sheets unless the physical size of the record or other circumstance makes this difficult, in which case the first page of the record only is marked. Reclassification date noted as appropriate.
a. Electronic file label	Classification identified on file label.	Classification identified on file label.
b. External label (portable storage media)	Classification identified on external label (optional within admittance controlled data center).	Classification identified on external label.
c. Video displays (CRTs)	Classification identified on first application screen.	Classification identified on each screen.
Disclosure Restrictions	At discretion of holder based upon need to know.	No disclosure to others outside information community unless permission has been received from the owner.
Access Control	Access limited to individuals authorized by holder.	Access limited to individuals authorized by owner. Each access must be logged.
d. Review of authorizations	12 months	6 months
e. Change passwords	3 months	3 months
Copying	No copying allowed.	Only with permission from owner. Owner may elect to provide copy.

(Continued)

TABLE 9.2 (*Continued*)

Action to Be Taken or Controlled	Classification Category	
	Company Restricted	**Company Confidential**
Mail a. Internal company mail b. External mail	At discretion of holder.	Only with permission from the owner. Owner may elect to provide copy.
	Double-wrap if mailed through U.S. Mail or other external mail service.	Double-wrap if mailed through U.S. Mail or other external mail service.
Electronic communication (Internal/External)	Only to or from secured terminals. Use secure communication link or encode data. Encoding technique must be approved by Information Security Services, Information Systems.	Only to or from secured terminals. Use secure communication link or encode data. Encoding technique must be approved by Information Security Services, Information Systems.
Storage	Locked storage.	Locked storage.
Travel	Carried within locked device.	Carried within locked device. (Limited travel when possible.)
Disposal/Destruction	Burn, shred or pulverize.	Burn, shred, or pulverize.

Physical records (e.g. paper documents, computer printouts, photographs) will be protected according to the minimum requirements defined below. The owner of the information may choose to supplement minimum requirements.

CHAPTER TEN

Computer, Telecommunications, and Systems Controls

 INTRODUCTION

Computer and telecommunications controls are an integral part of the company's internal control structure. The responsibility for implementing and enforcing these controls resides with application and system owners, users, and service providers. These standards apply universally to all company computing and telecommunications environments worldwide, which include personal computers, workstations, computer centers, and local area and wide area networks.

The internal controls described here should be discussed early in the IT planning process and culminate in the implementation of solid IT policies and procedures that allow the organization to have a secure IT environment.

Establishing internal controls that are part of IT policies and procedures benefits organizations of all sizes in various ways. First, internal controls help create a controlled IT environment that is compliant with company policies and regulatory requirements. Second, internal controls that are established as part of the planning process help IT departments meet the organization's technology needs more effectively and in a timely manner. Finally, IT policies and procedures help executive managers know the role IT plays within the

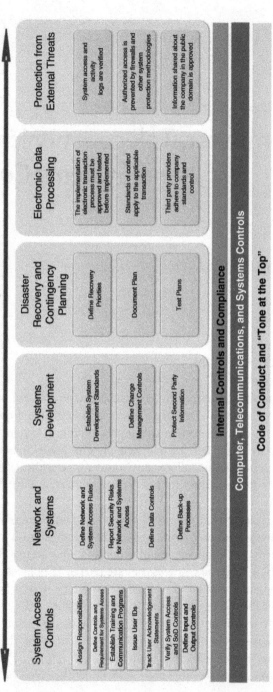

organization and how internal controls will be implemented to meet corporate strategic goals. Once established, internal auditors can use these policies and procedures as guidelines to examine the effectiveness of IT operations and assess whether their activities are compliant with internal regulations during audit reviews.

It is the company's policy that all employees have access to the information resources necessary to perform their job. It has also been a corporate policy that these resources be sufficiently controlled to provide high integrity, ensure availability, and minimize risk of disclosure, misuse, or loss by either accidental or intentional actions.

 ## PROCESS OVERVIEW

The diagram below suggests that the foundational elements of the processes that support computer, telecommunications, and systems controls are Internal Controls and Compliance, Controls, and Code of Conduct and "Tone at the Top."

 ## METRICS

Table of Metrics

Systems Metrics

- **Number of Systems with Known Vulnerabilities**—Systems that are vulnerable to threats and attacks.
- **Number of SSL Certificates Configured Incorrectly**—SSL Certificates provide secure, encrypted communications between a website and an Internet browser. SSL Certificates are typically installed on pages that require end-users to submit sensitive information over the Internet like credit card details or passwords.
- **Volume of Data Transferred Using the Corporate Network**—Usage of the corporate network.
- **Number of Users with "Super-User" Access Level**—Number of users with possible excessive access which could put the company at risk.
- **Number of Days to Deactivate Former Employee Credentials**—The time to deactivate a former employee's system access.
- **Number of Communication Ports Open During a Period of Time**—The number of communication ports open should correlate to the number of users.
- **Frequency of Review of Third-Party Accesses**—Determines how many third parties (non-employees) are accessing company systems.

Table of Metrics

- **Frequency of Access to Critical Enterprise Systems by Third Parties**—Determines how many third parties (non-employees) are accessing company enterprise or ERP systems.
- **Percentage of Business Partners with Effective Cybersecurity Policies**—Determines cybersecurity policy compliance.
- **Number of Cloud Applications Used**—Determines how many cloud applications are used by a company.
- **Number of SAE Reviews Conducted/Obtained**—Highlights the number of SAE 18 reviews conducted or results obtained for third-party services provided.

Process Metrics

- **Online Application Availability**—The percentage of time the application is functioning properly.
- **Batch SLAs Achieved**—The percentage of key batch jobs that finish on time.
- **Production Incidents**—The number of production problems by severity.

Delivery Metrics

- **Project Satisfaction**—The average score from post-project surveys completed by business partners.
- **Project Delivery**—The percentage of projects delivered on time.
- **Project Cost**—The percentage of projects delivered within the cost estimate.
- **Defect Containment**—The percentage of defects contained within test environments.
- **Value and Number of Compliance Issues**—Issues reported by fiscal period and the financial impact to the company.

Organizational Metrics

- **Attrition**—The percentage of employees who move to other jobs.
- **Performance Reviews**—The percentage of employees with current written reviews.

Financial

- **IT Budget Variance**—Actual costs compared to budgeted costs.
- **IT Resource Cost**—The average cost of a technology resource.

Business Continuity Metrics

- **Percentage of Downtime**—Percent of system and application not available.
- **Number of Days to Recovery**—The number of days to recover the application and ensure it is available to users.
- **Frequency of Business Continuity Plan Tests Performed**—How often business continuity plans are tested during a defined fiscal period.
- **Service Level Agreement (SLA) Performance**—How well a third party is performing and meeting SLA objections after recovery.

Table of Metrics

- **Operational Level Agreement (OLA) Performance**—Determine how well an internal department is performing after recovery.
- **Date of Last Plan Update**—The date of the last update to a business continuity plan.
- **Number of Cloud Computing Plans Reviewed/Obtained**—The number of cloud computing plans reviewed per a defined fiscal period.

 ## APPLICATION OF INTERNAL CONTROLS

Maintaining effective internal controls within key business process designs, business processes, procedures, and financial reporting is a responsibility shared by all employees. This section sets forth specific expectations for company managers and employees. These standards are intended to help ensure that a strong internal control environment exists throughout the company. They describe activities that, when implemented, can ensure company assets are protected, financial and other management reports are accurate, and there is compliance with company policies and other requirements.

These standards should be used to regularly self-assess current processes, system designs, and plans to ensure they have appropriate and sufficient controls. The Internal Audit and Internal Controls teams will be evaluating adherence to these standards in future internal control assessments.

 ## SAE 18

If your company is a service organization that performs outsourced services that affect the financial statements of another company, your organization will more than likely be asked to provide an SOC 1 Type II Report, especially if the user of your services is publicly traded.

Some example services that will require SAE 18 reporting include:

- Payroll Processing
- Loan Servicing
- Data Center/Co-Location/Network Monitoring Services
- Software as a Service (SaaS)
- Medical Claims Processor

SUB-PROCESSES

The specific sub-processes included in the computer systems controls process are:

10.1 Owners, Users, and Service Providers

10.2 Physical Security and Environmental Controls

10.3 Computer Access Control

10.4 Network Operations and Security Controls

10.5 Systems Development Methodology

10.6 Change Management

10.7 Computer and Telecommunications Backup for Production Restart/ Recovery

10.8 Disaster Recovery and Business Contingency Planning

10.9 Input Controls

10.10 Output Controls

10.11 Paperless Transactions, Electronic Commerce, and EDI

10.12 Non-Company Networks and Bulletin Boards

 10.1 OWNERS, USERS, AND SERVICE PROVIDERS

Introduction

Three distinct responsibilities—owner, user, and service provider—have been defined to assure that basic information protection policies are implemented. Although these roles may be separate, they are sometimes performed by the same individual.

Definitions

Owner—The company is the sole owner of information resources as well as other company assets. The term *owner* is a convention used to identify an individual who has approved management responsibility for acquiring and controlling the use and disposition of an information resource. Each information systems resource must have a defined owner. If more than one individual can be considered the owner of an informational resource, then one individual must be designated as the primary contact.

System owner—An individual with approved management responsibility for a physical computer or telecommunications system. A system owner may also be a service provider or may contract responsibility for operating and managing the system to another company unit or a vendor.

Application owner—An individual with approved management responsibility for a specific application, including application programs and data. If more than one individual can be considered the application owner, then one individual must be designated as the primary contact.

User—Individual or group of individuals authorized to use an information resource.

Service provider—Individual, department, or vendor who provides owners and users with information systems services and is responsible for the operation and maintenance and security of computing and telecommunications hardware and software.

Unattended—Out of visual range of the user.

The company unit or department managers are responsible for ensuring a system owner is assigned for all computer and telecommunications equipment, including computer centers, remote processing sites, local area networks, workstations, departmental and personal computers, and data storage sites.

Standard of Internal Control

10.1.1 **Assigned System and Application Owners.** Company units are responsible for ensuring an owner is assigned for each application. Systems shared among multiple departments or business groups, may have several application owners but there must be a primary contact. The company unit or department managers must maintain up-to-date lists of application owners and system owners.
Refer to risks: A-1, A-3, A-4, A-5

10.1.2 **Application Owner Responsibilities.** Application owners have the responsibility to:
a. Approve application requirements/design or application changes.
b. Assign security classifications.
c. Authorize access to application data files or formally approve others to authorize access on their behalf.
d. Acknowledge acceptance of additions or changes to applications.

e. Ensure that business recovery plans are prepared, including identification of all necessary backup files for both corporate and third party applications.

f. Ensure compliance with all local statutory requirements.

g. Ensure that supported versions of distributed system software are installed and used.

Refer to risks: A-2, A-7, A-8, A-10, A-21

10.1.3 **System Owners/Service Providers Responsibilities.** System owners/service providers have the responsibility to:

a. Provide a physical environment with safeguards against unauthorized removal or destruction of data or data processing equipment.

b. Provide system management controls to maintain operational integrity and security.

c. Arrange for the backup and retention of critical application data files and programs in secure third party locations where normal processing occurs.

d. Arrange for equipment and/or alternative computing facilities sufficient to meet established disaster recovery priorities.

e. Provide sufficient computer resources to respond to the computing needs of the users who operate systems at their facility, department, or local area network.

f. Ensure procedures exist to comply with agreements for use of licensed software.

g. Ensure virus detection software is installed, active, and up-to-date on equipment when it is used for business, engineering applications, product testing, and/or manufacturing processing.

h. Ensure compliance with all local statutory requirements.

i. Arrange for the approved system banner to be displayed as part of the logon process.

j. Escalate any issue regarding noncompliance with the internal control standards to management if it cannot be resolved with the system and application owner.

Refer to risks: A-2, A-6, A-9, A-10, A-12, A-21

10.1.4 **Approved IT Products and Services.** Where a global or regional contract is established for an IT service or product, that contract will be used unless an approval exception has been granted.

Refer to risks: A-9, A-12, A-14, A-15, A-16, A-17

10.1.5 **Documented Policies and Procedures.** Company units responsible for software development or maintenance are responsible for preparing and maintaining detailed data processing policies and procedures applicable to the application they are responsible for. The policies and procedures must include:

    a. Criteria for management approval of third party and corporate system changes to move software from a test to production status

    b. Documentation standards for system architecture, logical design, and physical design

    c. Software coding standards, which define program structure, guidelines for logic complexity, and data element naming conventions

  Refer to risk: A-11

10.1.6 **User Responsibilities.** A user has responsibility to:

    a. Use information resources only for authorized company business purposes. The use of these resources for non-business purposes, such as but not limited to, distributing chain letters and jokes, private business ventures, advertisements, etc., is prohibited. Like any company property, these resources and their use are subject to monitoring and/or inspection at any time.

    b. Protect all resources in his/her custody against accidental or unauthorized modification, disclosure, or destruction.

    c. Keep passwords secret, change them frequently, and establish ones that cannot be easily guessed.

    d. Never leave an active session unattended/unsecured.

    e. Notify supervision immediately if there is a suspicion or a possibility that the security of company information has been compromised or such an attempt has been made in violation of system access policies.

    f. Ensure that appropriate controls are utilized when becoming an owner. When systems are used in an environment outside the original owner's control, the user becomes the owner.

    g. Obtain management approval before using personal devices and applications to process company data or information.

    h. Ensure all software installed on company computers/devices is properly licensed. Illegal copies of software must not be received, made, used, or distributed.

    i. Obtain management approval before installing or executing software on company-owned computers.

> j. Ensure approved virus detection software is installed, active, and up-to-date on all workstations assigned for their use. At a minimum each workstation must be checked daily, or each time it is used if less than daily.
>
> k. Periodically back up computer data files, programs, and software to ensure continuity of business operations in the event of hardware, software, or application failure or an extended outage.
>
> l. Use only the access processes provided by regional company information systems infrastructure units to access computers connected to the company's internal network.
>
> m. Identify them on outgoing e-mail messages. Users must not use anonymous remailers for company business.
>
> n. Obtain management authorization before removing computer equipment and data files (including those removed for disposal) containing company information.
>
> **Refer to risks: A-9, A-10, A-12, A-18, A-19, A-20**

Risk If Standard Is Not Implemented

A-1 Applications, systems, and personal devices may not be properly maintained and controlled without owner sponsorship.

A-2 Changes and access to applications or systems may not be properly authorized.

A-3 IT personnel may seek approval for application or system changes from someone other than the business process owner.

A-4 Management personnel may change responsibilities without transferring ownership of applications or systems.

A-5 The responsibilities associated with operating and/or maintaining computing and telecommunications facilities may not be clearly defined.

A-6 Computer equipment may be damaged by fire or natural causes or intentionally damaged by unauthorized persons.

A-7 Backup files may not be available for processing in the event of a disaster.

A-8 The company's ability to conduct business may be significantly impaired in the event of a disaster at a computer or network site.

A-9 Adequate resources may not be available to meet business requirements and growth.

A-10 The company may be liable for misuse or unauthorized copying of proprietary software.

A-11 The responsibilities associated with operating and/or maintaining system software operations and application documentation may not be clearly defined.

A-12 Business, manufacturing, or engineering systems may become dysfunctional, resulting in productivity and revenue losses, or critical data could be destroyed.

A-14 Operational efficiency and reliability may be impaired and significantly disrupt processing.

A-15 Volume commitments established in contracts may not be reached.

A-16 The company may not receive the discounts appropriate for its total level of information technology purchases.

A-17 Duplicate infrastructures may be developed, increasing overall company costs.

A-18 Company information may be disclosed, lost, or contaminated, which may adversely affect the company's competitive position.

A-19 Passwords to user computer or network accounts may be disclosed and allow unauthorized access to data and programs.

A-20 Individual accountability may be lost.

A-21 Local statutory responsibilities may not be met, exposing the company to legal liabilities.

10.2 PHYSICAL SECURITY AND ENVIRONMENTAL CONTROLS

Introduction

Management may designate certain computing and telecommunications areas as requiring restricted access. Access to restricted computing and telecommunications areas must be limited to authorized individuals on a need-to-know basis. Examples of restricted areas are product design departments, computer centers, telecommunications access areas and switch rooms, and network file server locations.

Standard of Internal Control

10.2.1 **Restricted Access.** The following control techniques must be employed for these areas:

a. Physical access to computer and network hardware, software, data, and documentation must be specifically authorized by management and restricted to only those personnel requiring such access for performance of assigned functional responsibilities.

Refer to risks: B-1, B-2

b. All entrances/exits to restricted computing and telecommunications areas must be physically secured.

Refer to risks: B-1, B-2, B-3

c. All keys, keycards, badges, and combinations used to limit access to restricted computing and telecommunications areas must be confiscated and/or access denied by management upon employee termination or transfer. Access lists to these areas must be reviewed on at least an annual basis.

Refer to risks: B-1, B-2, B-3

d. All physical access to computer hardware, software, data, and documentation by suppliers and vendors must be specifically authorized. All suppliers and vendors must be supervised by authorized personnel.

Refer to risks: B-1, B-2

e. All removal of computer and telecommunications equipment and data files containing proprietary information must be specifically authorized by management, recorded, and reconciled. All data files removed must be handled in accordance with their classification.

Refer to risks: B-1, B-2

10.2.2 **Authorized Asset Removal.** All removal of computer equipment, telecommunications equipment, and data files (including those removed for disposal) containing company information must be specifically authorized by management. All data files removed must be handled in accordance with their security classification.

Refer to risks: B-1, B-2

10.2.3 **Environmental Requirements.** Physical computer and telecommunications sites must be prepared and maintained in accordance with the environmental requirements specified by the supplier for the equipment.

Refer to risks: B-4, B-5, B-6, B-7

10.2.4 **Regular Inventories.** Periodic inventories of computer and tele-communications software and hardware must be performed on a regular basis and reconciled.
Refer to risks: B-1, B-2, B-5

10.2.5 **Restricted Access to Consoles.** Main computer consoles and network/system management terminals must be accessible to only authorized operations personnel and all console activity must be recorded.
Refer to risks: B-2, B-3

10.2.6 **Secured Hardware.** Telecommunication and computer hardware must not be located in unsecured areas that would pose undue risk.
Refer to risks: B-1, B-2

10.2.7 **Fire Protection.** Fire detection, prevention, and extinguishing systems and equipment must be installed at computer hardware and telecommunications sites, accessible to trained operations personnel, and periodically tested according to company and code specifications.
Refer to risks: B-1, B-4, B-5, B-7

10.2.8 **Electrical Mishap Protection.** All computer and telecommunication hardware must be appropriately protected against electrical surges, water damage, and natural disasters based on a risk assessment.
Refer to risks: B-1, B-4, B-5, B-7

10.2.9 **Hardware Location.** Computer hardware and telecommunications sites must not be constructed or located near any combustible or hazardous areas.
Refer to risks: B-1, B-4, B-5, B-7

10.2.10 **Clean Hardware Sites.** Computer hardware and telecommunications sites must be kept clean and free from combustible materials and responsible personnel are to follow acceptable housekeeping rules. Office areas within these facilities must be avoided and allowed on an exception basis only.
Refer to risks: B-1, B-4, B-5, B-7

10.2.11 **Error Logs.** All computer and telecommunications hardware and software problems/errors must be recorded, monitored, and analyzed to ensure timely identification and correction.
Refer to risk: B-6

Risk If Standard Is Not Implemented

B-1 Computer and telecommunications hardware, software, data, and documentation may not be adequately protected from damage or theft.

B-2 Unauthorized use, disclosure, modification, destruction, or stealing of systems and data could occur.

B-3 Computer and telecommunications hardware may be used by unauthorized personnel to bypass normal security and operating controls and gain access to confidential systems and data.

B-4 Personnel may be subjected to unnecessary physical risk if environmental controls are not adequate.

B-5 Loss of critical data could occur due to improperly installed, maintained, or stored computer hardware and storage media.

B-6 Operational efficiency and reliability may be impaired and significantly disrupt processing.

B-7 Significant damage or destruction to computer and telecommunications hardware, software, and data could occur as a result of inadequate environmental monitoring and control systems.

 10.3 COMPUTER ACCESS CONTROL

Introduction

Computer access control applies to all information resources: desktops, servers, mainframes, networks, and so on. The objective of computer access control is to assure the integrity, availability, and confidentiality of company information and the facilities that process, store, or transmit such information.

System access controls reduce the risk of information being disclosed, contaminated, misused, or destroyed, whether by accidental or intentional means. It is based upon proper authorization and establishes a basis for internal control by enabling separation of responsibility both within and among owner, user, and service provider functions (see Section 10.1 for detail on roles/responsibilities of owner, user, and service provider). Restricting an individual's access to resources based upon "need to know" and establishing individual accountability are essential principles in achieving effective access and internal control. Refer to the definitions below to obtain additional details on computer access control.

Definitions

Access Control—One of the most important internal controls an organization of any size should establish is access control—the doorway to all IT systems and corporate resources. Access controls specify how the business will monitor its IT resources and how they should be used. The most commonly used access controls include user accounts, consisting of passwords and usernames; login and resource access rights; and the establishment of privileged system accounts.

Login and Access Requests—The username and password allow employees access to a company's network resources. As a result, companies must hold employees accountable for all activity associated with their user accounts. For example, employees should not share their passwords with anyone, write them down on paper, or store them in their computers or personal devices. If they reveal their password to IT support staff, systems must be reset to prompt the employee for a password change when the user logs into the system again.

Furthermore, the user account should be set up to allow employees three login attempts only. After the third failed login attempt, the system should disable the account. To reestablish the user account, the employee must contact the company's network administrator or customer service department. Finally, access requests to network resources should come from the employee's direct supervisor, and the company's IT policies and procedures should indicate who needs to implement all access requests.

Remote Access—Remote access extends the network's boundaries by enabling employees to use company resources when working outside the office. Remote access should occur through a remote server that allows the creation of user profiles. At least two types of profiles must be created: a normal user profile and a user profile for each system administrator. A normal user profile has no rights to perform system operations and is given to any non-IT employee who asks for remote access or works from a remote location. On the other hand, user profiles for system administrators must enable them to run system applications and tools remotely.

All remote access requests must come from the employee's supervisor and should specify the kind of access needed and the location where access will take place. In addition, remote access connections should use encryption, as well as a time limit for connections that are inactive for 30 minutes or longer or a company-defined period of time. Furthermore, remote access accounts should have a different username and password combination, as well as a password that changes for each login activity—a digital access card can be used for this.

Finally, the IT department needs to keep track of all remote access connections in a log or report. Auditors can use these best practices as a baseline when reviewing whether the IT department's operations are consistent with the company's strategic plan.

Single-Factor Authentication—Authentication methods based on "something you know" where the primary method of identifying the user is a password.

Two-Factor Authentication—Authentication or identification methods whose information, if captured, cannot be used by itself for unauthorized individuals to gain entry into a computer system or application. Two-factor authentication is based on "something you have plus something you know." It requires processing something that is unique to the individual and a PIN (Personal Identification Number) that ensures that the individual is indeed who they say they are. Time-dependent random number generators and cryptographic techniques are examples of such an authentication technique.

Owners/service providers of mainframe, midrange, and server computer equipment must ensure access control software is installed on the equipment when it is used for business, engineering, or research applications, product testing, and/or manufacturing processing. The access control software may be part of the computer operating system.

Standard of Internal Control

10.3.1 **Access Control Software.** At a minimum, access control software must perform the following functions:

   a. Data files and programs must be protected from unauthorized access and/or alteration, theft, or destruction;

   Refer to risks: C-l, C-2, C-3, C-4, C-9

   b. Unique user ID/password verification must be provided to establish individual accountability.

   Refer to risks: C-l, C-2, C-3, C-4, C-5, C-9, C-12, C-17

   c. Access control facilities must provide a means to segregate business functions. Segregating business functions should be done by accessing control software through use of groups and profiles.

   Refer to risks: C-l, C-2, C-3, C-4, C-5, C-11

d. Two-factor authentication must be used for access control to all computer-stored information classified as Company Confidential or Company Restricted, and for remote access to the company's network. In some cases, single-factor authentication is all that is needed. Strength of authentication should be driven by sensitivity of the information and the risk of its exposure. When single-factor authentication is implemented, passwords should be one-way encrypted. In addition, the software must automatically require passwords be established and changed in accordance with the following standards:

- Password must include at least three of the four following characters: (i) at least one numeric character; (ii) at least one special character (/, [,-,+,=,!,#, etc.); (iii) at least one lowercase character; and (iv) at least one uppercase character.
- A password must be a minimum of eight characters in length.
- A password must be changed at least every 60 days for general users, and 45 days for privileged or "super-users" (those with the ability to circumvent system security controls).
- After three unsuccessful password attempts, the user ID must be deactivated until reactivated by the security administrator or automated processes established by the security administrator and a report is generated to the security administrator.
- A password must not be reused within a certain time interval (two previous passwords).

Refer to risks: C-1, C-2, C-3, C-4, C-9, C-10, C-12

e. Access control software must have the ability to automatically create audit trail transactions showing significant security events such as unauthorized attempts (successful and unsuccessful) to access information resources, all access to Confidential Controlled data/programs, and all use of privileged or emergency user IDs.

Refer to risks: C-1, C-2, C-3, C-4, C-9, C-10

f. The ability to protect audit records from being disabled, modified, or deleted must be provided.

Refer to risks: C-1, C-2, C-3, C-4, C-9, C-10, C-12

Note: The password controls with respect to format, length, and expiration are only appropriate for internal applications and external applications that have access to proprietary information. This does not apply to external applications that contain publicly available information.

g. The ability to automatically log off terminals that remain inactive for an extended period of time (45 minutes maximum). At minimum inactive terminals that remain logged on after scheduled working hours must be logged off either automatically through software or manually. Where a workstation is configured to automatically require a password on power-up, the use of password-protected screensavers, screen locks, or new security technologies that may be introduced which force user re-authentication before work resumes may be used in place of automatic logoff during a user's assigned work hours.

Refer to risks: C-1, C-9, C-10, C-12, C-13, C-17

10.3.2 **Implementation of Access Controls.** Assigned owners of desktop/workstation equipment must ensure that the following access controls are in place:

a. Either physical or software access control must be installed on every desktop/workstation. For machines containing Confidential Controlled data, access control software must be used. For all other classification categories, a physical key lock is sufficient.

b. Confidential Controlled files must be encrypted on desktops/workstations; Company Restricted files must be encrypted if they leave company facilities (such as on a laptop).

c. File sharing must be controlled with access granted only on a need-to-know basis.

d. "Guest" accounts must be controlled such that individual accountability is not compromised and logging software must be installed to report on all access for machines containing Confidential Controlled data.

Refer to risks: C-1, C-2, C-5, C-9, C-10, C-12, C-18

10.3.3 **Security Administration Procedures.** Owners/service providers of computer equipment, in coordination with unit and department managers, must appoint security administrators. The security administrator function should be segregated from computer operations, systems development, and support when practical. Responsibility for managing and controlling the security administration function must remain with the company. Periodic reviews of accounts and privileges assigned by security administrators must be made by management. These procedures include:

a. Establishing each new user account with documented management approval. It is recommended to use the employee number as the user ID with a unique prefix assigned to each country whenever possible.
b. Granting access to production data files and programs with documented owner approval.
c. Controlling the use of software procedures (privileges) that bypass normal access security controls.
d. Defining, reporting, and investigating unauthorized access attempts in compliance with company/unit/department policies.
e. Monitoring continued compliance with security standards by regular reviews/audits of the facilities they administer.
f. Monitoring of computer accounts to detect any which have not been used for an extended period of time (12 months maximum) and verifying the continued need for them.

Refer to risks: C-7, C-8, C-9, C-10, C-13

10.3.4 **Transferred or Terminated Employees.** Security administrators, in coordination with Human Resources, must establish procedures to maintain computer accounts for users who are transferred within the company, and to deactivate employee computer accounts upon the employee's transfer or termination from the company on a timely basis. Security administrators have the authority to delete or activate accounts of terminated employees without reference to the owner or the owner's manager. Procedures must also be in place to detect active computer accounts assigned to terminated employees.
Refer to risks: C-14, C-15

10.3.5 **User Acknowledgment Statement.** Security administrators, in conjunction with supervisors, must ensure that each system user has a signed user acknowledgment statement on file. The statement must indicate that the user is familiar with and understands the corporate policy for use of information resources and they acknowledge their responsibility to: use the facilities, data, and information only for authorized company business purposes; access only the information for which they are authorized; protect the information accessed; and protect their password exclusively for their own use.
Refer to risk: C-16

10.3.6 **Use of Personal Equipment and Devices.** Security administrators, in conjunction with supervisors, must establish the conditions, policies, and procedures whereby personal equipment and software can be used for company business. At a minimum the following policies must be in place:

a. All software installed on an individual's personal equipment in order to facilitate processing of company business remains the property of the company.

b. The individual is personally responsible for protecting the software from license violation, including unauthorized copying.

c. Corporate standard virus protection software must be used on personal equipment used for company business.

d. It is the user's responsibility to verify that licensing conditions are met prior to installing on personal equipment and that conditions continue to be met as long as the software remains on the personal equipment.

Refer to risks: C-1, C-21

10.3.7 **Application Owner Responsibilities.** Application owners' responsibilities include:

a. Access to the application and its data to appropriate users must be authorized. Access should always be restricted on a need-to-know basis and is restricted to the extent information is required to satisfy specific job duties.

Refer to risks: C-11, C-17

b. Data files and programs must be classified in accordance to the company's Information Classification System (refer to Information Classification section). Corporate Security will assist in final decisions of classification.

Refer to risks: C-1, C-12, C-17, C-18

c. Computer-generated reports and online video screens containing confidential or sensitive information must be labeled with the proper company information classification.

Refer to risks: C-1, C-12, C-18

d. Confirmation must occur at least annually with user department management on the continued need for user's access. The confirmation process should be conducted with the assistance of the security administrator.

Refer to risk: C-19

10.3.8 **Signed Nondisclosure Statements.** Suppliers, contract programmers, and other non-company users must be informed of company information security policies and must sign nondisclosure agreements as required from company users before they are given direct access to the company's computer systems.
Refer to risks: C-1, C-12, C-17, C-18

10.3.9 **Segregation of Duties.** Computer systems or programs are considered in production status if relied upon by management for planning, conducting, recording, or reporting business, engineering, or manufacturing operations. Software for production systems may be developed by IT departments, end users, or vendors. Production systems may operate on mainframe, departmental, or personal computers or over wide area/local-area networks. The following controls must exist to protect production computer software and data files:

a. Every application and system must have an identified owner who has ultimate responsibility to satisfy application system control and audit requirements.
Refer to risks: C-1, C-10

b. Where systems are used in an environment outside the original owner's control, the user becomes the owner and has the responsibility to ensure that appropriate controls are utilized.
Refer to risks: C-1, C-6, C-9, C-12, C-13, C-17

c. Individual accountability is to be established for all systems activities and information processed (e.g. data content, programming, and systems operation).
Refer to risks: C-1, C-5, C-9, C-20

d. Data processing personnel directly supporting the system must be permitted access to application programs.
Refer to risks: C-1, C-6, C-9, C-12, C-17

e. Control and audit features are to be considered prior to purchase or licensing or, if company-developed, during the user requirement phase. These features are to be implemented at the time the system becomes operational.
Refer to risks: C-1, C-10

10.3.10 **Multiple Systems Access.** Supervisors must ensure access granted to multiple systems does not compromise segregation of duties.
Refer to risks: C-11, C-19

10.3.11 **User Password Responsibilities.** A user is accountable for all access and resulting actions that occur from the use of his or her password. A user must:

a. Protect a password as a personal possession.

b. Not share the password except on an emergency basis. When sharing has occurred, the user must establish a new password at the earliest opportunity.

c. Ensure that other individuals do not acquire his/her password by observing keyboard entry, access to written copy, overhearing, etc.

Refer to risks: C-1, C-5, C-9, C-12, C-18

10.3.12 **Assignment of User IDs.** In certain extraordinary circumstances it may be appropriate, due to business requirements, to assign a user ID to more than one individual. Such assignments are subject to the following:

a. Formal approval of a written business case by the application/data owner and regional security administration group.

b. Each user ID has a single named owner who accepts responsibility for all usage of the user ID and ensures that it is used only by authorized people.

c. The user ID assigned at a group level that the owner can effectively control.

d. The owner is required to maintain and update a list of all individuals sharing the ID and is able to produce this list on request.

e. The owner of the shared user ID ensures that a new password is assigned when one of the shared users no longer has business need for the account.

f. The shared user ID is not the owner's individual ID.

g. The shared ID is restricted only to access applications that were specified and approved in the business case.

h. Confirmation of the continued business need for the shared user ID is performed at least annually.

Refer to risks: C-1, C-5, C-9, C-12, C-18

Risk If Standard Is Not Implemented

C-1 Company information may be disclosed, lost, or contaminated, which may adversely affect the company's competitive position.

C-2 Computers that process business, manufacturing, and engineering systems transactions, and that perform product testing, may not have adequate access security software, resulting in access violations.

C-3 Computer access security software or operating systems may not provide adequate minimum protective or detective security controls.

C-4 Passwords to user computer or network accounts may be disclosed and allow unauthorized access to data and programs.

C-5 Individual accountability may be lost.

C-6 Inadequate segregation of duties may result from the combination of system accesses and manual duties.

C-7 Computer access security controls may not be implemented.

C-8 Security administrators may have conflicting duties that would allow them to change access security and system processing.

C-9 Access to production data files and programs may be granted without proper authorization.

C-10 Unauthorized access attempts may be made on a regular basis without detection.

C-11 Access to multiple systems by the same user could result in a lack of segregation of functions.

C-12 Sensitive information may be accessed and/or disclosed to unauthorized personnel.

C-13 Special access privileges may be granted that result in unnecessary or unauthorized access to production data files.

C-14 Terminated/transferred employees may gain access to and/or damage company data, disrupt normal business processing, or disclose sensitive information to outsiders.

C-15 System access by terminated/transferred employees or accounts assigned to terminated/transferred employees may not be detected.

C-16 System users may not understand their responsibilities with regard to use of information systems.

C-17 System users may be given access to data files and programs that are not required for their job functions.

C-18 Information stored on computer systems may not be properly protected.

C-19 Users may change job responsibilities but not change their system access requirements.

C-20 Engineering, manufacturing, or business applications may become dysfunctional, resulting in revenue and productivity losses, or critical data could be destroyed.

C-21 The company may be liable for misuse or unauthorized copying of proprietary software.

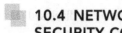

10.4 NETWORK OPERATIONS AND SECURITY CONTROLS

Introduction

The objectives of network operations and security controls include protection from unauthorized network use, protection against alteration and unauthorized use of information while in transit through the network, and maintenance of the integrity and reliability of network equipment and services. The scope of this section includes voice, data, video services, and network components.

Definitions

Backbone—A main cable or network segment used to connect smaller network subsets together into a larger logical network.

External Access—Access to company's networks from outside company premises. This includes accessing a company LAN or a PC on the corporate network from outside company premises.

Personal Identification—A unique, non-shared personal identifier that uses one or more of the following:

a. Network access user ID/password combination.

b. Devices carried by the users that are part of an automatic password changing system and identify the current network password. Such devices are commonly known as "smart cards."

c. Biometrics identifier such as thumbprint, voiceprint, retinal scans, etc.

Terminal or Computer Identification—A unique device ID (for either the computer or the terminal) that is electronically supplied on request to the host computer or access point that is being accessed. The ID is generated by special hardware in the device itself.

Terminal or Computer Location—A location that is known to be an authorized location (e.g. via a leased circuit with known endpoints in authorized locations).

WAN—Wide Area Network. A network segment that covers a larger area than a Local Area Network (LAN). Usually implies use of common carrier services.

Standard of Internal Control

10.4.1 **Documented Topology.** Service providers who operate communications networks must document and maintain descriptions of their physical and logical network topology.

Refer to risk: D- 1

10.4.2 **Approved Protocols and Services.** Only tested and approved protocols and services will be allowed over company backbone networks.
Refer to risks: D-1, D-2, D-3

10.4.3 **Network Management.** Network service providers must utilize configuration, performance, fault, accounting, and security management tools to monitor and manage networks.
Refer to risks: D-1, D-2, D-3, D-4, D-6, D-7

10.4.4 **Standardized Network Addresses.** Network addresses must be obtained and maintained as specified in the company network standards. If no standards exist, they need to be developed.
Refer to risks: D-2, D-3, D-7

10.4.5 **Information Encryption.** Users must ensure that any information is encrypted including e-mail, fax, voice, video, and data classified as Company Confidential when it is transmitted over the network. In other words, any information classified as Company Confidential must not be transmitted unless it is encrypted. Passwords must be encrypted during network transmission.
Refer to risks: D-l, D-4, D-5

10.4.6 **Defined Owners.** Each network component or service must have a defined owner.
Refer to risk: D-8

10.4.7 **Network Connection Authorization.** Every network connection must be authorized by the company unit requesting the connection and the owner of the network segment to which the connection is requested. Every network connection must be documented by the owner/service provider. Every network connection must adhere to Company Corporate and IT security standards and practices.
Refer to risks: D-1, D-4, D-5, D-9

10.4.8 **Accountability for Access.** Access to or actions through a network that would compromise the security of other units on the network are not to be permitted by any company unit. Company units that authorize a non-company person or unit to access the company's network are accountable for their actions.
Refer to risks: D-1, D-4, D-5

10.4.9 **Approved Firewalls/Routers.** Any network-to-network connections between the company and non-company networks will be through approved firewalls/routers.
Refer to risks: D-1, D-4, D-5, D-9

10.4.10 **Approval and Registration of External Access Points.** All external access points into company's network must be approved by the geographic Information Technology group. All external access points into the company's network must be registered with the IT group.
Refer to risks: D-1, D-4, D-5

10.4.11 **Accountability for Network Security.** The network service providers are responsible for monitoring the use of the network, preventing any security deficiencies, and notifying Information Security Services if any security deficiencies or misuse of the network are discovered. Additionally, the proactive corrective action taken to remedy the deficiencies or to prevent the misuse from continuing must also be monitored.
Refer to risks: D-1, D-2, D-3, D-4, D-5, D-6, D-9

10.4.12 **Cellular or Telephone Access (Bring Your Own Device).** Any system that requires an access code (usually a user ID and password combination) may only be accessed by cellular or portable telephones if:
a. The transmission in the cellular network is encrypted; and
b. Company Confidential information is not transmitted except as specified in 10.4.14.
Refer to risks: D-1, D-4, D-6

10.4.13 **Company Restricted or Company Confidential Voice Mail Messages.** Voice mail messages containing information classified as Company Restricted or Company Confidential should be identified as such at the beginning of the message.
Refer to risks: D-1, D-4

10.4.14 **Secured Transmission of Company Restricted or Company Confidential Information.** Company Restricted or Company Confidential information must not be discussed or transmitted using cellular telephones.
Refer to risks: D-1, D-4, D-6

Risk If Standard Is Not Implemented

D-1 The company's proprietary information may be disclosed or lost, which may adversely affect the company's competitive position.

D-2 Data may not be accurately or completely transferred.

D-3 Transmissions may not have adequate error correction.

D-4 Sensitive information may be accessed and/or disclosed to unauthorized personnel.

D-5 Proprietary information stored on computer systems may not be properly protected.

D-6 Proprietary data may be disclosed to unauthorized personnel during transmission.

D-7 Databases may not contain accurate and complete information after system failure.

D-8 Networks may not be properly maintained and controlled without network owner sponsorship.

D-9 Operational efficiency and reliability may be impaired and significantly disrupt processing.

 ## 10.5 SYSTEMS DEVELOPMENT METHODOLOGY

Introduction

All departments responsible for software development and maintenance must define and document standard methodologies that must be used in developing and maintaining application systems. These controls should be considered when selecting a third party application for a business solution to ensure that a defined development methodology is used.

Standard of Internal Control

10.5.1 **Standard Development and Maintenance Methodologies.** The methodology and formality employed should be appropriate for the size of the project.
Refer to risks: E-1, E-2, E-3, E-4

10.5.2 **System Development Methodology Requirements.** System development methodologies must include the following components:
a. Systems development projects must be segmented into measurable parts or phases with predefined deliverables to ensure the appropriate level of project tracking and control.
Refer to risks: E- 1, E-3

b. Project team roles and responsibilities must be clearly defined and documented.

Refer to risks: E-2, E-4

c. The system development project team, consisting of user, IT, and application owner personnel, must approve the completion of each major phase of development prior to progression to subsequent phases.

Refer to risks: E-3, E-4, E-5, E-6

d. Formal plans must be prepared for system development projects. Development and project plans must include activities that result in the following deliverables at a minimum:

■ A clear and accurate statement of business purpose and requirements for the proposed system, including the business environment in which it will function.

Refer to risks: E-2, E-5, E-6

■ A feasibility study identifying possible software solutions and cost/benefit analysis.

Refer to risk: E-5

■ A detailed logical and physical system design.

Refer to risk: E-6

■ Business process design that integrates system design with the business processes the new system is intended to support.

Refer to risks: E-1, E-4, E-5

■ The information confidentiality, integrity, availability, and audit features which are to be designed and incorporated into application systems.

Refer to risk: E-15

■ System and user acceptance testing that will adequately test each system function and condition defined by the detailed logical and physical design.

Refer to risks: E-7, E-8

■ Specifications for conversion to the proposed system that will ensure the integrity of processing procedures and data.

Refer to risk: E-9

■ User procedures that document both the manual and system-supported activities required to execute a business process, including how users interact with the system and how that interaction is controlled. User procedures should reasonably answer questions on system operation, error correction, and control.

Refer to risks: E-10, E-11, E-14

■ Operations documentation that details how to operate the application system. The documentation should include procedures for restarting the application in the event of hardware or software failure.

Refer to risks: E-12, E-13

■ Training to sufficiently enable users to independently operate and control system processing.

Refer to risk: E-14

e. Provisions must be made to have access to purchase software source code should the vendor discontinue support.

Refer to risks: E-10, E-12

Risk If Standard Is Not Implemented

E-1 Systems may be implemented which do not meet user requirements or comply with company software quality standards.

E-2 Roles and responsibilities may be unclear, resulting in increased development process times or system inadequacies.

E-3 Systems may be implemented without approval of the system design, proper testing, or conversion, resulting in erroneous processing.

E-4 Users may not actively participate in the development process, which could result in incorrect decisions during the design and testing phases.

E-5 Improper selection of data processing solutions to business problems may result from incomplete evaluation of alternatives.

E-6 The system design may not be properly documented and communicated, resulting in uncontrolled or erroneous processing.

E-7 Individual programs and the entire system may not be adequately tested or may not operate as intended resulting in erroneous processing.

E-8 Users may not participate in acceptance of the system. The system may not operate properly and may not meet their needs.

E-9 Data files may not be properly converted to the new system.

E-10 Users may not be able to recover from processing errors.

E-11 Users may not be able to process independently of IT or other personnel who developed the system.

E-12 Operations personnel may not be able to operate the system.

E-13 Operations and/or user personnel may not be able to recover from errors to continue business processing.

E-14 Improperly trained users may not be able to adequately operate and control the system.

E-15 Company information may be disclosed, misused, or lost, which may adversely affect the company's competitive position.

 ## 10.6 CHANGE MANAGEMENT

Introduction

Change management allows organizations to plan, schedule, implement, and track modifications to corporate activities. A formal change management process helps IT departments ensure that the implementation of system changes are aligned with business needs. Because of this, companies should document formal processes to implement changes in their IT systems. Specific areas to document include laboratory and staging areas, communication regarding changes, application development, and internal service-level agreements (SLAs).

Changes to any production environment, including software, cloud computing, hardware, and operating procedures, must be authorized, documented, and tested. These standards of control for the change management process should also be considered when working with a third party on the implementation of software for a business solution.

Definitions

Change Management—The reporting, tracking, and resolution of change requests and problem reports for all configuration items/units.

Promotion/Migration Management—The control of logical and physical movement of code between testing, quality assurance, and production.

Release Management—The notification and distribution of software.

Software—Includes all levels of software—application software, operating system software, middleware software, presentation management software, etc.

Status Reporting—The status of configuration items/units is recorded according to a documented procedure. This should enable the re-creation of an application from various revisions.

Version Control—The check-in/check-out or revision management of configuration items/units (e.g. process related documentation, software requests, code, operating system software, etc.)

Standard of Internal Control

10.6.1 **Documented Production Environment.** System and application owners must document whether their environment is a production environment.
Refer to risk: F-2

10.6.2 **Change Requests.** Requests for changes to the production environment must include a business purpose or business impact analysis and must be approved by the system and application owner(s) impacted.
Refer to risks: F-1, F-2

10.6.3 **IT Infrastructure, Service Provider, and Cloud Computing Reviews.** Requests for changes to the production environment must include an IT infrastructure impact analysis, which must be reviewed by the service providers impacted.
Refer to risk: F-8

10.6.4 **Tested Changes.** Changes to the production hardware and/or software environment must be tested. Tests must include sufficient conditions to ensure the new system configuration operates as intended. Testing must also include evidence that all requirements were tested to the satisfaction of the ultimate users of the system.
Refer to risks: F-3, F-4, F-5

10.6.5 **Financial Management Review.** If the system change will result in the creation of journal entries or changes in journal entry account distribution, the change must be approved by financial management.
Refer to risks: F-5, F-6

10.6.6 **Software Configuration Management.** Organizations or departments with responsibility for hardware or software must document and implement plans and procedures for software configuration management. Software configuration management includes version control, change, promotion/migration, and release management and status reporting.
Refer to risks: F-2, F-4

10.6.7 **System Development Methodology.** Organizations or departments with responsibility for hardware or software must follow an approved, documented system development methodology when making maintenance changes to the production environment. The methodology and formality employed should be appropriate for the size and impact of the project.
Refer to risks: F-4, F-7

10.6.8 **Documented Contingency Plans.** Organizations or departments with responsibility for hardware or software must document a contingency plan to be followed in the event the change to the production environment is not successful and there are issues with a third-party application.
Refer to risk: F-7

10.6.9 **System-wide Version Controls.** If distributed systems are designed with multiple copies of the same programs and data files on more than one computer, system-wide version controls must be developed to ensure proper versions of programs and data files are used throughout the system.
Refer to risks: F-1, F-3

10.6.10 **Changes to Vendor Supplied Source Code.** The chief information officer (CIO) must approve all changes to vendor-supplied source code where such changes are not fully supported by the vendor.
Refer to risks: F-2, F-3, F-4, F-9, F-10, F-11

Risk If Standard Is Not Implemented

F-1 Erroneous changes or changes resulting in improper use of the system may result from unauthorized system changes.

F-2 Personnel preparing the system change may not adequately evaluate the impact of the change on business processing.

F-3 Changes may not be properly tested and their implementation may result in erroneous system processing, impacting those who are dependent on the system, such as manufacturing, our customers, business units, local, state, and federal government agencies, etc.

F-4 Users and operations personnel may not be aware of system changes that could result in erroneous system processing.

F-5 Financial or operational records may be misstated.

F-6 Improper journal entries and allocations may result from the system change.

F-7 Users and operations personnel may not be able to recover from a system failure.

F-8 Personnel preparing the system change may not adequately evaluate the impact of the change on the IT infrastructure.

F-9 The vendor may no longer provide support.

F-10 When the vendor updates the source code, the source code changes may no longer be possible.

F-11 Whenever the vendor upgrades the source code, rework will be required to make the changes to the source code again.

 ## 10.7 COMPUTER AND TELECOMMUNICATIONS BACKUP FOR PRODUCTION RESTART/RECOVERY

Introduction

Organizations, service providers, or departments that operate computer or telecommunications equipment are responsible for ensuring that the appropriate system management processes are implemented in accordance with company policies and procedures. System management processes include, but are not limited to, restart/recovery, problem management, change management, security, and performance management.

Standard of Internal Control

10.7.1 **File Backup.** Computer and telecommunications data files, programs, and system software must be backed up regularly to ensure continuity of business operations in the event of a hardware, software, or application failure. The backup process is critical for those employees using personal devices.
Refer to risks: G-1, G-2

10.7.2 **File Retention in Accordance with Regulatory or Statuary Requirements.** Application owners are responsible for identifying data files that must be retained to comply with regulatory or statutory requirements, such as taxing authorities or government contracting agencies. Normally referred to as history files, they should be stored at a location not subject to the same peril as the processing site.
Refer to risks: G-3, G-4

10.7.3 **Managed Backup Files.** Owners/service providers of computer and telecommunications systems must maintain a system to record and track backup data files and other offline media for recovery and retention purposes.
Refer to risk: G-5

10.7.4 **Authorized Access.** Production backup information, including programs, data files, and supporting documentation, must be stored in a secure manner to ensure that unauthorized personnel cannot attain access (e.g. physically secured computer or telecommunications rooms, approved security filling cabinets, and wall units, etc.)
Refer to risk: G-6

10.7.5 **Documented Policies and Procedures.** Personnel responsible for computer and telecommunications operations must prepare and maintain policies, procedures, and instructions on the operation of the computer or telecommunications equipment and system software.
Refer to risk: G-7

Risk If Standard Is Not Implemented

G-1 Programs and information assets could be lost due to failure of hardware, software, application, or human error.

G-2 Files could be lost, erased, or reused in error.

G-3 Business data files (history files) may not be properly retained according to the records management policy and could subject the company to fines and penalties.

G-4 Data files retained for regulatory requirements may not contain complete and accurate data.

G-5 Backups may not be available and procedures may not be operating as management intended.

G-6 The ability to continue business operations in the event of an emergency may be impaired.

G-7 Procedures for the operation and control of computer systems may not be properly communicated or performed.

10.8 DISASTER RECOVERY AND BUSINESS CONTINGENCY PLANNING

Introduction

The objective of disaster recovery and contingency planning for computer systems and telecommunications is to ensure the continuance of the company's applications in the event of unanticipated computer processing disruptions such as operational failures or site disasters that destroy or prevent access to the computer or telecommunications equipment, data, and software.

The recovery plan is not intended to duplicate a normal business environment, but is intended to minimize the potential loss of assets and keep the company in business. Through decisive action, which is based on advanced planning, business disruptions and losses can be minimized. The only applications that may choose to be exempt from this standard are those that can be reproduced from other existing information, are not input to a critical application, or would incur more expense from following these standards than the application's worth is to the company in the event of destruction by a disaster.

Definitions

Business Continuity Plan—The business continuity plan is used by organizations of all sizes to detail how business will continue if a disaster or emergency occurs. The business continuity plan documents all business operational functions by department, employee, and supplier information, inventory, emergency procedures, and post-disaster plan.

Additionally, applications should be prioritized that are critical to the successful operation of the company and acceptable downtime should be determined when establishing business continuity plans. The business continuity planning process should encompass the steps needed if a disruption in business or a disaster occurs. The plan should consider the business process and IT impacts as well as the applications that are maintained in the cloud.

The following table is an example of a business continuity plan.

Business Process Considerations (the People)

---

1. **Document internal key personnel with backups.** These are key employees that are integral to the function of your business processes. A controller should identify the key employees by each business process. It's important to identify backups.
   - Consider which job functions are critically necessary every day. Think about who fills those positions when the primary job-holder is on vacation.
   - Make a list of all those individuals with all contact information, including business phone, home phone, cell phone, pager, business e-mail, personal e-mail, and any other possible way of contacting them in an emergency situation where normal communications might be unavailable.

Business Process Considerations (the People)

2. **Identify who can telecommute.** Some people in your company might be perfectly capable of conducting business from a home office.

3. **Document external contacts.** If you have critical suppliers, contractors, or consultants, build a special contact list that includes a description of the company (or individual) and any other absolutely critical information about them, including key personnel contact information. Include in your list people like attorneys, bankers, IT consultants, and solution providers. This list should include anyone that you might need to call to assist with various operational issues.

4. **Document critical equipment and access to ERP Systems.** Determine if a copy machine and fax are necessary if ERP access is not possible.

5. **Identify critical files and documents.** These include articles of incorporation, financial key supplier contracts, utility bills, banking information, critical HR documents, building lease papers, and tax returns. <u>**Key Point:**</u> Remember the requirements for HIPAA and GDPR.

6. **Identify your contingency location if needed.** This is the place you will conduct business while your primary offices are unavailable. Depending on the situation it could be a hotel or telecommuting may be a viable option.

7. **Make a "How-to."** It should include step-by-step instructions on what to do, who should do it, and how. Your organizations policies and procedures are critical. Public companies can use Sarbanes-Oxley documentation. Ensure that business processes are assigned to a "lead" person as suggested in step 1. Key processes should be prioritized.

8. **Put the information together.** A business continuity plan is useless if all the components are scattered all over the company. Each key process business should have an electronic folder (and backup) with all the key information. If necessary, the contents of the folder can be printed.

9. **Communicate.** Make sure everyone in your company is familiar with the business continuity plan. Hold mandatory training classes for each and every employee. Schedule refreshers periodically.

10. **Test the plan.** All business continuity plans should be tested to make sure all the key components have been identified and the plan can be executed. Schedule refreshers of tests of the plan periodically.

11. **Plan to update the plan.** No matter how good your plan is, and no matter how smoothly your test runs, it is likely there will be events outside your plan.

12. **Review and revise.** Every time something changes, update all copies of your business continuity plan and initiate the business continuity plan communication process again. With all the changes in technology, it's important to ensure that the plan is never outdated.

13. **Consider next steps.** Consider the next steps for recovery and identify what needs to happen to bring the organization, region, country, or division back online.

Contingency Planning—The prearranged plans and procedures that critical business functions will execute to ensure business continuity until computer and telecommunications facilities are reestablished following a disaster. The table below provides the process steps for developing an IT business continuity plan and can be used throughout the contingency planning process.

Developing the IT Business Continuity Plan

1. **Gather all relevant network infrastructure documents**, e.g. network diagrams, equipment configurations, databases.

2. **Obtain copies of existing IT, application listings, and network plans;** if these do not exist, proceed with the following steps. *Note:* Ensure that software as a service (SaaS) or cloud applications are also included in your continuity plan.

3. **Identify what management perceives as the most serious threats** to the IT infrastructure, e.g. fire, human error, loss of power, system failure.

4. **Identify what management perceives as the most serious vulnerabilities** to the infrastructure, e.g. lack of backup power, out-of-date copies of databases.

5. **Review previous history of outages and disruptions and how the firm handled them.**

6. **Identify what management perceives as the most critical IT assets.**

7. **Determine the maximum outage time management can accept if the identified IT assets are unavailable.**

8. **Identify the operational procedures currently used to respond to critical outages.**

9. **Determine when these procedures were last tested to validate their appropriateness.**

10. **Identify emergency response team(s)** for all critical IT infrastructure disruptions; determine their level of training with critical systems, especially in emergencies.

11. **Identify supplier emergency response capabilities;** if they have ever been used; if they were, did they work properly; how much the company is paying for these services; status of service contract; presence of SLA and if it is used.

12. **Compile results from all assessments into a gap analysis report** that identifies what is currently done versus what ought to be done, with recommendations as to how to achieve the required level of preparedness, and estimated investment required.

13. **Have management review the report and agree on recommended actions.**

14. **Prepare IT disaster recovery plan(s) to address critical IT systems and networks.**

15. **Conduct tests of plans and system recovery assets to validate their operation.**

16. **Update plan documentation to reflect changes.**

17. **Schedule next review/audit of IT business continuity plan capabilities.**

Critical Application—A critical business application is one that company must have to support major revenue activities, movement of goods to customers, a strategic manufacturing process, or to fulfill contractual or regulatory obligations. In addition, the application's availability is deemed by management to be vital to the continued functioning of company business. Examples of critical applications are: customer service support, order entry, inventory control, manufacturing resource planning, purchasing, warehouse control, quality assurance, and finance.

Disaster—A loss of computing or telecommunication resources to the extent that routine recovery measures cannot restore normal service levels within 24 hours, which impacts the company's business significantly.

Recovery—The restoration of computing and telecommunication services following an outage resulting from a disaster.

Disaster Recovery and Cloud Providers—Niel Nickolaisen, chief technology officer at O.C. Tanner Company, provides the following considerations for developing a disaster recovery plan with cloud providers. O.C. Tanner Company, an employee recognition company, develops strategic employee recognition and reward solutions that help people to accomplish and appreciate great work for Fortune 100 companies internationally. He recommends the following considerations.

1. **The provider must stratify the services provided into different categories.** Some services are so mission critical that they require redundancy. Other applications are mission critical but require recovery rather than redundancy.

2. **The cloud provider must have the ability to test recovery from a disaster.** Even if the corporate chooses not to do such tests internally, there should be available evidence that a provider has done it for others.

3. **The cloud provider must demonstrate no single points of failure.** The provider should have a recovery process which is the equivalent of backing up onto the same server. And as a recommended best practice, the provider should follow the same checklists and standards of internal control as recommended in this document.

4. **The cloud provider must be financially viable.**

Vital Business Assessment—A process required to determine what business functions and supporting applications are critical for the company to continue to conduct business in the event of a disaster.

Standard of Internal Control

10.8.1 **Recovery Priority.** Application owners must classify their application's recovery priority. This priority must be used by computer and telecommunications equipment owners/service providers to determine the sequence of restarting selected critical corporate and third party applications in the event of an unanticipated processing disruption. The priority assessment should include the following:

a. Conduct a vital business assessment to quantify the risk in terms of dollars, production volume, or other measurable terms due to partial or total loss of processing the application.

b. Assess the lead time between loss of application processing and adverse impact on company operations as part of determining acceptable downtime.

c. Obtain agreement from the company unit management on the classification as to critical or noncritical.

Refer to risks: H-1, H-2, H-3

10.8.2 **Alternative Equipment or Facilities.** The owners and service providers of computer systems and telecommunications, equipment and facilities, in coordination with application owners, are responsible for arranging for alternative equipment and/or computing facilities. Disaster recovery plans must include the following:

a. A determination of the most effective alternative processing method for both critical and noncritical applications. Alternatives include:

- Processing at another company site;
- Third-party solutions provided on cloud computing;
- Processing at a conditioned site maintained by a recovery site vendor; or
- Not processing applications until computer equipment and or sites are restored, normally reserved for noncritical operations only.

Refer to risks: H-1, H-2, H-3, H-4

b. A plan detailing IT and user personnel requirements and special skills needed in the event of an unanticipated processing disruption.

c. Storage of critical computer vital records, replacement forms, supplies, and documentation at an offsite storage facility. Storage at place of residence is not an acceptable alternative. Preference should be given to using a professional offsite vendor at a distance of 4 to 80 miles from storage of the original data.

Refer to risks: H-1, H-2, H-3, H-4

10.8.3 **Documentation and Testing.** Detailed disaster recovery plans must be documented and tested at least annually to ensure recovery can be accomplished. Where tests of the full disaster recovery plans are found to be impractical due to business conditions or the cost of testing, test plans must be developed and implemented to test portions of the plan. The alternative to a full test is a complete paper walk-through with an audit of the offsite vital records. Application owners must participate in the test to certify business recovery capability.

Refer to risks: H-1, H-4

10.8.4 **Annual Review of Disaster Recovery Plans.** System owners/service providers, in conjunction with application owners, must review and update the disaster recovery plan at least annually or more frequently when significant changes are made to the applications, hardware, or software.

Refer to risk: H-4

10.8.5 **Recovery Time Targets.** Owners/service providers responsible for disaster recovery arrangements must specify and publish to users the target times for recovery of:

a. Mission-critical functions

b. Normal service

Users must be informed that no service will be available during the specific recovery period.

Refer to risk: H-4

10.8.6 **Tested Disaster Recovery Plans.** Users are responsible for developing and testing their plans in conjunction with service providers to continue their business operations during the recovery period. Where the plan is to cease operations during this period, this fact must be documented.

Refer to risk: H-4

Risk If Standard Is Not Implemented

H-1 The company may incur a severe disruption of engineering, manufacturing, or business operations if computer or telecommunications equipment owners are not able to recover in the event of an unanticipated processing disruption. This risk could be further compounded by the lack of the correct vital records in the offsite storage facility.

H-2 Critical systems may not be recovered first.

H-3 The company could sustain substantial financial loss and regulatory fines if critical computer systems and equipment were severely damaged or destroyed.

H-4 The disaster recovery plans may not be effective, which would jeopardize the company's ability to continue its business.

 ## 10.9 INPUT CONTROLS

Introduction

This section recommends the controls for the manual input process into production systems or systems of record.

Standard of Internal Control

10.9.1 **Authorized Input.** All manually input or interfaced transactions must be properly originated and authorized and include evidence of authorization prior to processing.
Refer to risks: I-1, I-2, I-7

10.9.2 **Sufficient Edits and Validations.** Manually input or interfaced data must be subjected to sufficient edits and validations, including duplicate and completeness checks, to prevent or detect data input errors. Referential integrity must be enforced before processing a delete transaction.
Refer to risks: I-1, I-2

10.9.3 **Identified and Corrected Errors.** Manually input or interfaced data rejected by application system edit and validation procedures must be controlled to ensure that input errors are identified and corrected, and data is re-input to the system on a timely basis.
Refer to risks: I-3, I-6

10.9.4 **Audit Trails.** Application systems must provide an audit trail from the input transactions recorded by the system to the source transaction and originating user, third party or system. This should include the operator's identification, and the date and time of each transaction.
Refer to risks: I-4, I-5, I-7

Risk If Standard Is Not Implemented

I-1 Unauthorized transactions may be processed.

I-2 Invalid or erroneous data may be processed and affect operating and/or financial decisions.

I-3 Rejected input may not be corrected and re-input into the system, resulting in incomplete processing.

I-4 An adequate audit trail may not exist to provide a means of substantiating input transactions.

I-5 Financial and/or operating personnel may not be able to explain transaction activity or account balances.

I-6 Untimely correction of rejected items may result in incorrect records and financial statements.

I-7 Individual accountability cannot be established for all input transactions.

 ## 10.10 OUTPUT CONTROLS

Introduction

This section recommends the controls for the output process from production systems or systems of record.

Standard of Internal Control

10.10.1 **Audit Trails.** Application systems must provide audit trails which evidence:
   a. All input transaction data, including data received from other systems
   b. Additions or changes to master file or reference table data
   c. Internally generated transactions
      The retention period is determined by business and government requirements.
   Refer to risks: J-1, J-2, J-3

10.10.2 **Identified Transactions.** Application system audit trails should provide for unique identification of processed transactions to allow them to be traced and vouched through the system.
   Refer to risks: J-1, J-2, J-3

10.10.3 **Report Headings.** All online video screens or reports should include sufficient information to ascertain their origin, period covered, appropriate titles, completeness, and their information classification.
Refer to risks: J-l, J-2, J-3, J-4

10.10.4 **Distribution of Company Restricted and Company Confidential Information.** Owners/service providers and application system users must establish and implement procedures to ensure that recipients of Company Restricted and Company Confidential reports are appropriately advised of their personal responsibility to promptly collect and secure these materials.
Refer to risk: J-4

10.10.5 **Records Management.** Data files, data storage media, and computer reports containing Company Restricted and Company Confidential information must be controlled and properly destroyed after their useful lives.
Refer to risk: J-4

Risk If Standard Is Not Implemented

J-1 Application systems may not produce adequate audit trail, input, or processing reports to control processing.

J-2 Erroneous or unauthorized changes to system data may not be detected.

J-3 System audit trails may not be adequately generated or maintained.

J-4 Company Restricted and Company Confidential information may be unintentionally disclosed to the detriment of the company.

 ## 10.11 PAPERLESS TRANSACTIONS, ELECTRONIC COMMERCE, AND EDI

Introduction

Paperless transaction processing refers to a business operation in which electronically processed or stored information replaces the traditional paper trail of evidence. Paperless processing control provisions, like those for a manual processing environment, are concerned with the authorization, accuracy, completeness, and timeliness of transactions. Thus, all relevant business process and application controls apply to all parts of the electronic exchange, including telecommunications (internal and external networks), translation, application interface, and administration.

Definitions

EDI—Electronic Data Interchange (EDI) is the transfer of structured data, by agreed message standards, from one computer system to another, using an electronic means.

Electronic Commerce—Doing business electronically.

Paperless Transactions—Any transaction conducted via an electronic means. This could include but is not limited to fax, phone, voice response, e-mail, etc.

Trading Partner—Any organization with which a trading relationship is established. A trading partner can be a third-party company or an internal company organization.

Trading Partner Agreement (TPA)—An agreed code of conduct between parties involved in electronic commerce. It applies only to the electronic interchange of data and not to the substance of the message transmitted. It deals with questions of security, verification, and authentication of the communicating parties. The purpose of a TPA is to provide a set of rules that set out minimum standards with which parties trading electronically will comply.

Standard of Internal Control

10.11.1 **Authorization Integrity.** Paperless transactions must include evidence of proper authorization. Effective controls must be in place to ensure the integrity of all electronic authorizations.
Refer to risk: K-1

10.11.2 **Authentic Transaction Sources.** Controls must be in place to ensure the authenticity of the transaction source. The authentication and security requirements must be defined and agreed to by the company and its trading partners (internal or external). It is the responsibility of the business process owner initiating the transaction(s) to classify the data and ensure that the appropriate control and security requirements are met.
Refer to risk: K-2, K-7

10.11.3 **Timely Exchange of Transactions.** The service provider, whether external or internal, is responsible for implementing system controls to ensure that paperless transactions are exchanged within the period of time agreed to by the business process owner.

Refer to risks: K-4, K-5, K-8

10.11.4 **Transaction Integrity and Accuracy.** The integrity and accuracy of paperless transactions must not be altered by either internal or third parties.

Refer to risk: K-2

10.11.5 **Transaction Integrity and Audit Trails.** Each component in the paperless processing system, from manual entry and computer operations to application edits and system security, must encompass the controls necessary to ensure transaction integrity. In addition, there must be adequate audit trails at key points in the transmission path to provide verification of such integrity and security.

Refer to risk: K-2

10.11.6 **Records Management.** Retention of paperless transactions must be consistent with the corporate records management policy. Retention of electronic transactions may require managing to ensure that documents are available, authentic, and reproducible.

Refer to risk: K-3

10.11.7 **Trading Partner (Third Party) Agreements.** For paperless transactions involving non-company entities, TPAs must be established and approved prior to the initiation of such processing. TPAs must be approved by the appropriate legal department and should identify the controls for transaction processing as well as trading partner responsibilities, terms and conditions, and corresponding liabilities. In the event a TPA cannot be established, the decision to operate without an agreement must be documented and approved by the director of the company unit initiating the transaction(s). The documentation must include acceptance of the risks associated with operating without a TPA. The company unit initiating the transaction(s) is responsible for ensuring that a TPA or exception is obtained and kept on file.

Refer to risks: K-4, K-9

10.11.8 **Value-Added Networks.** Where value-added networks (VANs) are utilized, operational, recovery, security, and legal liabilities for the integrity of company information must be contractually defined.

Refer to risk: K-9

10.11.9 **Approval Electronic Transaction Processing.** Each system, such as invoicing, ordering, or remitting payments between the company and suppliers, customers, or contract services, must be approved by IT and the business process owner.
Refer to risks: K-5, K-6

Risk If Standard Is Not Implemented

K-1 Transactions may not be legitimate, introducing the risk of fraudulent processing and legal liabilities.

K-2 Transaction authenticity or integrity may not be assured, decreasing the reliability of the information and also introducing the risk of fraudulent or erroneous processing.

K-3 Paperless records may not be retained, or securely held, thus introducing risk of information loss and possible regulatory penalties.

K-4 The company may be liable for delayed transactions.

K-5 Company information may be disclosed, lost, delayed, or contaminated, which may adversely affect the company's competitive position.

K-6 Business data may be transmitted without proper data processing or accounting controls, resulting in erroneous orders, payments, or purchases exposing the company to fraud and financial risk.

K-7 Sensitive information may be disclosed to unauthorized parties.

K-8 Delayed transactions may introduce the risk of legal liabilities to the company.

K-9 Responsibilities may be unclear, causing the company to be unnecessarily liable for system failure or transaction loss and unable to resolve disputed items, resulting in revenue loss or increased liability.

10.12 NON-COMPANY NETWORKS AND BULLETIN BOARDS

Introduction

A legitimate business may exist for accessing non-company networks and bulletin boards, which are defined as networks and bulletin boards, which are not sponsored or controlled by company. While these networks can provide the company with a great deal of valuable information, they also greatly increase the risk of exposing the company's computing resources to individuals outside the company, computer viruses, Trojan horses, logic bombs, and other acts of computer sabotage. Authorization to use non-company networks and bulletin boards for business purposes is dependent on a legitimate business need and the approval of the user's management.

Vulnerability and Threat Management

One of the main reasons data controls are established is to manage potential software and hardware risks. During the IT planning process, organizations should consider the following guidelines:

1. IT departments should implement a documented process for receiving software updates and security patches from vendors.
2. Companies should draft a test and implementation plan that defines how patches and updates will be conducted, and follow established change management protocols.
3. Organizations should consider conducting an ethical attack at least once per year to verify system vulnerabilities, especially if an external website is available to the public. The ethical attack can be performed by a third-party vendor or the IT department.
4. Software and hardware applications should undergo an ethical attack before production.

Definitions

Computer Virus—Program that contains software instructions necessary to make replicas of itself and insert these instructions in the execution path of other programs without the knowledge or permission of the user.

Firewalls and Intrusion Detection Systems (IDSs)—In many companies, firewalls serve as the main defense against intruders and act as a gateway for all inbound and outbound network connections. IDS software, on the other hand, helps keep track of network activities. Because of their importance, internal auditors working in small and mid-size companies should recommend that IT departments implement the following protocols to enhance their use of firewall and IDS tools:

1. All external Internet protocol connections must take place through the firewall.

2. The firewall should be set up with a default "deny-all" configuration, give access as needed, and document all access requests.
3. Firewall and IDS configuration changes must follow the change management process.
4. All change requests must be reviewed by the security staff and approved by senior management staff prior to implementation.
5. All firewall and IDS alarms should be logged and archived daily.

Many security breaches can be prevented by using data security protocols like the ones described above. Incorporating these best practices can help small and mid-size companies ensure that internal controls that safeguard the integrity and privacy of their information are in place.

Freeware—Software available through computer bulletin boards and networks at no cost. Patches and drivers are not included in this category.

Isolated Environment—An environment not connected to a network.

Logic Bomb—Code imbedded in a program that is executed if certain conditions are met. The purpose of this code is to commit computer sabotage.

Shareware—Software available through computer bulletin boards and networks at a fee that is payable after downloading the software.

Trojan Horse—A program that masquerades as a legitimate program but in reality harbors code that could inflict serious damage to the user's computer.

Standard of Internal Control

10.12.1 **Direct Interactive Links.** Direct interactive links between the company host and non-company host systems, used for transfer and remote execution of commands, are allowed only if initiated and controlled by the company.
Refer to risks: L-1, L-2

10.12.2 **Direct Non-interactive Links.** Direct non-interactive links that are used for mail, message, and data file transfer are allowed only if incoming and outgoing traffic over these links is controlled by the company.
Refer to risks: L-1, L-2

10.12.3 **Activity Logs.** Logging of activity via standard accounting procedures must be established wherever possible for the purpose of producing audit trails, and must include logons, logoffs, attempts to access, and CPU time. In addition, file transfers must be logged and should include date, time of transfer, routing information, and file size, wherever possible.
Refer to risks: L-2, L-3, L-4, L-5, L-6

10.12.4 **Freeware and Shareware Software.** Management is responsible for establishing and operating processes to control the acquisition and use of freeware and shareware. These processes must ensure that:

   a. Only software or data required for legitimate business purposes and approved by management is downloaded.
   b. A cost-versus-risk assessment is performed and management accepts the risks.
   c. Under no circumstances is software designed to remove or circumvent security controls (e.g. password hackers) downloaded.
   d. Any license conditions are complied with and royalties or other product use payments made.
   e. Appropriate records are maintained of what software has been obtained and where it is used.
   f. Software is thoroughly tested in an isolated environment for both expected and possible unexpected results before being used in a company network or shared computing environment.
   g. The agreement of the service provider is obtained before such software is installed.

   Refer to risks: L-7, L-8

10.12.5 **Payments Made by Purchasing.** Any payments required for third party applications and licenses must be made through purchasing.
   Refer to risks: L-9, L-10, L-15

10.12.6 **Copyright Restrictions.** All copyright restrictions on copyrighted materials and any publicly available software must be obeyed. Illegal copies must not be received or used.
   Refer to risks: L-10, L-15

10.12.7 **Approved Distribution of Company Restricted and Company Confidential Information.** Company data and information classified as Company Restricted or Company Confidential should not be transmitted or received except in extraordinary cases and then only by using encryption techniques approved in advance of the transmission.
   Refer to risks: L-2, L-11

10.12.8 **Access to Non-Company Networks and Bulletin Boards.** Non-company networks and bulletin boards may be accessed only for company business purposes. Users may not use non-company networks and bulletin boards for private purposes.
   Refer to risks: L-12, L-13, and L-14

10.12.9 **"One Face to the Customer."** When posting to bulletin boards and Internet Usenet groups, or participating in an e-mail discussion group through mail-list services, users should consider the company's "One Face to the Customer" effort, which emphasizes the importance of speaking to our customers and business partners with a single, unified message.
Refer to risks: L-13, L-14

10.12.10 **Unauthorized Access.** Users should not attempt to access computing resources on non-company networks and bulletin boards for which they do not have authorization.
Refer to risks: L-15, L-16

10.12.11 **Anonymous Remailers.** Users must not use anonymous remailers, or take any other action to attempt to disguise the regular identification attached to outgoing e-mail messages.
Refer to risks: L-13, L-14

10.12.12 **Accurate Representation of Positions and Responsibilities.** Users should not represent in their electronic communications that they hold positions or have responsibilities within the company that are different from their actual positions.
Refer to risks: L-13, L-14

10.12.13 **Intranet Usage.** Web page written for distribution over company's intranet must not contain information classified as Company Restricted unless it is encrypted during transmission and requires two-factor authentication.
Refer to risks: L-1, L-2

Risk If Standard Is Not Implemented

L-1 Unauthorized use, disclosure, modification, or destruction of systems and data could occur.

L-2 Company information may be disclosed or lost, which may affect the company's competitive position.

L-3 Computers that process business, manufacturing, and engineering system transactions, or that perform product testing, may not have adequate access security software.

L-4 Computer access security software or operating systems may not provide adequate minimum protective or detective security controls.

L-5　Passwords to user computer accounts may be disclosed and allow unauthorized access to data and programs.

L-6　Unauthorized access attempts may be made on a regular basis without detection.

L-7　Programs and/or command files containing destructive code such as computer viruses, Trojan horses, logic bombs, etc. may be introduced into company computing resources.

L-8　Implementation of the software may result in erroneous system processing.

L-9　The source of the software may not be legitimate.

L-10　Copyright law or a standing licensing agreement, which the company has with a vendor, may be violated.

L-11　Sensitive information may be accessed and/or disclosed to unauthorized personnel.

L-12　Adequate computing resources may not be available to meet business requirements.

L-13　Communications may not accurately depict the company, its business activities, its products, or its services.

L-14　Communications may not be consistent and properly representative of the company.

L-15　Company may be liable for misuse or unauthorized copying of proprietary material.

L-16　The company may be liable for the misuse of computer resources.

CHAPTER ELEVEN

Protection of Assets: Human, Physical, and Intellectual

 INTRODUCTION

This section includes the functions necessary for all members of management to effectively fulfill their responsibility to secure the company's assets and employees, maximize profitability, and enhance the maintenance of business continuity. All policies, procedures, and practices implemented to fulfill these standards must be based on compliance with local laws and practices that may be specific to a particular site or business process. (e.g. Payroll, Treasury, Accounts Payable, etc.)

 PROCESS OVERVIEW

The diagram below suggests that the foundational elements that support the protection of human, physical, and intellectual assets are Internal Controls and Compliance, Security Framework, and Code of Conduct and "Tone at the Top."

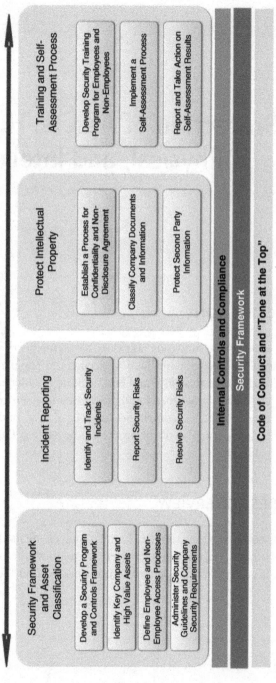

 **METRICS**

Table of Metrics

Security Metrics

- Number of Corporate Facilities
- Number of Security Policies, Standards, Procedures, and Metrics with Committed Owners
- Percentage Compliance with Security Policies, Standards, Procedures, and Metrics
- Company Employee Security Awareness Level
- Number and Severity of Findings in Audit Reports and Self-Assessments
- Number of Internal Controls Identified
- Percentage of Internal Controls Tested
- Number of Security Incidents Reported per Fiscal Period
- Time Lag Between Incident and Detection
- Number of Nuisance Alarms
- Security Cost as a Percentage of Total Company Revenue
- Number of Safety Hazards Proactively Identified and Eliminated annually
- Number of Failed Responses to Issues Identified by Security

Intellectual Property

- Number of Background Checks Conducted for New Hires
- Time Spent per Employee in the Innovation Process
- Cost to Support Innovation Initiatives
- Number of New Products, Services, or Inventions Generated Annually
- Revenue Generated from Sales of Products Using Patented Assets
- Revenue Opportunities Generated from Licensing New Products
- Revenue Loss from Violations of Non-Disclosure Agreements

 APPLICATION OF INTERNAL CONTROL

All policies, procedures, and practices implemented to fulfill these standards must be based on compliance with local laws and regulatory requirements and practices that may be specific to a particular site or company unit.

SUB-PROCESSES

The specific functions in this section are:

11.1 Security Framework

11.2 Perimeter Security

11.3 Interior Security

11.4 Protecting Intellectual Property

11.1 SECURITY FRAMEWORK

Introduction

Management must designate a specific employee (or employees) to be responsible for the administration, maintenance, and implementation of the local security program and implement a tracking and reporting process for reporting and correcting issues.

Standard of Internal Control

11.1.1 **Security Program Administration.** Management must designate a specific employee (or employees) to be responsible for the administration, maintenance and implementation of the local security program.
Refer to risks: A-2, A-5

11.1.2 **Physical Security Personnel.** Management should ensure that security personnel or those providing security functions are appropriately prepared for discharging their responsibilities by:
   a. Having a documented training program, including any specialized training that is appropriate for the site or company unit
   b. Consistently and uniformly applying and supporting security procedures
   c. Having a written agreement, consistent with these standards and approved by the Legal, Risk Management, and Worldwide Corporate Security, that defines performance expectations whenever contract guard services are being used
   d. Conducting a pre-employment and drug screening process (e.g. interview of references, criminal records check, and confirmation of education and prior employment) in accordance with appropriate national and local laws
Refer to risks: A-2, A-4, A-5, A-8

11.1.3 **Security Guidelines.** These standards must be used to form the basis of all security programs. All security guidelines and procedures must be maintained and available to all affected employees. All policies and procedures related to security must be submitted to corporate security for approval. Issues arising from this approval process will be referred to the director of corporate security for resolution.
Refer to risks: A-2, A-3, A-5, A-6, A-7

11.1.4 **Incident Reporting.** Management will develop procedures for documenting and reporting incidents (e.g. fraud, theft, embezzlement, or unlawful or unethical practices or conditions) that result in the actual or potential loss of company assets. Additionally, serious operational security incidents or high-profile losses must be reported promptly to corporate security. The reporting process must be linked with the company's Security Incident Reporting System to provide updates to corporate security and, through internal audit, provide updates to the board of directors.
Refer to risks: A-2, A-5, A-6, A-7

11.1.5 **Security and Related Forums.** Security and related personnel will participate with corporate security in formally established geographic and/or divisional security forums to discuss security issues, risks, and appropriate countermeasures.
Refer to risks: A-2, A-5, A-8

11.1.6 **Identification of Key Assets.** Management will develop and implement an annual process for identifying the key assets entrusted to their organization. The process should include discussions with other appropriate organizations (e.g. technical and business intelligence, other organizations involved in the business process). The assets considered should include physical assets, information systems, intellectual property, and proprietary information. An asset should be considered as key if the loss of or inability to use the asset would significantly impact revenue or the ability to meet customers' needs and/or maintain a competitive position. The characterization of critical assets should include:
a. Description
b. Function in the business (how asset is used)
c. Why the asset has value (e.g. essential for operations, competitive advantage)
d. Description of the form(s)
e. Who uses the asset

    f. Where the asset is located

    g. How access to or use of asset is controlled

    h. How security is maintained

    i. Recovery process in the event the asset is compromised, destroyed, or stolen

    Refer to risks: A-5, A-6

11.1.7 **Key Asset Security.** The process for identification should also include controlled distribution of this confidential information to appropriate personnel to ensure consistent and comprehensive awareness of those assets which require special security consideration. The identification of these assets will be the basis of the entire risk profile and the business continuity plan.

    Refer to risks: A-5, A-6

Risk If Standard Is Not Implemented

A-2 Security for company employees and visitors may be inadequate.

A-3 The disaster/emergency plans may not be effective.

A-4 Improperly trained security personnel may not be able to adequately respond to a situation/incident requiring their involvement.

A-5 Company assets, such as product, property, material, and technology, may be stolen, damaged, or otherwise compromised.

A-6 Unauthorized access to and/or disclosure of proprietary information could adversely affect the company's competitive position and reputation.

A-7 The company's ability to conduct business may be significantly impaired.

A-8 Security response to major incidents may be slow and ultimately impede resolution.

 11.2 PERIMETER SECURITY

Introduction

In defining perimeter security, all company and subsidiary locations (including any unimproved or apparently unused land), whether leased or owned, must display appropriate notice(s) identifying the premises as company property with access and activities restricted to company business.

Standard of Internal Control

11.2.1 **Identification of Company Property.** The placement and wording of the notices(s) should be appropriate and consistent with any applicable lease provisions and with local legal requirements regarding trespassing and liability statutes.
Refer to risks: B-1, B-5, B-8

11.2.2 **Physical Security Measures.** All facilities used by company must be designed to protect against unauthorized entry, theft, property damage, and injury to personnel. Techniques shall be consistent with the standards and may include but are not limited to:
a. Electronic access control
b. Intrusion detection system
c. Interior detection
d. Protective fencing for utilities, electrical substations, chemical storage, communication equipment, and other vital areas
e. Exterior protective lighting that provides daylight visibility of CCTV recordings
f. Local remote alarm system monitoring
g. Security personnel as required
h. Alarm and emergency response capabilities
i. Key asset areas afforded increased protection
Refer to risks: B-1, B-2, B-3, B-4, B-5, B-6

11.2.3 **Employee Access.** Employee access to sites and facilities shall be controlled. These controls shall be by visual acceptance (Security Officer, Reception, or site-responsible person) of the employee's corporate identification badge or by Electronic Access Control. Site procedures for controlling company employee access shall address the following issues:
a. Days and hours when access is permitted
b. Business justification for being onsite
c. Use of non-disclosure and confidentiality agreements
Refer to risks: B-1, B-2, B-4

11.2.4 **Non-Employee Access.** Non-employees (e.g. contractors, contract employees, joint venture employees, company retirees, visitors, subsidiary employees, or suppliers) shall have business justification for entering the site, shall be granted explicit access authorization, and shall have controlled access to the site. Site procedures for controlling non-employee access must address the following issues:

a. Days and hours when access is permitted
b. Business justification for being onsite
c. Use of non-disclosure and confidentiality agreements
d. Company host responsibility for non-employee's access to the site
e. Authorized personnel who can grant non-employee access to a specific site

Refer to risks: B-1, B-2, B-3, B-4, B-5, B-6, B-7

11.2.5 **Property Control Procedures.** The intent of this standard is to describe specific standards related to controlling physical assets while individuals are entering and leaving the premises. Management will establish property control policies and procedures including:

a. Paper or electronic removal documentation with sufficient information (e.g. asset number, individual charged with responsibility, time period asset will be off-premises) to account for the whereabouts of corporate assets assigned to individual employees
b. Paper or electronic documentation that tracks non-company assets (e.g. tools and equipment) that are brought on premises to ensure accountability for the asset when it is removed from the premises
c. Inspection procedures appropriate for the site to assist in the safeguard of assets
d. An audit process to verify the effectiveness of controls

Refer to risk: B-2

Risk If Standard Is Not Implemented

B-1 Unauthorized or unlawful entry may be attempted or made into company premises without detection.

B-2 Company assets, such as product, property, material, and technology, may be stolen, damaged, or otherwise compromised.

B-3 Records and data may be destroyed, stolen, or altered by unauthorized individuals.

B-4 Unauthorized access to and/or disclosure of proprietary information could adversely affect the company's competitive position and reputation.

B-5 Security for company employees and visitors may be inadequate.

B-6 The company's ability to conduct business may be significantly impaired.

B-7 Required documentation of non-employee access to company property will not be maintained.

B-8 Inability to respond to security incidents.

 ## 11.3 INTERIOR SECURITY

Introduction

A person shall be in possession of only one company-issued corporate identification badge. Persons who have not been issued permanent identification shall be issued a visitor/temporary badge for entry to company sites and facilities. Temporary identification badges may also be issued to employees and non-employees who are not immediately in possession of their permanent badge. Visitor/temporary identification badges shall have the holder's name or a number designation that is traceable to the holder. When entering a company site facility, the company-issued identification may only be used by the person whose name and image (if applicable) are printed on the badge. Identification badges must be visible at all times while on company property.

Standard of Internal Control

11.3.1 **Identification Badges.** Management shall implement procedures for issuance of identification badges for site access control (e.g. visual or electronic) to all employees and non-employees. There shall be only two groups of identification badges used for access control: photographic permanent and daily visitor/temporary. Permanent photo identification badges shall be produced by the company security system and include on their face the badge holder's image, name, and company. Identification badges may include electronic data, corporate logos, insignias, and designations.
Refer to risks: C-1, C-2, C-3, C-4, C-5

11.3.2 **Identification Badges (Cont'd).** A web page titled "Company Issued Identification Badges" is available and contains more detailed information, including graphic displays of corporate badges.
Refer to risks: C-1, C-2, C-3, C-4, C-5

11.3.3 **Access to Sensitive Areas.** Company-issued corporate identification badges shall be used in conjunction with an access control program suitable for reducing loss of assets and minimizing risk in sensitive areas. Identification badges may have electronic data or special insignias for controlled access to these areas, including labs, data centers, and stockrooms.
Refer to risks: C-1, C-2, C-3, C-4, C-5

11.3.4 **Control Over High-Value Assets.** Management will maintain a program to ensure that high-value assets potentially vulnerable to theft (e.g. raw materials and finished products) are appropriately controlled and secured through all phases of the supply chain, including receipt, manufacturing, storage, and delivery. The program will include:

a. Identification of all high-value assets
b. An inventory tracking system that tracks all high-value assets from receipt to delivery to the customer
c. Physical security measures that ensure high-value assets are protected from unauthorized access from receipt until delivery to the customer
d. Pre-access screening controls to include background investigations and drug screening (these controls need to follow company-defined denial criteria)
e. Information system security controls to prevent unauthorized access (access must be based on business need)
f. In-transit inventory control and reconciliation processes that occur within the time specified by authorized company policy
g. A negative variance escalation process that includes security and management
h. A counting process to ensure objectivity
i. A disaster recovery process which ensures alternative high-value assets are available
j. Designation of responsibilities/segregation of duties
k. Subcontractor controls to prevent unauthorized access to high-value assets
l. Supplier-owned inventory controls
m. A self-audit process that defines areas of improvement and associated corrective actions

Refer to risks: C-2, C-3

Risk If Standard Is Not Implemented

C-1 Unauthorized persons may enter property.

C-2 Company assets, such as product, property, material, and technology, may be stolen, damaged, or otherwise compromised.

C-3 Security for employees and visitors may be inadequate.

C-4 Unauthorized access to and/or disclosure of proprietary information could adversely affect competitive position and reputation.

C-5 Records and data may be destroyed, stolen, or altered by unauthorized individuals.

 ## 11.4 PROTECTING INTELLECTUAL PROPERTY

Introduction

Management must ensure that corporate-level non-disclosure agreements are in place and updated as appropriate for all vendors, partners, suppliers, and select customers. Management must ensure that all employees and non-employees working on company-owned or -leased facilities that have access to company intellectual property complete an approved non-disclosure or confidentiality agreement prior to having access.

Management must ensure the entire workforce is aware of the importance of protecting intellectual property and safeguarding company proprietary information, and can correctly identify the intellectual property used in their work.

Standard of Internal Control

11.4.1 **Confidentiality Agreements.** Management must ensure that corporate-level non-disclosure agreements are in place and updated as appropriate for all vendors, partners, suppliers, and select customers. These agreements must be renewed where appropriate.
Refer to risks: D-1, D-2, D-3, D-6, D-7

11.4.2 **Training and Awareness.** Management must ensure the entire workforce is aware of the importance of protecting intellectual property and safeguarding company proprietary information, and can correctly identify the intellectual property used in their work.
Refer to risks: D-1, D-2, D-3, D-7, D-8

11.4.3 **Handling and Using Intellectual Property.** Management must implement departmental policies and procedures to ensure workers handling intellectual property minimize their vulnerability to destruction, manipulation, and/or loss.
Refer to risks: D-1, D-2, D-3, D-5, D-6

11.4.4 **Information Storage.** Proprietary information must be secured and stored to preclude unauthorized or casual disclosure at all times and in all places (e.g. offsite as well as onsite).
Refer to risks: D-1, D-2, D-3, D-7, D-8

11.4.5 **Disposal of Proprietary Materials.** All locations will provide a secure means for the collection and/or safe destruction of proprietary waste materials and storage media. Destruction must ensure that the material is destroyed beyond reconstruction and recognition.
Refer to risks: D-1, D-2, D-3, D-4

11.4.6 **Classification of Information.** Sensitive and proprietary information will be marked in accordance with current company classification guidance provided by corporate security under information security.
Refer to risks: D-3, D-5

11.4.7 **Protection of Second Party Information.** All workers have an obligation to protect second-party information marked confidential and proprietary materials/data in the same manner Company Confidential information is protected.
Refer to risks: D-1, D-3, D-5

11.4.8 **Self-Assessments.** Management will conduct periodic self-assessments of their operation to ensure that all confidential materials, including hard and electronic copies, are being managed in accordance with Corporate Proprietary Safeguarding procedures.
Refer to Risks: D-1, D-2, D-3, D-4, D-5, D-6

Risk If Standard Is Not Implemented

D-1 Company assets, such as product, property, material, and technology may be stolen, damaged, or otherwise compromised.

D-2 Records may be destroyed, stolen, or altered by unauthorized persons.

D-3 Unauthorized access to and/or disclosure of proprietary information could adversely affect the company's competitive position and reputation.

D-4 Laws and government regulations may be violated resulting in fines, penalties, lawsuits, or contingent liabilities.

D-5 The company's ability to conduct business may be significantly impaired.

D-6 The company's ability to demonstrate ownership and control of its intellectual assets is weakened.

D-7 Competitive advantage is weakened.

D-8 Reputation as a high-tech leader is weakened if the company cannot demonstrate the security and integrity of data as required by regulatory compliance requirements.

CHAPTER TWELVE

The Insurance Process

INTRODUCTION

The insurance process includes the functions necessary for all members of management to effectively fulfill their responsibility to safeguard the company's assets and employees, maximize profitability, and enhance the effectiveness of the business continuity plan.

PROCESS OVERVIEW

The diagram below suggests that the foundational elements for the insurance process are Internal Controls and Compliance, Company Insurance Coverage and Business Continuity, and Code of Conduct and "Tone at the Top."

METRICS

Table of Metrics

- Number of Corporate Facilities
- Number of Business Critical Facilities

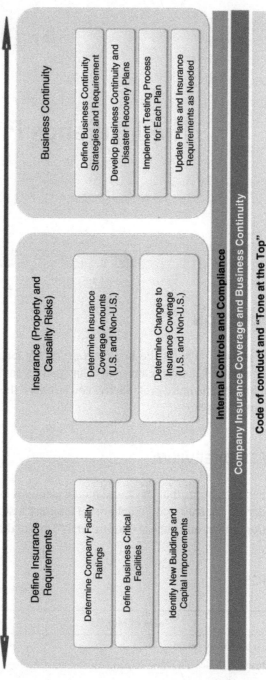

Insurance and Business Continuity

Define Insurance Requirements

- Determine Company Facility Ratings
- Define Business Critical Facilities
- Identify New Buildings and Capital Improvements

Insurance (Property and Causality Risks)

- Determine Insurance Coverage Amounts (U.S. and Non-U.S.)
- Determine Changes to Insurance Coverage (U.S. and Non-U.S.)

Business Continuity

- Define Business Continuity Strategies and Requirement
- Develop Business Continuity and Disaster Recovery Plans
- Implement Testing Process for Each Plan
- Update Plans and Insurance Requirements as Needed

Internal Controls and Compliance

Company Insurance Coverage and Business Continuity

Code of conduct and "Tone at the Top"

Table of Metrics
■ Value of Insurance Policy per Facility
■ Number of Insurance Policies Reviewed Annually
■ Number and Value of Changes to Current Insurance Policies
■ Number of Business Continuity Plans Developed
■ Number of Business Continuity Plans Tested Annually
■ Number of Business Continuity Plans Updated Annually

 ## APPLICATION OF INTERNAL CONTROLS

In management's selection of procedures and techniques of control, the degree of control implemented is a matter of reasonable business judgment. The common guideline that should be used in determining the degree of internal controls implementation is that the cost of a control should not exceed the benefit derived. However, there is a minimum set of controls that should exist in a normal business environment. The internal control standards listed here represent the minimum controls to be implemented for the insurance process.

 ## SUB-PROCESSES

The specific functions of the insurance process are:

12.1 Protection Against Physical Damage and Other Accidents

12.2 Insurance (Property and Casualty Risks)

12.3 Business Continuity

 ## 12.1 PROTECTION AGAINST PHYSICAL DAMAGE AND OTHER ACCIDENTS

Introduction

The company's facilities will be maintained in accordance with the relevant protection standards based upon business criticality, all life/safety standards, and regulatory guidelines. New company facilities will be designed to include highly protected risks (HPR) specifications based on business criticality.

Standard of Internal Control

12.1.1 **Capital Improvements.** All plans for significant capital improvements or plant modifications must be reviewed by company's fire protection engineers prior to the submission of a capital appropriation request, to assure compliance with company's protection standards.
Refer to risks: A-1, A-2, A-3

12.1.2 **Facility Ratings.** Efforts will be made to control the maximum foreseeable loss (MFL) and probable maximum loss (PML) within the standards set by the corporate risk management process.
Refer to risks: A-1, A-2, A-3

12.1.3 **Business Critical Facilities.** Company's owned or leased business critical facilities will be maintained in accordance with HPR standards as defined by the insurance industry.
Refer to risks: A-1, A-2, A-3

Risk If Standard Is Not Implemented

A-1 If protection is not adequate, an accident can cause significant loss of life, assets, and business.

A-2 If protection is not adequate, the company can face significant regulatory penalties and fines.

A-3 If protection is not adequate, the company can sustain significant reputation damage.

12.2 INSURANCE (PROPERTY AND CASUALTY RISKS)

Introduction

Insurance coverage against property and casualty risks will be designed to protect the company's shareholders from significant financial loss and to meet all legal and regulatory requirements. All insurance in the United States will be purchased by the corporate risk management department, with the exception of U.S. workers' compensation insurance, and the cost will be allocated in compliance with corporate policies and procedures.

Corporate risk management will be made aware of changes (e.g. acquisitions, divestiture, new businesses, plant modifications, asset dispositions, significant losses, etc.) occurring within the corporation and its units to assure that insurance coverage adequately addresses risk exposures.

Standard of Internal Control

12.2.1 **Coverage Amount.** Insurance coverage against property and casualty risks will be designed to protect the company's shareholders from significant financial loss and to meet all legal and regulatory requirements.
Refer to risks: B-1, B-2

12.2.2 **Insurance Decisions.** All decisions regarding the design and scope of insurance programs, with the exception of the U.S. Workers' Compensation program, will be made by the Corporate Risk Management department in compliance with corporate policies and procedures. Decisions related to the design and scope of the company's U.S. workers' compensation program will be made by corporate environmental, health, safety, and security (EHS&S).
Refer to risks: B-1, B-2, B-3

12.2.3 **U.S. Insurance Purchases.** U.S. workers' compensation insurance will be purchased through corporate EHS&S and the cost will be allocated to the appropriate business units.
Refer to risks: B-1, B-2, B-3

12.2.4 **Non-U.S. Insurance Purchases.** All insurance outside the United States will be either purchased by, or coordinated with policies arranged by, corporate risk management. In cases where other insurance is required for statutory, legal, or contractual reasons, it will be in compliance with corporate policies and procedures and subject to prior review by corporate risk management. If the cost for such insurance is paid for by the corporate risk management department, it will be allocated in compliance with corporate policies and procedures.
Refer to risks: B-1, B-2, B-3

12.2.5 **Changes to Insurance Coverage.** Corporate risk management will be made aware of changes (e.g. acquisitions, divestiture, new businesses, plant modifications, asset dispositions, significant losses, etc.) occurring within the corporation and its units to assure that insurance coverage adequately addresses risk exposures.
Refer to risks: B-1, B-2

Risk If Standard Is Not Implemented

B-1 Existing insurance coverage may be inadequate or even canceled, subjecting shareholders to excessive loss.

B-2 Excessive insurance may be purchased, resulting in overpayment of insurance premiums. This could increase overhead expense and adversely affect competitive position.

B-3 Duplicate insurance coverage could cause significant delays in recovering insurance payments and could significantly impede cash flow.

12.3 BUSINESS CONTINUITY

Standard of Internal Control

12.3.1 **Business Continuity Strategies.** Each global business unit will develop and maintain documented business continuity strategies to assure that critical products and/or services continue to flow unimpeded to customers in case of a disaster.
Refer to risk: C-1

12.3.2 **Disaster Recovery and Contingency Plans.** Each key site, as defined by the business continuity strategy, must maintain documented sending, receiving, disaster recovery, and contingency plans.
Refer to risk: C-2

12.3.3 **Plan Testing Standards.** All plans must conform to corporate risk management testing and documentation standards and policies.
Refer to risk: C-2

Risk If Standard Is Not Implemented

C-1 An inadequate strategy may cause irreparable harm to market share, resulting in a significant financial loss to our shareholders.

C-2 Inadequate plans may cause a significant delay in implementing the business continuity strategy and damage to the company's reputation and competitive advantage resulting in a significant loss of business.

CHAPTER THIRTEEN

Environmental, Health, and Safety (EH&S)

 INTRODUCTION

It is corporate policy to carry out business activities in a manner consistent with sound EH&S Policies and Standards. According to Wikipedia, environmental, health and safety (EH&S) is the discipline and specialty that studies and implements practical aspects of environmental protection and safety in the workplace. In simple terms it is what organizations must do to make sure that their activities do not cause harm to anyone and adhere to regulatory requirements.

 PROCESS OVERVIEW

The diagram below suggests that the foundational elements that support EH&S requirements are Internal Controls and Compliance, EH&S Compliance, and Code of Conduct and "Tone at the Top."

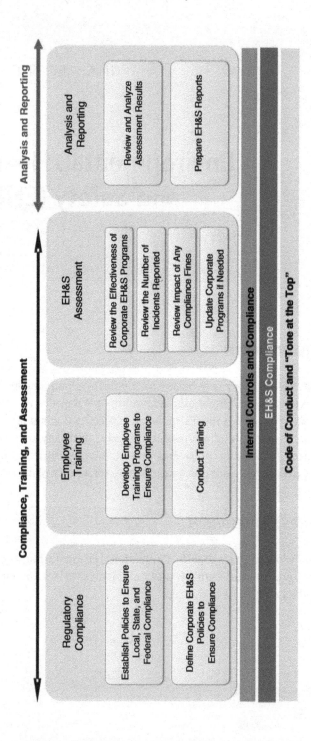

 METRICS

Table of Metrics

- **Number of EHS&S Assessments Conducted Annually**—Number of assessments completed on an annual basis.
- **Number of Risks Identified by Operating Unit**—As a result of the assessment process, these are the number of risks identified by company operating units.
- **Number of Compliance Issues Identified**—The number of compliance issues identified per the assessment process.
- **Number of Compliance Issues Mitigated**—The number of compliance issues resolved and mitigated.
- **Value of Compliance Fines Paid (by Agency)**—The value of compliance fines and who they were paid to.
- **Number of Training Sessions Conducted**—The number of EH&S training session conducted per defined fiscal period.
- **Percentage of Employees Trained**—The percentage of employees out of the total company employee base who have completed EH&S training.

APPLICATION OF INTERNAL CONTROL

Regulatory requirements play an important role in EH&S discipline and EH&S managers must identify and understand relevant EH&S regulations, the implications of which must be communicated to executive management so the company can implement suitable measures. Organizations based in the United States are subject to EH&S regulations in the Code of Federal Regulations, particularly CFR 29, 40, and 49. EH&S management is not limited to legal compliance and companies should be encouraged to do more than is required by law, if appropriate.[1]

SUB-PROCESSES

The specific function in this section is:

13.1 General Controls

---

[1]Wikipedia, "Environment, Health and Safety," accessed January 3, 2019, https://en.wikipedia.org/wiki/Environment,_health_and_safety.

13.1 GENERAL CONTROLS

Standard of Internal Control

13.1.1   **Policy.** EH&S policy will be established and documented by the corpo-rate EH&S management team.
Refer to risks: A-1, A-2, A-5, A-7

13.1.2   **Management Systems.** Each operating unit will establish a management system comprised of programs and procedures to meet corporate EH&S standards. The management system will be based on defined EH&S risks and impacts to the business.
Refer to risks: A-1, A-2, A-3

13.1.3   **Laws and Regulations.** Compliance with EH&S laws and regulations is the responsibility of each operating unit.
Refer to risks: A-1, A-2, A-3, A-4, A-6, A-7

13.1.4   **EH&S Standards.** All operating units must conform to the applicable corporate EH&S standards.
Refer to risks: A-1, A-2, A-3, A-5, A-6, A-7

13.1.5   **Assessments.** An assessment of EH&S hazards and risks will be con-ducted at all operating units. Assessment findings will be documented and communicated to the operating unit management team. The EH&S department will audit major installations and operating units based on risk and historical performance.
Refer to risks: A-1, A-2, A-3, A-4, A-5

13.1.6   **Notification.** Notification requirements are identified in corporate EH&S standards and will be followed based on the specific details of each EH&S incident.
Refer to risks: A-1, A-2, A-3, A-4, A-6, A-7

13.1.7   **Training.** EH&S training of employees is the responsibility of the operating unit. Specific training requirements are identified in the EH&S standards.
Refer to risks: A-1, A-2, A-3, A-4, A-5, A-6, A-7

13.1.8   **Acquisitions and Divestitures.** The EH&S department must be given timely notification of plans to acquire or divest property, businesses, or other assets. As appropriate the EH&S department will notify the operating unit in charge of such actions of potential EH&S liabilities which may result and recommended methods for mitigation.
Refer to risks: A-1, A-2, A-4, A-6, A-7

Risk If Standard Is Not Implemented

A-1 Improper considerations could contribute to environmental or employee harm or loss of significant corporate assets.

A-2 Government laws and regulatory requirements may be violated.

A-3 Civil criminal penalties, and fines against the company and/or individual employees may occur.

A-4 Debarment or suspension from receiving government contracts may occur.

A-5 Critical decisions may be based on erroneous information.

A-6 May negatively impact corporate reputation and brand image.

A-7 Can result in non-value-added cost to the business.

CHAPTER FOURTEEN

Customer Services

INTRODUCTION

All customer services policies will comply fully with all other company policies. The policy contact, working with the policy sponsor, ensures the achievement of the intended results of the policy and that the policy is accurate and up to date.

Customer support center personnel should be highly knowledgeable and able to satisfy customer requests quickly while providing quality service.

PROCESS OVERVIEW

The diagram below suggests that the foundational elements that support the customer service process are Internal Controls and Compliance, Customer Service Processes and Controls, and Code of Conduct and "Tone at the Top."

METRICS

Table of Metrics

Customer Service

- **Customer Satisfaction Rating (CAS)**—This is a commonly used key performance indicator to track how satisfied customers are with your organization's products and/ or services.

297

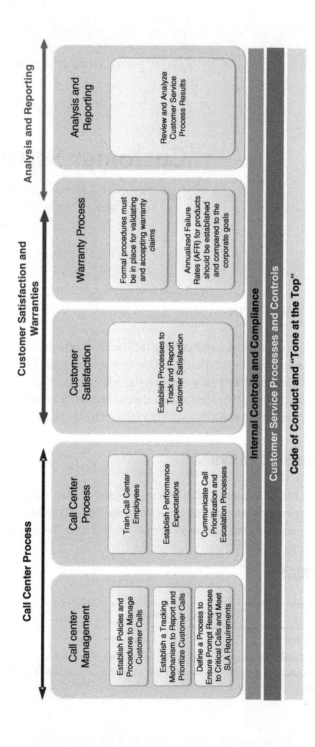

Table of Metrics

- **Number of Calls Received**—Number of calls received per period.
- **Response Time to Call (by Type)**—Time to respond to an open issue.
- **Number of Open "Tickets"**—Number of open issues or tickets per period.
- **Customer Effort Score (CES)**—CES is a single-item metric that measures how much effort a customer has to exert to get an issue resolved, a request fulfilled, a product purchased/returned, or a question answered. The idea is that the customer will be more loyal to brands that are easier to do business with. By focusing on reducing customer effort, you'll create a better experience for your customer.
- **Customer Churn (Attrition)**—Customer churn, also known as customer attrition, in its most basic form, is when a customer chooses to stop using your products or services.

Warranties

- **Warranty Cost per Unit**—Total Warranty Cost/Number of Units.
- **Warranty Cost as % of Sales**—Annual Warranty Cost/Annual Sales
- **Supplier Recovery**—Supplier Recovery/Total Warranty Cost
- **Warranty Contribution Rate**—Warranty Cost for a Specific Area/Total Warranty Cost
- **Claim Frequency**—Number of Claims/Number of Units

 ## APPLICATION OF INTERNAL CONTROL

In management's selection of procedures and techniques of control, the degree of control implemented is a matter of reasonable business judgment. The common guideline that should be used in determining the degree of internal controls implementation is that the cost of a control should not exceed the benefit derived. There is a set of controls that should exist in a normal business environment. The internal control standards listed here represent the minimum controls to be implemented within the customer services process.

 ## SUB-PROCESSES

The specific sub-processes included are:

14.1 Policy

14.2 Call Center Management

14.3 Warranty

14.4 Support Sales

14.1 POLICY

Introduction

All customer services policies will comply fully with all other company policies and standards. The policy contact, working with the policy sponsor, ensures the achievement of the intended results of the policy and that the policy is accurate and up to date.

Standard of Internal Control

14.1.1 **Customer Services Policies.** The policy contact is responsible for the maintenance, renewal, and technical content approvals of the policy. A policy takes effect as of the date of the last approval signature or at a specifically defined date after the last approval. Each policy expires two years after its last approval. Policies will be removed from the policy system only with the approval of the policy contact and sponsor.
Refer to risk: A-9

14.1.2 **Packaged Services.** Only packaged services combining two or more offers may have a package discount applied. Packaged services are priced at the sum of the pieces and may be discounted within the range of 0% to 15%. The discount must be approved by the appropriate manager, identified in the package guideline, who reviews both a business justification and a company market risk analysis which specifically addresses the following four areas: relevant market mix, proprietary product to price reduction, market presence, and market impact.
Refer to risk: A-1

14.1.3 **Maintenance Service.** The company must provide maintenance services (e.g. warranty) for a specified minimum length of time after the date of last sale of the product as defined.
Refer to risk: A-1

14.1.4 **Notice of Discontinuation of Service.** The company must provide its customers with no less than one year advanced notice of intent to discontinue standard maintenance services as a result of changing business demands.
Refer to risk: A-2

14.1.5 **Exceptions to Commitment Terms and Conditions.** Exceptions to the commitment terms and conditions policy, such as commitment to provide or make available customized or extended hardware maintenance services beyond the periods authorized by this policy, must be approved with the appropriate level of management within the company. **Refer to risks: A-3, A-4**

14.1.6 **International Allowances.** All deviations that decrease the price of a product or offering, or an enhancement in service delivery coverage or product features without corresponding increase in price, must only be granted if there is competitive pressure. It must be documented and communicated to the impacted countries/territories within two weeks. These international allowances should not be made if appropriate country/territory managers are able to agree and approve individual country allowance requests consistent with existing policies and their own country policies and practices. **Refer to risk: A-5**

14.1.7 **Service Provider Contracts.** Contracts with service providers must include terms specifically defining record retention policies. **Refer to risk: A-1**

14.1.8 **Call Center Personnel.** Customer service training for call center personnel should occur. Subject matter experts should be available and used as a technical escalation point as needed. **Refer to risk: A-1**

14.1.9 **Customer Identification Requirements.** A single customer registration and identification process should be used for dealing with all aspects of electronic interactions with customers. Customers should be able to uniquely identify themselves anytime and feel acknowledged without continuously having to identify themselves. **Refer to risk: A-1**

14.1.10 **Call Tracking Requirements.** Commitments made to customers should be a closed-loop process where all commitments to customers (e.g. callbacks, onsite, availability of information, etc.) in the case of an event/request should provide a tracking and notification capability so that full awareness is possible. Notifications of missed or potentially missed commitments should roll up the chain of command until the commitment is honored. **Refer to risk: A-1**

Risk If Standard Is Not Implemented

A-1 The company and its service partners may not honor commitments, resulting in poor customer satisfaction, lost customer loyalty, or higher costs.

A-2 Reduced customer satisfaction.

A-3 Unauthorized repair costs may be incurred.

A-4 Unauthorized product maintenance may occur.

A-5 Lack of documentation for price deviations or service delivery coverages may result in fraudulent or inappropriate service transactions.

A-9 Customer service policies may not be properly maintained.

14.2 CALL CENTER MANAGEMENT

Introduction

To ensure good customer service as required by company policy, call centers will be established and managed to exceed service expectations, established metrics, and internal controls.

Standard of Internal Control

14.2.1 **Customer Satisfaction Surveys.** Service quality surveys/customer satisfaction surveys should be conducted after completion of service work.
Refer to risk: B-1

14.2.2 **Service Fulfillment Center Contracts.** Contracts should be in place with all Service Fulfillment Centers (SFC) to ensure reasonable and attainable metrics are established to meet or exceed contractual fill rates. The contract should also hold SFCs financially accountable for contractual fill rates when the metric falls below a certain threshold.
Refer to risk: B-1

14.2.3 **Gray Market.** A zero tolerance policy toward any employee's participation in acts leading to company product being diverted into the gray market should be in place. The following conduct should be expected of all employees: due diligence on all requests for special discounts whether for a customer, reseller, or distributor by ensuring the discount is necessary and a good business decision before agreeing to reduce the company's margin on any product; a check

for indicators that product may be flowing to the gray market from ongoing special discount programs; and the reporting of any suspicious activity as soon as it appears. Report any incident or suspected incidents of gray market activity to your manager immediately, and notify the Cross Border Program Office via e-mail or voicemail.
Refer to risk: B-2

14.2.4 **Service Center Security.** Alarm systems should be installed on all doors and windows, including a duress alarm with shunting capabilities. These systems should be tested on a regular basis to ensure they are in proper working order. A corporate-approved security video system should also be installed and checked on a regular basis to ensure proper working order. Security tapes should be reviewed on a regular basis.
Refer to risk: B-3

14.2.5 **Service Center Safety.** Exits should be clearly marked with proper signage, and emergency processes and phone numbers should be properly posted. Smoke and/or fire detectors should be located in service center areas, and fire extinguishers should be properly tagged and inspected on a regular basis.
Refer to risks: B-3, B-4

14.2.6 **Service Center Access.** If key or access cards are used to gain entry, access codes should be changed frequently and records should be maintained of which employees have keys.
Refer to risk: B-5

14.2.7 **Handling of Cash.** If cash transactions are processed at the service center, the use of a safe is required. Access to the safe should be restricted. Employees who handle cash should be bonded, and the cash drawer should be reconciled at the end of each day to the point-of-sale (POS) system reports. The cash should then be placed in the safe until pickup by the armored car service.
Refer to risks: B-3, B-6

14.2.8 **Training.** All company service center employees should be properly trained on the Code of Business Conduct, Retail Sales Procedures, Point-of-Sales systems, Travel/Business Expenses, Inventory Control, Emergency Procedures, Security, and Financial Procedures.
Refer to risk: B-7

Risk If Standard Is Not Implemented

B-1 Reduced customer satisfaction.

B-2 Loss of profit margin.

B-3 Assets may not be properly safeguarded.

B-4 The company could sustain substantial financial loss and regulatory fines if inventory and equipment were severely damaged or destroyed.

B-5 Unauthorized access to service centers may be obtained.

B-6 Loss of revenue due to acceptance of insufficient funds checks, improperly processed credit card transactions, mishandling of cash sales, or unauthorized refunds.

B-7 Employees may not be properly trained, resulting in financial risks to the company.

14.3 WARRANTY

Introduction

All company product warranties should be supported consistently throughout the customer base without regard to the country of origin or the point of original product purchase. Exceptions may exist within specific countries as dictated by law and competitive practices.

Standard of Internal Control

14.3.1 **Product Warranty Support.** The customer willingness to accept the warranty terms from the country of origin, exclusive of legal limitations, is the overriding determinant where areas of inconsistency exist.
Refer to risk: C-1

14.3.2 **Warranty Service Pricing.** Company customer services product management and development is responsible for the price negotiations for warranty service pricing based on the costs and market-based prices associated with delivering product warranties.
Refer to risk: C-2

14.3.3 **Warranty Procedures.** Formal procedures must be in place for validating and accepting warranty claims. These procedures should

include processing only those claims for which a broken part and documentation is provided. Also, only those parts with a valid serial number should be processed.
Refer to risk: C-3

14.3.4 **Warranty Claims.** Dealers should be credited only for warranty claims that are submitted with the broken part.
Refer to risks: C-3, C-4

14.3.5 **Customer Service Training.** Company service personnel should have a full understanding of the company's warranty terms and the overall returns process.
Refer to risks: C-3, C-5

14.3.6 **Scrap Disposal Contracts.** Written contracts should be in place with all third-party vendors for the disposal of goods.
Refer to risks: C-6, C-7

14.3.7 **Annualized Failure Rates.** Annualized Failure Rates (AFR) for products should be established and compared to the corporate goals, after a product has been in production for a predetermined number of months, to determine if the product has performed above or below the corporate goal. This will determine in a timely manner whether corrective actions need to be taken with regard to engineering, design, or component part replacement that could prevent the contamination of an entire family or model.
Refer to risks: C-8, C-9

14.3.8 **Warranty Claim Threshold.** An average warranty claim threshold for monitoring warranty claims should be established by management. This threshold should assist in identifying potential abuses by service dealers and determining when dealers should be approached regarding their warranty claims.
Refer to risk: C-3

14.3.9 **Serial Numbers.** High-value components used in the company's assembly process, regardless of the manufacturer, including displays, system boards, and memory-related components, should have serial numbers. Serialization for parts over a certain dollar amount should be etched or otherwise permanently affixed to the part to prevent tampering (no adhesive tags should be used). Procedures should include validation of the part serial number prior to warranty claim processing.
Refer to risks: C-3, C-5

14.3.10 **Warranty Policy.** Policies and procedures must be in place establishing guidelines for providing end-users with a level of warranty on all company-branded products. Customer services must deliver the level of service required to support the product warranty. These services will be delivered to end-users who hold a valid company warranty. End-users are customers who will use the final product and do not include selling partners, distributors, VARs, integrators, and other channel partners.
Refer to risk: C-3

14.3.11 **Revenue Recognition.** Assurance warranties provide the customer with assurance that the related product will function as the parties intended because it complies with agreed-upon specifications. Service warranties provide the customer with a service in addition to the assurance that the product complies with agreed-upon specifications. Revenue recognition methods will vary depending on which type of warranty is offered. The following are excerpts from ASC 606 clarifying general situations:

- If a customer has the option to purchase a warranty separately (for example, because the warranty is priced or negotiated separately), the warranty is a distinct service because the entity promises to provide the service to the customer in addition to the product that has the functionality described in the contract. In those circumstances, an entity should account for the promised warranty as a performance obligation.
- If a warranty, or a part of a warranty, provides a customer with a service in addition to the assurance that the product complies with agreed-upon specifications, the promised service is a performance obligation. If an entity promises both an assurance-type warranty and a service-type warranty but cannot reasonably account for them separately, the entity should account for both of the warranties together as a single performance obligation.

Refer to risk: C-10

14.3.12 **Tracking of Parts and Spares In Transit.** Online and electronic means used for customers to check the status regarding shipment of parts and spares must provide a paper trail of activities and actions.
Refer to risks: C-1, C-11

14.3.13 **Documentation.** Complete and accurate documentation should be filed with all warranty and exchange claims requiring the form. These forms should include part numbers and customer information for performing various quality and other verification procedures. **Refer to risks: C-3, C-7**

Risk If Standard Is Not Implemented

C-1 Low customer satisfaction resulting from untimely product repair returns.

C-2 The company may incur unnecessary costs related to product management and development due to poor price negotiation and cost/market analysis.

C-3 The company may incur fraudulent or unnecessary warranty costs.

C-4 Service provider disputes may arise.

C-5 Fraudulent returns may go undetected.

C-6 Disposed goods may be reentered into the returns process or be sold into the gray market.

C-7 The company's ability to control dealer and third-party maintainer service levels may be compromised.

C-8 Engineering may not take timely corrective actions if the product performance is not measured against the corporate standard.

C-9 Management may not be able to evaluate its business model to determine overall effectiveness.

C-10 Incorrectly stated financial statements.

C-11 Transaction authenticity or integrity may not be assured, decreasing the reliability of the information.

 14.4 SUPPORT SALES

Introduction

Guidelines for customer sales and refunds should always be followed and properly posted to ensure visibility.

Standard of Internal Control

14.4.1 **Refunds.** The manager should approve all refunds and complete records should be maintained of all refunds.
Refer to risk: D-1

14.4.2 **Support Revenue.** Revenue is one of the most important measures used by investors in assessing a company's performance and prospects. However, previous revenue recognition guidance differs in Generally Accepted Accounting Principles (GAAP) and International Financial Reporting Standards (IFRS).
Refer to risk: D-2

14.4.3 **Check Processing.** All checks for purchases over a certain dollar threshold should be approved through TeleCheck. Checks should then be endorsed with "Deposit Only" and the store account number.
Refer to risk: D-1

14.4.4 **Credit Card Transactions.** Credit card transactions should be reconciled daily to the (point of sale) POS Systems. All credit card transactions should be verified before processing and stored in a safe after store hours. Customer signatures for credit card purchases should be verified with the signature on the back of the card.
Refer to risks: D-1, D-3

Risk If Standard Is Not Implemented

D-1 Loss of revenue due to acceptance of insufficient funds checks, improperly processed credit card transactions, mishandling of cash sales, or unauthorized refunds.

D-2 Improperly stated financial statements.

D-3 Customer credit card information may not be properly safeguarded.

CHAPTER FIFTEEN

Professional Services (PS)

 INTRODUCTION

Professional services (PS) offerings are available in many different industries. These services include lawyers, advertising professionals, architects, accountants, financial advisers, engineers, and consultants. As a basic control, all PS business opportunities must be planned and implemented in compliance with corporate policies. PS policies and standards do not override company policies.

This section focuses on sub-processes that support the offering of customized, knowledge-based services to clients in the technology industry.

 PROCESS OVERVIEW

The diagram below suggests that the foundational elements that support the professional services processes are Internal Controls and Compliance, Professional Service Controls, and Code of Conduct and "Tone at the Top."

Professional Services

Policies and Procedures and Bids
- Develop and Implement Policies and Procedures
- Respond to Bids and Opportunities
- Track Bids and Opportunities
- Establish Budget for Opportunities

Program Management
- Develop Project Plans for Established Methodology
- Report Expenses
- Track Costs and Budgets
- Report Project Status

Order Management and Fulfillment
- Order Certification
- Capitalization of Software
- Order Administration
- Create the Customer Invoice
- Ensure Customer Satisfaction

Internal Controls and Compliance

Professional Services Controls

Code of Conduct and "Tone at the Top"

METRICS

Table of Metrics

- **Number of PS Bids Issued per Year**—Indicates the number of bids issued or responded to per year.
- **Number of PS Contracts Initiated Annually**—Indicates the number of contracts or bids won on an annual basis.
- **Number of PS Bids Lost per Year**—Indicates the number of bids lost on an annual basis.
- **Number of Employees per Project**—Determines the average number of employees assigned to a single project.
- **Employee Attrition/Retention**—Shows the attrition and retention trends for PS employees.
- **Customer Satisfaction Rating**—Determines customer satisfaction.
- **Employee Satisfaction Rating**—Reflects employee satisfaction and can be a driver of employee attrition and retention.
- **Annual Revenue per Billable Consultant**—Indicates the annual revenue generated by a billable consultant.
- **Annual Revenue per PS Employee**—Tracks the revenue by PS employees.
- **Year-over-Year Revenue Trends**—This metric reflects the sales effectiveness and the demand for skills offered by a company on an annual basis.
- **Billable Utilization**—Billable utilization is a major indicator of opportunity and workload balance and is a metric to determine expansion of the workforce.
- **Number of Projects Over Schedule**—Shows the number of projects that were delivered over the committed schedule.
- **Number of Projects Discontinued**—Tracks the number of projects discontinued during a defined fiscal period.
- **Value of Projects Discontinued**—Tracks the value of projects discontinued during a defined fiscal period.
- **Value of Project Overrun**—Determines the total value of project overruns.
- **Profit Margin per Project**—Shows the profit margin per project.
- **Profit Loss per Project**—Indicates the profit loss per project.

 ## APPLICATION OF INTERNAL CONTROLS

In management's selection of procedures and techniques of control, the degree of control implemented is a matter of reasonable business judgment. The common guideline that should be used in determining the degree of internal controls implementation is that the cost of a control should not exceed the benefit derived.

There is a minimum set of controls that should exist in a normal business environment. The internal control standards listed here represent the minimum controls to be implemented within the PS process.

SUB-PROCESSES

The specific sub-processes included in the professional services process are:

15.1 General Controls

15.2 Opportunity-Bid Process

15.3 Program Management

15.4 Customer-Order Management

15.1 GENERAL CONTROLS

Introduction

Policies and procedures will be developed to support the company's PS business with proper training, internal controls, and risk management processes. Adequate procedures must be implemented to effectively monitor and document fulfillment of training requirements.

Standard of Internal Control

15.1.1 **Policies and Procedures.** Exemptions from compliance to a PS policy or standard can only be granted through a waiver request. Procedures must be in place to ensure that budgets are developed and approved to support the PS business plan throughout the company.
Refer to risks: A- 1, A-2, A-3

15.1.2 **PS Information Access.** All official worldwide PS information including policies, guidelines, and standards should be maintained in a single repository and the information should be made available to all employees.
Refer to risks: A-1, A-2, A-3

15.1.3 **Employee Training.** Each PS business unit must develop, document, and monitor training requirements, including frequency, for PS personnel. The business unit management must ensure all PS personnel receive adequate training and encourage and measure personnel participation in professional certification programs.
Refer to risks: A-2, A-4, A-5, A-6

15.1.4 **Customer Feedback.** A worldwide customer feedback program should be implemented to measure performance. This feedback information should be used to improve the quality of services provided, increase business performance, and gain competitive advantage through improved levels of customer satisfaction.
Refer to risk: A-2, A-4, A-5, A-6

Risk If Standard Is Not Implemented

A-1 Internal business controls may be circumvented or may not be followed.

A-2 The company's competitive position or reputation could be adversely affected.

A-3 Mismanaged business practices may result in low profitability and affect continuity of business operations.

A-4 Inability to deliver quality service or meet program standards/milestones may result in legal penalties initiated by the customer.

A-5 Engagement performance falls below expectations, leading to loss of customer satisfaction.

A-6 Loss of future business opportunities affecting revenue and profitability of the PS division.

15.2 OPPORTUNITY-BID PROCESS

Introduction

All PS business opportunities require project approval. Waiver requests to use different reporting tools are subject to approval by PS worldwide operations.

Standard of Internal Control

15.2.1 **Opportunity Tracking.** Once an opportunity has been reported, it should not be removed from the tracking system until it is recorded as certified or lost, withdrawn by the customer, or not bid based on a company decision or due to an approved administrative correction.
Refer to risks: B-1, B-2, B-3

15.2.2 **Opportunity Tracking Data.** The information requirements for tracking and reporting new business opportunities within PS should be clearly established and followed.
Refer to risks: B-1, B-2, B-3

15.2.3 **Bid Budgeting.** A program budget must be established for bid of PS programs. These budgets must include all costs associated with the program bid effort that are incurred during the proposal development and contract negotiation process, including labor effort of the proposal team; travel and accommodation equipment; bid bonds; external purchases of services such as outside counsel, products, and supplies; benchmarking; and demonstration or proof of concept costs that are not charged to the customer.
Refer to risks: B-4, B-5, B-6

15.2.4 **Bid Budgeting Responsibility.** The opportunity manager must prepare the bid budget and obtain approval prior to the expenditure of any effort and cost to prepare the proposal response. The opportunity manager is responsible for managing proposal spending against the established budget.
Refer to risks: B-4, B-5, B-6

15.2.5 **Pricing and Costing for Bids.** Consistent and uniform pricing and costing methodologies must be established for all professional service opportunities. The pricing and costing standards must be adhered to by all individuals engaged in the preparation of PS bids. Actual cost factors unique to each country/region must be documented and applied at the country operating unit level.
Refer to risks: B-6, B-7, B-8, B-9

15.2.6 **Due Diligence.** Adequate procedures must be established to ensure a quality and appropriate due diligence for all customer programs/opportunities. A consistent process for due diligence plans should be established in order to achieve required profitability, risk avoidance, and control. The due diligence plan should be completed and available for the respective proposal.
Refer to risks: B-2, B-10, B-11, B-12

15.2.7 **Client Success Program.** All significant PS wins and client success information should be identified and made readily available to PS and the rest of the company so that they can be offered to potential clients, partners, the media, and analysts. Every significant PS account should be referenceable to shorten future sales cycles and enable everyone to meet the primary goal to close profitable business.
Refer to risks: B-13, B-14, B-15, B-16

Risk If Standard Is Not Implemented

B-1 Business opportunities are not recognized and captured in time, negatively affecting revenue and market share position of the company.

B-2 Price and terms negotiations cannot be leveraged, which may adversely affect profitability in customer transactions.

B-3 The company's business reputation and competitive advantage may be adversely affected.

B-4 Unauthorized or unacceptable proposal costs are incurred by personnel managing the opportunity/bid process due to lack of a monitoring tool.

B-5 Unplanned/excessive costs may negatively impact program revenue and profitability.

B-6 Mismanagement of opportunity/bid process may affect profitability as well as lead to inefficiency within the professional services business.

B-7 Assessment of fines and/or penalties may result.

B-8 Different prices and costing methodologies create pricing difficulties locally, and possibly globally. In addition, different prices for the same product to similar customers may be illegal and result in penalties to the company.

B-9 Prices may be reduced and/or costs disallowed due to noncompliance, defective pricing, and/or inadequate supporting documentation for reported costs.

B-10 Services may be sold to an unauthorized customer or to an unacceptable credit risk.

B-11 The PS division and the company may face unexpected business and legal risks in customer transactions.

B-12 Unforeseen business characteristics of the client are not considered when setting program expectations by PS and the customer.

B-13 No immediate visibility and recognition for success of client projects.

B-14 The company does not use client wins as an immediate and inexpensive form of marketing.

B-15 Lack of knowledge transfer and shared learning within PS may lead to loss of future business opportunities.

B-16 Lack of visibility with financial analysts and the company's board of directors.

15.3 PROGRAM MANAGEMENT

Introduction

A written project plan is required for all projects and subprojects. Project planning activities should begin after initial meetings with the customer and continue throughout the life of the project. The project plan must be maintained to reflect current information and past performance. Planning activities must address the scope, effort, resources, responsibilities, budget schedule, and, if applicable, selling strategy and due diligence processes. The results from project planning must establish baselines upon which proposals are made, contracts are settled, changes are controlled, and performance is measured.

Standard of Internal Control

15.3.1 **Quality Program Methodology.** The company's quality program methodology) must be used for project planning, management, and delivery of PS programs. Alternative methods can be used for customer-specific reasons, but must be documented in the project plan and approved accordingly.
Refer to risks: C-3, C-4, C-8

15.3.2 **Project Planning.** Industry and project management professional standard techniques should be employed in the development of work breakdown structures.
Refer to risks: C-1, C-3, C-4, C-6, C-8

15.3.3 **Budgeting.** A program budget must be established for delivery of all PS programs. The program budget must include: revenue, based on a milestone/period schedule; cost, based on a work breakdown schedule; and a risk contingency commensurate with the applicable risk rating. The budget should also satisfy revenue recognition requirements. Budgets must include revenue and cost for:
- Service delivery effort based on labor cost standards, including program management
- Company hardware and software products
- Travel equipment and supplies
- Direct administrative expenses, performance bonds, FRCPM, or other delivery-related incentives
- Third-party services and products
- Acceptance testing, warranty, and maintenance support
- Risk contingency
- Other related costs

Refer to risks: C-1, C-2

15.3.4 **Budgeting Responsibility.** The opportunity manager must prepare the program budget and obtain approval before the expenditure of any effort and cost for program delivery, and obtain approval for change orders. The opportunity manager is responsible for managing the delivery effort against the program budget for revenue, margin, and cash flow.
Refer to risks: C-1, C-2

15.3.5 **Project Identification.** Once a bid investment approval has been received, all customer projects and each contractual milestone must be identified by a unique identifier and provided to project administration system in the required format.
Refer to risks: C-3, C-4, C-5

15.3.6 **Contract Documents.** A detailed Service Level Agreement (SLA) or Statement of Work (SOW) together with a Functional Specification (or customer requirements documents) must be developed and included in the original contract which determines the baseline against which scope changes will be managed. If the SLA, SOW, or other documents are not completed prior to execution, the contract must provide a process for their completion.
Refer to risks: C-1, C-3, C-4, C-6, C-7, C-8

15.3.7 **Project Tracking.** All customer projects must be tracked and reported for actual revenue, cost, direct assets, and liabilities.
Refer to risks: C-9, C-10

15.3.8 **Time Recording.** All PS employees in a worldwide or field practice are required to record their effort on a weekly basis unless prohibited by local law. Information to be recorded includes:
   a. Company employee ID
   b. Fiscal-week-ending or specific date of activity
   c. Activity code (Attendance/Absence type)
   d. Program Component Identifier (PCI) or the Work Breakdown Structure (WBS) ID
   e. Actual hours worked or absent
   f. Business unit segment code
      The direct supervisor of the employee or contractor and the direct supervisor of work performed are responsible for accuracy of time recorded.
Refer to risks: C-9, C-11

15.3.9 **Revenue and Expense Tracking.** Revenue activities include order entry, invoicing, revenue recognition, deferral entries, and revenue adjustments. All direct expenses associated with a customer program or project must be tracked to that program or project, at a minimum, by program milestone and organizational unit.
Refer to risks: C-9, C-11, C-12, C-13, C-14

15.3.10 **Discontinuance of Service.** Proper procedures must be established and implemented to evaluate and validate customer programs over $100K that may be forecasted to be in a loss position. Adequate loss provisions for such customer projects must be established and properly communicated after appropriate due diligence via professional, technical, and financial review is conducted. All projects that are currently carrying a loss provision or have just entered into a loss position must report their financial status, including a monthly improvement plan, utilizing standard exception reports. Project reporting should be made by the Program Manager to the Country/Region Practice and Finance Managers.
Refer to risks: C-3, C-6, C-9, C-13

15.3.11 **Change Control Management.** All changes in the scope of customer projects, whether initiated by the customer, company, or company's third-party subcontractors, must be recorded in a change control log and should:
a. Follow the QPM Change Control Technique (or other customer required process).
b. Be managed to ensure that the company is fully compensated for any changes.
c. Achieve customer satisfaction.

Changes that result in an increase or decrease of effort, cost, or price of the end solution must be reported at their full gross price. Any reduction from that price must be reflected as an allowance as defined by the appropriate allowance policy.

The project manager and the customer must approve all changes. Any significant changes requiring an amendment to the contract must be approved by the appropriate level according to established policies.

The company and the customer shall each designate a single point of contact to manage the change process. Approved project changes must be documented in the SLA, SOW, functional specification, and/or the acceptance test specification. A contract amendment (scope change), signed by both parties, is required if the requested change results in any of the following:

a. An increase or decrease in contract revenue
b. A change in payment terms
c. A schedule change for contract deliverables
d. Any other change to the company's or the customer's rights, duties, or obligations under the contract which could affect the company's ability to perform or be compensated for services provided

Refer to risks: C-1, C-3, C-4, C-6, C-7, C-8

15.3.12 **Engagement File.** Every customer engagement should have an engagement file that is maintained throughout the engagement. The engagement file must be available for review per audit and legal requirements and should be archived after completion of the project for the number of years based on corporate and local legal and record management requirements.

Refer to risks: C-3, C-4, C-6

15.3.13 **Security of Customer Engagement Information.** All customer engagement information, including financial statements, schedules, work breakdown structures, contracts, sales strategies, negotiation strategy, technical solution documentation, and any other documents that may be applicable to the project, must adhere to company's security classification standards.

Refer to risks: C-14, C-15

15.3.14 **Communication.** Formal procedures should be developed and implemented to communicate and manage internal product dependencies within the company, which are critical to the future functionality of a client project.

Refer to risks: C-3, C-4

15.3.15 **Resource Sourcing.** The engagement manager is responsible for sourcing the resource requirements of the engagement. The engagement manager should negotiate the length of the engagement with the manager of the practice providing resources. The lending manager should receive expense relief at a standard cost per hour established by country based on job code. The lending manager must be given full credit toward his/her chargeability goal when the assignment is billable to a customer.

Refer to risks: C-3, C-4, C-9

15.3.16 **Project Status Reporting.** A defined process should be established to ensure consistent and regular monthly status reports as well as a standard electronic status information flow, as required, are communicated to all levels of PS management. The project status report should be maintained by the project manager and submitted to their manager for review.
Refer to risks: C-3, C-4, C-6

Risk If Standard Is Not Implemented

C-1 Engagement contracts may be executed at prices and/or terms and conditions that do not adequately cover program costs.

C-2 Unplanned/excessive costs may negatively impact program revenue and profitability.

C-3 Assessment of fines or penalties and loss of reputation may result from unmet service milestones.

C-4 Customer dissatisfaction may result.

C-6 The company could be held responsible for the negligence, errors, or omissions of another party, resulting in financial loss to our shareholders.

C-7 If the contract is not consistent regarding liability provisions, it can be unenforceable.

C-8 The company's competitive position or reputation could be adversely affected.

C-9 Inaccurate costs or revenues are recorded against customer projects and negatively impact profitability.

C-10 Intentional errors or misappropriations of assets could go undetected.

C-11 Unauthorized costs may be included, and funds may be misappropriated.

C-12 Information contained in the corporate accounting records may be inaccurate, and the financial statements may not be fairly stated.

C-13 Financial decisions made by company management may be erroneous due to the use of inaccurate or inconsistent financial data.

C-14 Contract prices may be reduced and/or costs disallowed due to noncompliance, defective pricing, and/or inadequate supporting documentation for reported costs.

C-15 Unauthorized use of confidential customer information may result in legal penalties and could adversely affect the company's reputation and competitive position.

15.4 CUSTOMER ORDER MANAGEMENT

Introduction

All orders specifying professional services require approval. Orders and de-certifications of orders must be written and communicated to the order entry organization in a standard and timely manner. All allowances granted must be approved by PS management prior to commitment to the customer. All engagements must be priced using a consistent pricing model which establishes the standard price for the engagement. Each country must establish a standard billing rate for fee-based services used in calculating the standard price.

Standard of Internal Control

15.4.1 **Order Certification.** Orders for multiyear services are certified for the first year's dollar amount initially and on a quarterly basis thereafter, until the order is completely certified.
Refer to risks: D-1, D-2, D-3, D-4, D-5

15.4.2 **Order Administration.** A standard format for processing orders must be developed and implemented, including all data elements necessary for order processing as well as data needed by professional services for downstream reporting.
Refer to risks: D-1, D-2, D-3, D-4, D-5

15.4.3 **Order Decertification.** An order must be de-certified if:
a. The customer cancels the order.
b. Any unused funds for PS services remaining on the customer's purchase order after completion of services have not been used within 12 months of the date of the purchase order.
c. The customer purchase order has expired.
d. No additional business is expected against the customer purchase order.
   All de-certifications must be approved by the applicable or designee. The approver must confirm that the services being canceled have not already been delivered.
Refer to risks: D-1, D-2, D-3, D-4, D-5

15.4.4 **Price Allowances.** The PS engagement must be priced according to the standard pricing policy before allowances are computed.
Refer to risks: D-6, D-7, D-8

15.4.5 **Pricing.** Any discounts or allowances can be documented, approved, and subtracted from the standard price to determine the bid price. No clients can be engaged on a contingent payment basis (i.e., payment based on client results) unless an exception approval is obtained according to policy.

Refer to risks: D-6, D-7, D-8

15.4.6 **Sub-contracting.** All partnership agreements with third-party companies must be reviewed and approved using company approval requirements.

Refer to risks: D-2, D-4, D-6, D-9, D-10

15.4.7 **Service/Product Delivery Without a Purchase Order.** No services or products should be delivered to a customer prior to execution of a contract and receipt of a purchase order. A billable letter of intent approved by the legal department is acceptable in a limited number of cases, until a final contract can be signed. A legally binding and billable agreement is acceptable in place of a PO, but this is not recommended. All exceptions must be properly approved according to established authorization levels and approval policies.

Refer to risks: D-1, D-3, D-4, D-5

15.4.8 **Capitalized Software.** Costs related to the development of software used in customer projects should be treated as a cost of delivering that project, reflected against project revenue, and should not be capitalized unless prior approval has been received. As a starting point to appropriately capitalize software development costs, it is important to determine the proper guidance. Under U.S. GAAP, two potential sets of major rules may apply when determining whether software development costs should be capitalized or expensed.

One set of rules (FASB Accounting Standards Codification (ASC) Topic 985, Software) is designed for software costs that the entity intends to sell or lease. These rules, commonly referred to as the software capitalization rules for external-use software, are the primary focus of this article. The other set of rules (ASC Topic 350, Intangibles—Goodwill and Other) governs software that the entity does not intend to sell or lease. These rules commonly are referred to as the software capitalization rules for internal-use software.[1]

Refer to risks: D-11, D-12

---

[1]Ryan P. Bouray, CPA, and Glenn E. Richards, CPA, "Accounting for External-Use Software Development Costs in an Agile Environment," *Journal of Accountancy*, March 12, 2018, accessed January 3, 2019, https://www.journalofaccountancy.com/news/2018/mar/accounting-for-external-use-software-development-costs-201818259.html.

15.4.9 **Invoicing.** Standard company invoicing procedures must be established for all billable customer contracts worldwide, regardless of whether PS generated the invoices directly or has an agreement with another business entity. Proper controls should include approval of manual invoices, establishing metrics and monitoring invoicing timelines, quarterly tracking, and taking corrective action when necessary **Refer to risk: D-6, D-9, D-13, D-14, D-15**

15.4.10 **Accounts Receivable.** Standard policies and control procedures must be established and followed for maintaining customer accounts receivable balances. PS and finance management must implement a system of management reporting and review to assist in monitoring customer accounts.
Refer to risks: D-12, D-13

15.4.11 **Customer Dispute Resolution.** PS management must implement procedures and standards for preventing and resolving customer disputes in a manner designed to increase customer loyalty, increase profitability, and minimize legal exposure.
Refer to risks: D-6, D-7, D-10, D-11

Risk If Standard Is Not Implemented

D-1 Customer programs delivery may be performed without a valid customer commitment.

D-2 Terms and conditions agreed upon by both parties are not adequately documented and result in disputes.

D-3 Products or services may be sold to an unauthorized customer or to an unacceptable credit risk, resulting in uncollectible accounts.

D-4 Orders may be accepted and processed at prices and/or terms and conditions that are not acceptable to management.

D-5 Sales/orders may be lost, destroyed, or altered. Confidential information may be used to the detriment of the company.

D-6 Customer dissatisfaction may result.

D-7 Assessment of fines and/or penalties may result.

D-8 Different prices of product to similar customers could create pricing difficulties locally and possibly globally. In addition, different prices for the same product to similar customers may be illegal and result in penalties to the company.

D-9 The company could be held responsible for negligence, errors, or omissions, resulting in financial loss to our shareholders.

D-10 The company's competitive position or reputation could be adversely affected.

D-11 Inaccurate costs or revenue are recorded against customer projects and negatively impact profitability.

D-12 Intentional errors or misappropriations of assets could go undetected.

D-13 Sales transactions may be incorrectly prepared, and/or billings and other terms may be misstated.

D-14 Sales transactions may have occurred but may not have been billed and/or recorded.

D-15 Misappropriation of assets or intentional errors could occur. Examples include the following:
   a. Products or services may be shipped or provided but not billed.
   b. Shipments or services provided may be billed but not recorded in the accounting records.
   c. Products or services may be billed and recorded but not shipped or provided.

CHAPTER SIXTEEN

Entity-Level Controls

 INTRODUCTION

The tone at the top sets the integrity of a company, directs the behavior of employees, and is the basis for an organization's ethical environment. When those at the top display greed and overlook or even support fraudulent activities, it is logical to expect the entire company to follow that lead.

For example, Enron's environment was known to be based upon a "trading mentality." By contrast, a tone at the top that makes it top priority to do the right thing for employees, customers, and other stakeholders creates a company-wide environment of openness and honesty that not only builds a fine reputation for its integrity, but also often brings about positive financial results.

 PROCESS OVERVIEW

The diagram below suggests that the foundational elements that support the requirements for entity-level controls are Internal Controls and Compliance, Corporate Policies, Code of Conduct and "Tone at the Top," and the COSO Framework.

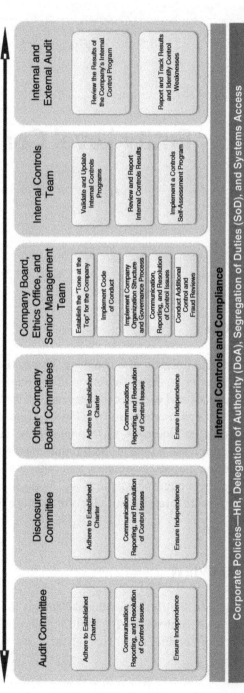

METRICS

Table of Metrics

- **Number and Type of Issues Reported in the Ethics "Hot Line"**—Tracks issues identified by employees using the ethics "hot line."
- **Number of Noncompliance Issues Reported by Type and Organization**—Tracks noncompliance issues by type and company organization.
- **Number of Internal Control Self-Assessments Completed**—Indicates the number of self-assessments completed within a defined fiscal period.
- **Number of Entity-Level Control Surveys Completed**—Indicates the number of surveys completed within a defined fiscal period.
- **Response Rate per Each Entity-Level Control Issue Identified**—Determines the response rate for each survey issued.
- **Number of Issues Reported by the Entity-Level Control Survey**—Determines the number of issues reported by respondents of the entity-level control survey.
- **Internal Control Issues by Type**—Identifies the number of control issue by type.
- **Number of Control Self-Assessments Completed per Period**—Identifies the number of control self-assessments completed by defined physical period.
- **Number of Internal Audits Executed**—Number of audits conducted by the internal audit team.
- **Average Length of Service per Board Committee Member**—Indicates the average length of service for a board committee member.
- **Number of Corporate Policy Violations by Type**—Tracks the number of corporate policy violations by type (e.g. Delegation of Authority (DoA) or Segregation of Duties (SoD).

APPLICATION OF INTERNAL CONTROLS

When assessing the effectiveness of entity-level controls, programs and functions that should be evaluated include ethics programs, management controls, the audit and disclosure committees, and departments such as internal auditing, internal controls, law and public policy (LPP), and compliance. Although a number of external parties, such as the external auditors and regulators, clearly contribute to achieving organizational objectives, they are not part of the entity's system of internal control.

Entity-level controls determine how effective internal controls are working at the organization level. Unlike activity-based controls, entity-level controls focus on the governance and control environment of the entity. The concept of entity-level controls is somewhat complicated since these controls focus on the corporate level. They are referred to as "soft" controls and can be tested using the standards of internal control defined in this section or executing an entity-level controls level to a selection of employees.

SUB-PROCESSES

16.1 Compliance and Compliance Screening

16.2 Internal Controls Roles and Responsibilities

16.3 Entity Management Controls

16.4 Audit Committee Controls

16.1 COMPLIANCE AND COMPLIANCE SCREENING

Introduction

What is corporate compliance? Simply put, corporate compliance is the process of making sure your company and employees follow the laws, regulations, standards, and ethical practices that apply to your organization.

Effective corporate compliance will cover both internal policies and rules and federal and state laws. Enforcing compliance in corporate policy will help your company prevent and detect violations of rules. This can save your organization from fines and lawsuits. Corporate compliance also lays out expectations for employee behavior, helps your staff stay focused on your organization's broader goals, and helps operations run smoothly.[1]

Key Point: Compliance screening and regulatory requirements used to be the concerns of financial institutions. Now all organizations and global corporations are accountable for compliance screening programs, ongoing internal controls, and applicable due diligence programs to ensure that suppliers, customers, and even employees are not terrorists, enemies of the United States, money launderers, or Medicare and Medicaid fraudsters.

The table below indicates which industry should be paying attention to a specific regulatory requirement. The table also indicates which financial processes are impacted.

---

[1]Power DMS, "What Is Corporate Compliance and Why It's Important," accessed January 6. 2019, https://www.powerdms.com/blog/what-corporate-compliance-is-why-compliance-is-important/.

Compliance Requirement	Industries and Organizations	Financial Processes
1. Foreign Corrupt Practices Act (FCPA)	All	Payroll, T&E, AP
2. Office of Foreign Asset Control (OFAC)	All	Payroll, T&E, AP, AR
3. Bureau of Industry and Security (BIS)	Global Companies	Payroll, T&E, AP
4. System for Award Management Security (SAM)	Government Contractors	Payroll, T&E, AP
5. Office of the Inspector General (OIG)	Health Care	Payroll, T&E, AP
6. The Sarbanes-Oxley Act of 2002	Generally Public Companies	Payroll, T&E, AP, AR, and GL
7. U.S. Sentencing Guidelines	All	Payroll, T&E, AP, AR, and GL
8. International ACH Transactions (IAT)	Global Companies	Payroll, T&E, AP, AR
9. U.S. Patriot Act and Consumer Identification Program (CIP)	Financial Institutions	Payroll, T&E, AP, AR
10. Standards for Attestation Engagements (SSAE-16)	Organizations Providing Services	Payroll, T&E, AP, AR, and GL
11. Anti–Money Laundering (AML)	All	AR, AP, T&E, and Payroll
12. Know Your Customer (KYC)	All	AR
13. UK Bribery Act Regulations	Global Companies	AP, T&E

Standard of Internal Control

16.1.1 The company has established a compliance program with company-wide screening requirements for each business process and location.
Refer to risks: A-1, A-2, A-3, A-4, A-5, A-6, A-7, A-8, A-9, A-10

16.1.2 The scope and objectives of the compliance program are clear and articulated to key affected company parties and employees.
Refer to risks: A-1, A-2, A-3, A-4, A-5, A-6, A-7, A-8, A-9, A-10, A-11

16.1.3 The compliance program has a business plan that specifies objectives, staffing, and budget requirements.
Refer to risks: A-1, A-2, A-3, A-4, A-5, A-6, A-7, A-8, A-9, A-10, A-11

16.1.4 The compliance organization receives updates from each disclosure and audit committee meeting.
Refer to risk: A-8

16.1.5 Possible compliance violations reported via the ethics line are communicated to the compliance and finance organizations.
Refer to risk: A-8

16.1.6 The compliance group periodically evaluates the risk of noncompliance and criminal conduct.
Refer to risk: A-8

16.1.7 Establish clear responsibility for the compliance program and the screening requirements for each specific business process.
Refer to risks: A-1, A-2, A-3, A-4, A-5, A-6, A-7, A-8, A-9, A-10, A-11

16.1.8 Adequate resources are established for the compliance program.
Refer to risks: A-1, A-2, A-3, A-4, A-5, A-6, A-7, A-8, A-9, A-10, A-11

16.1.9 Establish standards and procedures to prevent and detect violations of law.
Refer to risks: A-9, A-10, A11

16.1.10 Communicate standards of conduct and procedures to prevent and detect violations of law and regulatory compliance requirements.
Refer to risks: A-9, A-10, A11

16.1.11 Senior management and the board oversee a compliance program for the company and ensure the effectiveness of the compliance program.
Refer to risks: A-1, A-2, A-3, A-4, A-5, A-6, A-7, A-8, A-9, A-10, A-11

Risk If Standard Is Not Implemented

A-1 The company would not have a centralized organization to identify, manage, and report compliance issues.

A-2 Employees and stakeholders are confused as to the where to look for guidance of compliance and how to raise issues.

A-3 If a business plan is not in place, the objectives, deliverables, and resources for the compliance program are not specified.

A-4 Lack of reporting may impact the company's future business dealings with government agencies.

A-5 Compliance screening does not take place and issues are not reported, prioritized, and addressed.

A-6 Without a timely view of the legal risks that a company faces, the compliance program may be addressing the wrong risks.

A-7 Without clear responsibility for the compliance program, business and legal risks to the company are not identified, risks would not be evaluated in a formal and consistent manner, policies may be promulgated from a parochial perspective that does not consider the enterprise perspective, policies are inconsistent across the enterprise, employees do not receive necessary training, and the effectiveness of the policy and training is never processed.

A-8 A compliance program with inadequate resources is at the risk of being ineffective. An ineffective compliance program is less likely to be able to prevent and detect violations of law. An ineffective compliance program subjects the company to greater risk of criminal, civil, or administrative enforcement action.

A-9 Without standards of conduct and procedures, employees may not be aware of the laws, policies, and regulations that govern their activities.

A-10 Standards of conduct, screening requirements, and procedures that are not communicated are less likely to be followed.

A-11 The absence of an effective compliance program could subject the company to additional criminal, legal, financial, and reputational risk.

16.2 INTERNAL CONTROLS ROLES AND RESPONSIBILITIES

Introduction

As important as an internal control structure is to an organization, an effective system is not a guarantee that the organization will be successful. An effective internal control structure will keep the right people informed about the organization's progress (or lack of progress) in achieving its objectives. As a standard, the organization with overall responsibilities for the internal control and remediation is critical to the success of the program

Standard of Internal Control

16.2.1 A charter is in place to establish the direction and roles and responsibilities of the internal controls and remediation process. A charter specifies the level of independence required for the internal controls function.
Refer to risks: B-1, B-3

16.2.2 An organizational structure is in place that ensures coverage of internal controls for the company. Staffing levels for the internal controls team are appropriate to ensure coverage of all areas.
Refer to risks: B-1, B-3

16.2.3 The internal controls team has the credentials and attends training as required.
Refer to risks: B-1, B-3

16.2.4 The internal controls team is assigned by defined financial cycles and business processes as approved by the controller and CFO.
Refer to risk: B-4

16.2.5 The internal controls team integrates business processes with IT to ensure that process controls are mapped to system controls and functionality.
Refer to risk: B-5

16.2.6 There is a defined process for the implementation of corporate policies.
Refer to risks: B-6, B-7, B-8

16.2.7 As a corporate policy cornerstone, the Delegation of Authority (DoA) policy has been approved and the deployment of the policy is documented and approved. Additionally, updates are made through a defined process.
Refer to risks: B-6, B-7, B-8

16.2.8 An internal controls policy is documented and communicated throughout the company. Accountability for the internal controls environment and control activities are well defined.
Refer to risks: B-6, B-7, B-8

16.2.9 There is a formal status reporting and remediation process.
Refer to risk: B-9

16.2.10 Executive management receives communication on the status of the SOX 404 project and the controls environment as requested.
Refer to risk: B-9

16.2.11 The internal controls team provides SOX 404 training and communication sessions on a monthly to quarterly basis.
Refer to risk: B-9

16.2.12 There is a linkage between the internal controls team, internal, and external audit to ensure control risks are addressed and remediation activities are coordinated.
Refer to risks: B-8, B-11

16.2.13 The internal control team uses project management processes as prescribed through the Project Management Institute (PMI).
Refer to risks: B-8, B-9, B-11, B-12

16.2.14 The internal controls team is apprised of changing risks and conditions as defined by the compliance officer, and the internal–external audit teams.
Refer to risks: B-1, B-2

Risk If Standard Is Not Implemented

B-1 Duplication of efforts within the team and with other control groups could arise. If the level of independence is not well defined, conflicts of interest could arise.

B-2 Key controls may not be identified for all areas of the company and staffing levels may not be adequate to ensure coverage.

B-3 The correct level of expertise may not be in place to meet the objectives of the team charter.

B-4 Financial (process) cycle coverage may not be complete.

B-5 Significant IT systems may not be included in the project scope, resulting in key controls not being identified, tested, or remediated.

B-6 Corporate policies may not be in place or not updated in a timely manner.

B-7 The DoA policy is not approved or communicated, causing policy violations by improper approvals.

B-8 Internal controls requirements across the organization are not communicated and accountability is unclear.

B-9 Status reporting will not be timely and accurate. Management will not be updated if there are project or control risks.

B-10 Training is not updated and delivered in a timely manner.

B-11 Remediation of internal and external issues is not addressed in a timely manner.

B-12 Documentation may not be completed in a standard format.

16.3 ENTITY MANAGEMENT CONTROLS

Introduction

Entity-level controls are internal controls that help ensure that management directives pertaining to the company are implemented, tested, remediated, and appropriately updated. Management of a company must ensure that risk is identified and mitigated with the proper controls and organizational structure.

Standard of Internal Control

16.3.1 Board committees exist as required or where warranted by the need for more in-depth or directed attention to particular matters.
Refer to risks: C-1, C-2, C-3, C-4, C-5, C-6, C-7, C-8

16.3.2 The sufficiency and timeliness with which information is provided to board or committee members allow monitoring of management's objectives and strategies, the entity's financial position and operating results, significant business risks, and terms of significant agreements.
Refer to risks: C-1, C-2, C-3, C-4, C-5, C-6, C-7, C-8

16.3.3 The board of directors establishes and supports the appropriate "tone at the top."
Refer to risks: C-1, C-2, C-3, C-4, C-5, C-6, C-7, C-8

16.3.4 The board or committee takes action as a result of its findings, including special investigations as needed.
Refer to risks: C-1, C-2, C-3, C-4, C-5, C-6, C-7, C-8

16.3.5 Adequate documented risk and controls exist to assess that management move carefully, proceeding only after carefully analyzing the risks and potential benefits of any venture.
Refer to risks: C-1, C-2, C-3, C-4, C-5, C-6, C-7, C-8

16.3.6 Management exhibits appropriate attitude toward the accounting functions and concerns about the reliability of financial reporting and safeguarding of assets.
Refer to risks: C-1, C-2, C-3, C-4, C-5, C-6, C-7, C-8

16.3.7 There is regular frequency of interaction between senior management and operating management, particularly when operating from geographically remote locations.
Refer to risks: C-1, C-2, C-3, C-4, C-5, C-6, C-7, C-8

16.3.8 Management's attitudes and actions toward financial reporting, including disputes over application of accounting treatments and policies, is appropriate with requirements.
Refer to risks: C-1, C-2, C-3, C-4, C-5, C-6, C-7, C-8

16.3.9 The entity's organizational structure is appropriate, and facilitates its ability to provide the necessary information flow to manage its activities in the company.
Refer to risks: C-1, C-2, C-3, C-4, C-5, C-6, C-7, C-8

16.3.10 Formal job descriptions and responsibilities are in place that define the tasks for key positions in the company.
Refer to risks: C-1, C-2, C-3, C-4, C-5, C-6, C-7, C-8

16.3.11 There are adequate analyses of the knowledge and skills needed to perform job requirements.
Refer to risks: C-1, C-2, C-3, C-4, C-5, C-6, C-7, C-8

Risk If Standard Is Not Implemented

C-1 The board of directors does not adhere to COSO objectives.

C-2 There are no standards of internal control and fiscal timeliness are delayed and/or weak.

C-3 Management's guidelines and standards do not exist and/or are not communicated effectively throughout the company.

C-4 There is no follow-up to open issues at board meetings to ensure remediation.

C-5 Management's business decisions do not receive proper review and/or standards do not exist to enable an effective and timely review.

C-6 Management's guidelines and standards do not exist and/or are not consistent with financial objectives.

C-7 The organizational structure impedes the business objectives.

C-8 There is no review process to ensure compliance of standards in place.

 ## 16.4 AUDIT COMMITTEE CONTROLS

Introduction

The audit committee's role includes: the oversight of financial reporting; the monitoring of accounting policies; the oversight of any external auditors; regulatory compliance; and discussion of risk management policies with management. The audit committee may approve the company's annual internal audit plan and is usually apprised of any suspicions of fraud reported via the ethics hotline process.

Standards of Internal Control

16.4.1 There is a process in which critical employee issues are raised to the audit committee
Refer to risks: D-1, D-5, D-9, D-13, D-17, D-21, D-22

16.4.2 The CFO possesses the required knowledge and expertise and complies with the company's code of ethics and business conduct.
Refer to risk: D-2

16.4.3 There is appropriate level of involvement and interaction with external auditor, including the audit committee's role in the appointment, retention, and compensation of the external auditor.
Refer to risks: D-3, D-11, D-27, D-28

16.4.4 The external audit plan is reviewed and approved by the audit committee.
Refer to risks: D-3, D-4, D-10

16.4.5 The audit committee complies with SEC rules.
Refer to risk: D-5

16.4.6 Internal auditor plans are reviewed and approved by the audit committee.
Refer to risk: D-6

16.4.7 The audit committee adopts and fosters an environment to promote ethical behavior.
Refer to risks: D-8, D-21

16.4.8 The ethics and code of conduct team interacts with the audit committee.
Refer to risks: D-8, D-21

16.4.9 The audit committee reviews audit proposals from other firms and adheres to term limitations established for external auditors.
Refer to risks: D-10, D-11

16.4.10 The audit committee nomination process satisfies the independence requirements.
Refer to risks: D-12, D-17, D-18, D-27

16.4.11 Outside compensation for the audit committee is disallowed.
Refer to risks: D-12, D-17, D-18, D-27

16.4.12 The audit committee chairman has assigned term limitations.
Refer to risks: D-12, D-17, D-18, D-27

16.4.13 Communication with the audit committee to the CFO and CEO occurs on an ongoing basis and significant findings and issues are addressed.
Refer to risk: D-13

16.4.14 Earnings press releases are discussed with the audit committee prior to being released to the public relations department.
Refer to risk: D-14

16.4.15 There is an appropriate level of involvement and interaction with internal audit, including the audit committee's line of authority, budgeting, and staffing of internal audit.
Refer to risks: D-11, D-15

16.4.16 The charter for internal audit is reviewed and approved by the audit committee.
Refer to risks: D-11, D-15

16.4.17 The audit committee is composed of business executives who possess the knowledge and experience necessary to effectively carry out their roles and responsibilities.
Refer to risks: D-16, D-20, D-24, D-27, D-28

16.4.18 An audit committee charter serves as a framework to the board and its committees; the audit committee complies with the directives of the charter.
Refer to risks: D-20, D-24, D-27, D-28

16.4.19 There is a review of the performance of the audit committee.
Refer to risks: D-16, D-20, D-24, D-27, D-28

16.4.20 Issues that arise out of the ethics and code of conduct process are presented to the audit committee.
Refer to risks: D-9, D-13, D-21, D-24

16.4.21 The audit committee initiates additional investigations on any issues reported through the ethics investigation process, and has access to financial statements and plans.
Refer to risks: D-9, D-13, D-21, D-24

16.4.22 Management's report on internal controls and the external auditor's attestation report are reviewed with the audit committee on an annual basis. Both are discussed with external auditor management.
Refer to risk: D-23

16.4.23 The audit committee reviews the roles of the disclosure committee.
Refer to risks: D-21, D-24

16.4.24 Meetings with the chief financial officer (CFO) and/or accounting officers, internal auditors, and external auditors are held frequently and timely.
Refer to risk: D-25

16.4.25 As a part of corporate governance requirements, compensation committee issues are reviewed by the audit committee.
Refer to risk: D-27

16.4.26 The committee serves in an oversight role to the public reporting of the company's financial statements.
Refer to risks: D-14, D-26

16.4.27 Related-party transactions do not present a conflict of interest.
Refer to risk: D-27

16.4.28 Audit committee roles and responsibilities are clearly defined and articulated to the audit committee prior to voting.
Refer to risk: D-28

16.4.29 The audit committee reviews the audit committee charter before voting that the charter is final.
Refer to risk: D-28

Risk If Standard Is Not Implemented

D-1 Employee issues are not identified and raised to the audit committee.

D-2 The CFO lacks the required knowledge and experience.

D-3 There is a lack of appropriate level of interaction with the external auditor.

D-4 External audit performs unapproved work.

D-5 SEC and IFRS rules are not followed.

D-6 Internal auditor plans are not reviewed by the audit committee.

D-8 The audit committee fails to demonstrate the company's ethics and business conduct message.

D-9 Ethics concerns are not identified or addressed.

D-10 Independence of external auditors and term limitations are not defined.

D-11 Independence is impaired.

D-12 The audit committee chairman is in place for a longer term than planned.

D-13 Communication of significant findings and issues does not occur on a frequent basis and issues are not communicated to the CFO and CEO.

D-14 Earnings press releases are not communicated as required.

D-15 The charter for internal audit is not approved by the audit committee.

D-16 The committee fails to meet the knowledge and experience requirements.

D-17 The committee fails to keeps abreast of current developments.

D-18 The committee fails to meet the continuing education requirements.

D-19 Audit committee may not be in compliance with the audit committee charter.

D-20 Performance issues could arise within the audit committee.

D-21 Issues raised by the ethics investigation process are not raised as required by Section 301 of SOX which calls for companies to have a process in place for investigating questionable audit and accounting practices.

D-22 Investigation and access to information does not occur in a timely manner.

D-23 Communication of the internal controls report and the attestation process does not occur.

D-24 Disclosure committee obligations are not reviewed by the audit committee. Disclosures will not occur in a timely manner as required by Section 302 of SOX.

D-25 Meetings may not be held in a timely manner in order to address key issues.

D-26 Financial statements are not reviewed by the audit committee prior to public release.

D-27 A conflict of interest exists, resulting in the best interest of the company being at risk.

D-28 There may be questions on the roles and responsibilities of the audit committee and its charter.

Glossary

Access Controls These are the procedures and controls that limit or detect access to critical network assets to guard against loss of integrity, confidentiality, accountability, or availability. Access controls provide reasonable assurance that critical resources are protected against unauthorized modification, disclosure, loss, or impairment.

Account Number Defines the accounting transaction type for the transaction and includes a system-generated number tied to a company's chart of accounts.

Accounts Payable Business processes supporting the functions of issuing payment for property, goods, and services. Sub-processes include supplier, authorization processes, invoicing processing and payment, freight analysis, and account reconcilement and process analysis.

Accounting Policy Basic concepts, assumptions, policies, methods, and practices used by a company for maintaining accounting principles and summarization into financial statements as prescribed by GAAP. A policy can be described as *what* needs to happen to ensure that accounting cycles are working within boundaries of internal control.

Accounting Procedure The routine steps in processing accounting data during an accounting period. In sequence, (1) occurrence of the transaction, (2) classification of each transaction in chronological order (journalizing), (3) recording the classified data in ledger accounts (posting), (4) preparation of financial statements and (5) closing of nominal accounts. A procedure ensures that a policy is properly executed and explains *how*. Other procedures or policies will be referenced if applicable.

Accruals Accruals are adjustments for (1) revenues that have been earned but are not yet recorded in the accounts, and (2) expenses that have been incurred but are not yet recorded in the accounts. The accruals need to be added via adjusting entries so that the financial statements report these amounts.[1]

---

[1] Accounting Coach, "What Are Accruals," accessed January 1, 2019, https://www.accountingcoach.com/blog/what-are-accruals.

ACH Credit An ACH credit is like depositing money in an account. In an ACH credit transaction, the individual/originator/business/agency instructs the financial institution to credit an account with money. The payment is then made via the ACH to the respective account. ACH credit payments are sometimes called "push payments" because the payer initiates the transaction by "pushing" the funds to the recipient's account.

ACH Debit For example, a customer wants to pay an electric bill via ACH debit. The customer is the originator of the transaction, and his bank is the Originating Financial Depository Institution (ODFI). The customer authorizes his bank, the ODFI, to send money from his account to the recipient's upon the recipient's request. ACH debit transactions are sometimes called "pull payments" because they are initiated by the recipient "pulling" funds from the payer's account.

ACH Payment ACH is an acronym for "Automated Clearing House." The ACH network is responsible for transferring money from bank to bank in a "paperless" transaction.

Audit Committee The audit committee's role includes: the oversight of financial reporting; the monitoring of accounting policies; the oversight of any external auditors; regulatory compliance; and discussion of risk management policies with management. The audit committee may approve the company's internal annual internal audit plan and is usually apprised of any suspicions of fraud reported via the ethics hotline process.

Best Practices Implementation of the highest quality, most advantageous, repeatable processes achieved by applying the experiences of those with the acquired skill or proficiency.

Business Continuity Planning Process of developing advance arrangements and procedures that enable an organization to respond to an event in such a manner that critical business functions continue with planned levels of interruption or essential change.

Business Continuity Program An ongoing program supported and funded by management to ensure business continuity requirements are assessed, resources are allocated, and recovery strategies and procedures are completed and tested.

Cardholder Agreement A cardholder agreement is a document given to credit card holders that details the rights and responsibilities of both the cardholder and the issuer.

Change in Accounting Principle When a company adopts an alternative generally accepted accounting principle to a previously used principle to account for the same type of transaction or event, that action is called a change in accounting principle. The term *accounting principle* includes not only accounting principles and practices but also the methods of applying them. The initial adoption of an accounting principle in recognition of events or transactions occurring for the first time or that were previously immaterial in their effect is not considered a change in accounting principle. A change in accounting principle differs from a change in accounting estimate in that a change in accounting estimate results when new events occur, more experience is acquired, or additional information is obtained that affects the previously determined estimate.

Change in Payment Terms Approved changes to the duration of credit period (without financial penalty) extended to suppliers by the company and/or the company to its customers, which creates additional exposure.

Check 21 The Check Clearing for the 21st Century Act (Check 21) is a federal law that took effect on October 28, 2004, and gives banks and other organizations the ability to create electronic image copies of consumers' checks, in a process known as check truncation.

Company Confidential This classification applies to information intended for use within the company or to further its business endeavors. Material classified this way requires protection because of its personnel, technical, or business sensitivity. Unauthorized release or loss of this information can reasonably be expected to harm the company's business or internal operations.

Company Restricted This classification applies to strategic, corporate-level information providing the company significant future competitive advantage or causing serious harm to the company's image, stock price, or market share if disclosed.

Compensating Control A compensating control, also called an alternative control, is a mechanism that is put in place to satisfy the requirement for a security measure that is deemed too difficult or impractical to implement at the present time. In the payment card industry (PCI), compensating controls were introduced in PCI DSS 1.0, to give organizations an alternative to security requirements that could not be met due to legitimate technological or business constraints.

Computer Virus A program that contains software instructions necessary to make replicas of itself and insert these instructions in the execution path of other programs without the knowledge or permission of the user.

Contingency Plan A set of measures to deal with emergencies caused by failures due to human action or natural disasters.

Contingency Planning The prearranged plans and procedures that critical business functions will execute to ensure business continuity until computer and telecommunications facilities are reestablished following a disaster.

Continuity of Service and Operations Set of controls and contingency measures to ensure that when unexpected events occur, critical services and operations continue without interruption or are promptly restored.

Contra Revenue Contra revenue is a deduction from the gross revenue reported by a business, which results in net revenue. Contra revenue transactions are recorded in one or more contra revenue accounts, which usually have a debit balance (as opposed to the credit balance in the typical revenue account).[2]

[2]Accounting Tools, "Contra Revenue," posted November 17, 2017, accessed January 1, 2019, https://www.accountingtools.com/articles/what-is-contra-revenue.html.

Copy Any information that is duplicated and is used for reference purposes only. Copies are normally kept for a short period of time and are never sent to offsite storage. Each employee/contractor and business unit is responsible for disposing of their copies within the time frame specified under the column "Copy Retention Maximum" as specified on a records retention schedule.

Cost Center The designated accounting location, in which costs are incurred, defined as a sub-unit of a legal entity and in some cases the business unit depending on how the business unit code is utilized. All cost centers are assigned to a legal entity; however, only some cost centers may be assigned to business units. It is distinguished by an area of responsibility, location, or accounting method.

Cost Management Financial processes that support cost accounting, inventory accounting, and cost analysis.

Critical Application A critical business application is one that company must have to support major revenue activities, movement of goods to customers, a strategic manufacturing process, or to fulfill contractual or regulatory obligations. In addition, the application's availability is deemed by management to be vital to the continued functioning of company business. Examples of critical applications are: customer service support, order entry, inventory control, manufacturing resource planning, purchasing, warehouse control, quality assurance, and finance.

Critical Processes Business processes that if disrupted or made unavailable for any length of time will have a significant negative impact on the success of the business.

Data Model Establishes data definitions and processes for reference, ensures data rules are utilized, and provides a schematic view of the underlying components comprising the data that drives the financial function.

Disaster A loss of computing or telecommunication resources to the extent that routine recovery measures cannot restore normal service levels within 24 hours, which impacts the company's business significantly.

EDI Electronic Data Interchange (EDI) is the transfer of structured data by agreed message standards from one computer system to another using an electronic means.

Electronic Commerce Doing business electronically.

Entity Level Controls Entity-level controls have a pervasive influence throughout all organizations. If they are weak, inadequate, or nonexistent, they can impact material weaknesses relating to an audit of internal control. Week entity-level controls can also lead to material misstatements in the financial statements of the company. The presence of material misstatements could result in receiving an adverse opinion on internal controls and a qualified opinion on the financial statements.

Enterprise Resource Planning (ERP) System An ERP is an integrated business process management software that allows an organization to use a system of integrated applications to manage the business and automate many back-office functions related to technology, services, and human resources.

Financial Architecture The structure in which components, processes, and systems for a finance function are organized and integrated.

Fixed Assets A fixed asset is a long-term tangible piece of property that a firm owns and uses in its operations to generate income. Fixed assets are not expected to be consumed or converted into cash within 1–2 years. Fixed assets are known as property, plant, and equipment (PP&E). They are also referred to as capital assets.

Freeware Software available through computer bulletin boards and networks at no cost. Patches and drivers are not included in this category.

General Accounting Financial processes that support the fiscal close, general accounting, and intercompany processes.

Highly Significant Transaction A transaction that could reasonably result in a 10% or greater variance in revenues or would result in a 5% or greater variance in the net worth (assets minus liabilities).

HIPAA The acronym that stands for the Health Insurance Portability and Accountability Act, a U.S. law designed to provide privacy standards to protect patients' medical records and other health information provided to health plans, doctors, hospitals, and other health-care providers. The implementation of HIPAA security rule ensures that this data is protected.

Hire to Retire (H2R) Process Hire to Retire (H2R) is a human resources process that includes everything that needs to be done over the course of an employee's career with a company from hiring to termination or retirement.

Isolated Environment An environment not connected to a company's network.

Internal Controls The integrated framework approach defines internal control as a "process, effected by an entity's board of directors, management, and other personnel, designed to provide reasonable assurance regarding the achievement of objectives in the following categories: (A) reliability of financial reporting, (B) effectiveness and efficiency of operations, and compliant with applicable laws and regulations."

Intrusion Unauthorized access to any resource owned or operated by the company.

Intrusion Detection The process of collecting and analyzing information to identify incidents of misuse or intrusion.

Logic Bomb Code imbedded in a program that is executed if certain conditions are met. The purpose of this code is to commit computer sabotage.

Material Weakness A significant deficiency, or combination of significant deficiencies, that result in more than a remote likelihood that a material misstatement of the annual or interim financial statements will not be prevented or detected.

Maximum Foreseeable Loss (MFL) Maximum foreseeable loss is a reference to the largest financial hit a policyholder could potentially experience when insured property has been harmed or destroyed by an adverse event, such as a fire.

National Institute of Standards and Technology (NIST) NIST is the National Institute of Standards and Technology, a unit of the U.S. Commerce Department.

Formerly known as the National Bureau of Standards, NIST promotes and maintains measurement standards. It also has active programs for encouraging and assisting industry and science to develop and use these standards.[3]

Net Income Net income is equal to net earnings (profit) calculated as sales less cost of goods sold, selling, general and administrative expenses, operating expenses, depreciation, interest, taxes, and other expenses.

Non-Records Any tangible information that does not typically contain data pertaining to or originated by the company. Materials are typically used as reference or research tools by the staff and include such items as newspapers, periodicals, brochures, public and Internet information, and toolkits.

Office of Record Any business unit that is assigned responsibility for maintaining "official" company records.

Official Records These records are those which are required to be kept to meet statutory, regulatory, or contractual requirements, and those kept pursuant to good business practice for periods of time as specified in the corporate records retention schedule.

Organizational Controls Should cover all aspects of a company's activity without overlap, and be clearly assigned and communicated.

- Responsibility should be delegated down the level at which the necessary expertise and time exists.
- No single employee should have exclusive knowledge, authority, or control over any significant transaction or group of transactions.
- Agreeing realistic qualitative and quantitative targets strengthens responsibility.
- The structure of accountability depends upon continuing levels of competence of employees in different positions and the development of competence so that responsibility and reporting relationships can be regrouped in more efficient ways.

Paperless Transactions Any transaction conducted via an electronic means such as an electronic purchase order, invoice, or payment.

Payment Type A payment is the trade of value from one party (such as a person or company) to another for goods, or services, or to fulfill a legal obligation. The most commonly used payment methods include cash, check, or debit card, credit card, wire, or ACH payments. Payments may also take complicated forms, such as stock issues or the transfer of anything of value or benefit to the parties. In U.S. law, the payer is the party making a payment while the payee is the party receiving the payment. In trade, payments are frequently preceded by an invoice or bill.

---

[3]National Institute of Standards and Technology (NIST), "Definition: NIST (National Institute of Standards and Technology), accessed January 13, 2019, https://searchsoftwarequality.techtarget.com/definition/NIST.

P-Card A purchasing card (also abbreviated as PCard or P-Card) is a form of company charge card that allows goods and services to be procured without using a traditional purchasing process. In the UK, purchasing cards are usually referred to as procurement cards. Purchasing cards are usually issued to employees who are expected to follow their organization's policies and procedures related to P-Card use, including reviewing and approving transactions according to a set schedule (at least once per month). The organization can implement a variety of controls for each P-Card; for example, a single-purchase dollar limit, a monthly limit, merchant category code (MCC) restrictions, and so on. In addition, a cardholder's P-Card activity should be reviewed periodically by someone independent of the cardholder.

Payment Card Industry (PCI) Security Standards Council The PCI Security Standards Council is a global forum for the ongoing development, enhancement, storage, dissemination, and implementation of security standards for account data protection.

Policy Controls Are the general principles and guides for action that influence decisions. They indicate the limits to choices and the parameters or rules to be followed by a company and its employees. Major policies should be reviewed, approved, and communicated by senior management. Policies are derived by:
- Considering the business environment and process objectives.
- Identifying the potential categories of risks that the environment poses toward achievement of the objectives.

Probable Maximum Loss (PML) This is the maximum loss that an insurer would be expected to incur on a policy. PML is most often associated with insurance policies on property, such as fire insurance, and represents the worst-case scenario for an insurer.

Procedure Controls Prescribe how actions are to be performed consistent with policies. Procedures should be developed by those who understand the day-to-day actions.

Process A systematic series of actions directed to some end; a continuous action or operation taking place in a definite manner.

Process Flow A process flow communicates the actual process currently in place to support a business process. It is a picture of the flow and sequence of work steps, tasks, or activities and will include the flow or sequence of steps throughout the process; the person responsible for each task; and the decision points and their impact on the flow of work.

Procure to Pay (P2P) Procure-to-pay is a term used throughout the industry to designate a specific subdivision of the procurement process. The procure-to-pay systems enable the integration of the purchasing department with the accounts payable department. Some of the largest players of the software industry agree on a common definition of procure-to-pay, linking the procurement process with accounts payable processes.

Profit Center An area of responsibility for which an independent operating profit is calculated.

Project Management Project management applies operational, business, and management knowledge to the identification of project activities that are required to complete deliverables within timelines and cost estimates.

Project management is the application of knowledge, skills, tools, and techniques to project activities to meet project requirements. Project management is accomplished through: (1) Initiating, (2) Planning, (3) Executing, (4) Controlling, and (5) Closing. A communication process should be in place to ensure that project results are shared and updated throughout the life of the project.

Project Management Institute (PMI) Founded in 1969, PMI delivers value for more than 2.9 million professionals working in nearly every country in the world through global advocacy, collaboration, education, and research and is the leading not-for-profit professional membership association for the project management profession.

Recovery The restoration of computing and telecommunications services following an outage resulting from a disaster.

Remote Deposit Remote deposit is the ability of a bank customer in the United States and Canada to deposit a check into a bank account from a remote location, such as an office or home, without having to physically deliver the check to the bank. This is typically accomplished by scanning a digital image of a check into a computer, then transmitting that image to the bank. The practice became legal in the United States in 2004 when the Check Clearing for the 21st Century Act (or Check 21 Act) took effect, though not all banks have implemented the system.

Review Controls Include an ongoing self-assessment process as required by the Sarbanes-Oxley Act of 2002. A self-assessment is a series of questions that validate the effectiveness of the control environment. A self-assessment must be conducted every fiscal quarter; in some situations the manager of the operating unit may elect to conduct a self-assessment test more frequently. It is imperative that all weaknesses found in the testing process are remediated through a corrective action and follow-up process.

Revenue Revenue is the amount of money that a company actually receives during a specific fiscal period, including discounts and deductions for returned merchandise. It is the top line or gross income figure from which costs are subtracted to determine net income.

Revenue Recognition Revenue is one of the most important measures used by investors in assessing a company's performance and prospects. However, previous revenue recognition guidance differs in Generally Accepted Accounting Principles (GAAP) and International Financial Reporting Standards (IFRS)—and many believe both standards were in need of improvement.

On May 28, 2014, the FASB and the International Accounting Standards Board (IASB) issued (press release) converged guidance on recognizing revenue in contracts with customers. The new guidance is a major achievement in the Boards' joint efforts to improve this important area of financial reporting.

Presently, GAAP has complex, detailed, and disparate revenue recognition requirements for specific transactions and industries, including, for example, software and real estate. As a result, different industries use different accounting for economically similar transactions.

The objective of the new guidance is to establish principles to report useful information to users of financial statements about the nature, amount, timing, and uncertainty of revenue from contracts with customers. The new guidance:

- Removes inconsistencies and weaknesses in existing revenue requirements
- Provides a more robust framework for addressing revenue issues
- Improves comparability of revenue recognition practices across entities, industries, jurisdictions, and capital markets
- Provides more useful information to users of financial statements through improved disclosure requirements
- Simplifies the preparation of financial statements by reducing the number of requirements to which an organization must refer[4]

Risk Assessment/Analysis Process of identifying the risks to an organization, assessing the critical functions necessary for an organization to continue business operations, defining the controls in place to reduce organization exposure, and evaluating the costs for such controls. Risk analysis often involves an evaluation of the probabilities of a particular event.

Risk Management Risk management is an increasingly important business driver since company stakeholders have become much more concerned about risk. Risk may be a driver of strategic decisions, it may be a cause of uncertainty in the organization, or it may simply be embedded in the activities of the organization

SSAE 18 SSAE 18 is a series of enhancements aimed to increase the usefulness and quality of SOC reports, now superseding SSAE 16 and SAS 70. The changes made to the standard this time around will require companies to take more control and ownership of their own internal controls around the identification and classification of risk and appropriate management of third-party vendor relationships. These changes, while not overly burdensome, will help close the loop on key areas where industry professionals noted gaps in many service organizations' reports. The key changes are:

1. Service organizations will need to implement a formal Third Party Vendor Management Program.

---

[4]Financial Accounting Standards Board (FASB), "Why Did the FASB Issue a New Standard on Revenue Recognition," accessed January 1, 2019, https://www.fasb.org/jsp/FASB/Page/ImageB ridgePage&cid=1176169257359.

   2. Service organizations will need to implement a formal Annual Risk Assessment process.[5]

Sarbanes-Oxley 2002 The act can be divided into three main points:

1. The scope of an external audit firm has been restricted in which CPAs no longer have the right to set standards for their practice.
2. There are new duties for boards of directors in general and for audit committees in particular. Corporate governance provisions include a required code of ethics or standards of business conduct.
3. There are new requirements for the CEO and CFO. Each SEC filing (10K and 10Q) stating that:
   a. The report fairly represents in all material respects the company's operations and financial condition.
   b. The report does not contain any material misstatements or omit to state a material fact necessary in order to make the statements made, in light of the circumstances under which the statements were made, not misleading.
   c. The report containing financial statements complies with Section 13(a) or 15(d) of the Securities and Exchange Act of 1934.
   d. The company's control system is in place and effective.

Segregation of Duties (SoD) This control is one of the most important controls that your company can have. Adequate SoD reduces the likelihood that errors (intentional or unintentional) will remain undetected by providing for separate processing by different individuals at various stages of a transaction and for independent reviews of the work performed. The SoD control provides four primary benefits: (1) the risk of a deliberate fraud is mitigated as the collusion of two or more persons would be required in order to circumvent controls; (2) the risk of legitimate errors is mitigated as the likelihood of detection is increased; (3) the cost of corrective actions is mitigated as errors are generally detected relatively earlier in their lifecycle; and (4) the organization's reputation for integrity and quality is enhanced through a system of checks and balances.

Shareware Software available through computer bulletin boards and networks at a fee that is payable after downloading the software.

Significant Deficiency This is a single control deficiency, or combination of control deficiencies, that adversely affects the company's ability to initiate, authorize, record, process, or report external financial data reliably. There is more than a remote likelihood that a misstatement of the company's annual or interim financial statements that is more than inconsequential will not be prevented or detected.

---

[5]Statement on Standards for Attestation Engagements 16 (SSAE 16), "The SSAE 18 Audit Standard (Updates and Replaces SSAE-16)," accessed January 13, 2019, https://www.ssae-16.com/soc-1-report/the-ssae-18-audit-standard/.

Standards of Internal Control The standards define a series of internal controls that address the risks associated with key business processes, sub-processes and entity-level processes.

Super-User A user of an ERP with special privileges needed to administer and maintain the system or a system administrator. The special privileges may include the ability to process a financial transaction and make changes in the general ledger to modify the transaction. "Super-user" privileges must be monitored to ensure that access rights are not used to incorrectly modify or falsify a transaction resulting in risk to the company.

Supervisory Controls These are situations in which managers ensure that all employees understand their responsibilities and authorities, and the assurance that procedures are being followed within the operating unit.

T&E According to Concur, the term *T&E* stands for "travel and expense." These phrases (*T&E, travel*, and *expense*) are often used when talking about a major operational cost for businesses, which devote on average 10% of their budgets to T&E.

Threat Any circumstance or event that could harm a critical asset through unauthorized access, compromise of data integrity, denial or disruption of service, or physical destruction or impairment.

Time-Sensitive Processes Business processes that can only be interrupted or made unavailable for a short time and must be a restoration priority.

Trading Partner Any organization with which a trading relationship (buyer and seller) is established. A trading partner can be a third-party company or an internal company organization.

Trojan Horse A program that masquerades as a legitimate program but in reality harbors code that could inflict serious damage to the user's computer.

Two-Factor Authentication Two-factor (2FA) or multifactor authentication (MFA) is an additional security layer for your business—helping to address the vulnerabilities of a standard password-only approach.

Vital Business Assessment A process required to determine what business functions and supporting applications are critical for the company to continue to conduct business in the event of a disaster.

Vital Records Records considered absolutely essential to the continuation or reconstruction of an organization. Vital records help establish the legal and financial position of the company, and are critical to preserving the rights of the organization, its employees, customers, and stockholders. In addition, any record that would be cost prohibitive to recreate could also be considered a vital record. Under no circumstances should an original vital record remain onsite.

Vulnerability A flaw in security procedures, software, internal system controls, or implementation that may affect the integrity, confidentiality, accountability, or availability of a system, data, or services.

Vulnerability Assessment An examination of the ability of a system or application, including current security procedures and controls, to withstand assault. A vulnerability assessment may be used to identify weaknesses that could be exploited and to predict the effectiveness of additional security measures to protect information resources from attack.

Work Instruction A work instruction is a step-by-step document that depicts the actions needed to complete an activity at the transaction level and is a detailed document that may include keystroke information. This is a very detailed "how-to" document.

Addendum—
Additional Tools

 EXAMPLE INTERNAL CONTROLS POLICY

Introduction and Scope

Internal controls are the structured means used to obtain reasonable assurance of achieving the company's objectives, and include responsibilities to all stakeholders, which are employees, customers, and suppliers. Internal controls are integral to managing the business and are a requirement of the Sarbanes-Oxley Act of 2002. The scope of this policy is worldwide.

Internal Controls Requirements

- Internal controls must be applied within an operating unit in an effective and efficient manner and provide reasonable assurance that the operating unit will meet its objectives.
- Internal controls objectives are achieved through the competence and integrity of personnel, the independence of their assigned function, their understanding of prescribed procedures, and the effectiveness of monitoring accepted risk.
- The effectiveness of an internal controls system is dependent upon the following factors:
- The tone set by senior management is the most important aspect contributing to the ongoing success of the internal controls system.
- Managers and employees must understand the internal controls system. Internal controls should be understood, supported, and promoted throughout the company.

- Continued appropriateness of the method of communication among employees is a key dependency. Impediments to necessary communication should be minimized.
- Adequate time and resources should be made available for the business operation to maintain and review internal controls.

The Internal Control Environment

A control environment is comprised of the following elements:

- Integrity and ethical values
- Commitment to competence
- Board of Directors and Audit Committee
- Management's philosophy and operating style
- Organizational structure
- Assignment of authority and responsibility
- Human Resources policies and procedures

The Internal Control Process

The overall control system must be geared to changes in risk within the business environment. In relation to any particular risk, there are four strategies to choose from:

1. Terminate the activity;
2. Transfer the risk to another party;
3. Reduce the risk by instituting the appropriate internal controls; and/or
4. Accept the risk (where no further effective and efficient controls are possible).

In summary, an internal controls system supports the operating unit's objectives in the following categories:

- Effectiveness and efficiency of operations and resources
- Reliability of financial and operational reporting
- Compliance with policies, procedures, applicable laws, and regulations
- Safeguarding assets from fraud or waste

Control Mechanisms

- **Organizational Controls** should cover all aspects of the company's activity without overlap, and be clearly assigned and communicated.

- Responsibility should be delegated down to the level at which the necessary expertise and time exist.
- No single employee should have exclusive knowledge, authority, or control over any significant transaction or group of transactions.
- Responsibility should be strengthened by agreeing to realistic qualitative/quantitative targets.
- The structure of accountability should be based on continuing levels of employee competence in different positions, and the development of competence so that responsibility and reporting relationships can be regrouped in more efficient ways.
- **Policy Controls** are the general principles and guides for action that influence decisions. They indicate the limits to choices and the parameters or rules to be followed by the company and its employees. Major policies should be reviewed, approved, and communicated by senior management. Policies are derived by:
  - Considering the business environment and process objectives
  - Identifying the potential categories of risks that the environment poses toward achievement of the objectives
- **Procedure Controls** prescribe how actions are to be performed consistent with policies. Procedures should be developed by those who understand the day-to-day actions that will be subject to the procedures, and those that understand the policies that the procedures are required to implement.
- **Examples of Supervisory Controls** are situations in which managers ensure that all employees understand their responsibilities and authorities, and the assurance that procedures are being followed within the operating unit.
- **Review Controls** include an ongoing self-assessment process as required by the Sarbanes-Oxley Act of 2002. A self-assessment is a series of questions that validate the effectiveness of the control environment. A self-assessment must be conducted every fiscal quarter. In some situations, the manager of the operating unit may elect to conduct a self-assessment test more frequently. It is imperative that all weaknesses found in the testing process are remediated through a corrective action and follow-up process.

Roles and Responsibilities

- **Management:** The chief executive officer (CEO) is ultimately responsible for setting the "tone at the top" that affects integrity and ethics that are required for a positive control environment.

- **Board of Directors:** Management is accountable to the board of directors, which provides governance, guidance, and oversight.
- **Internal Auditors:** Internal auditors play an important role in evaluating the effectiveness of control programs, and contribute to ongoing effectiveness. Because of organizational position and authority in an entity, an internal audit function plays a significant monitoring role.
- **Other Personnel:** The internal controls system is the responsibility of everyone in an organization and should be an explicit or implicit part of everyone's job description. All employees should be responsible for communicating upward problems in operations, non-compliance with the code of conduct, or other policy violations or illegal actions.

 ## EXAMPLE DELEGATION OF AUTHORITY (DoA) POLICY

Introduction and Scope

The company's board of directors (The Board) approved this Delegation of Authority (DoA) policy on (XXXX. XX, XXX). The Board will review the DoA on an annual basis and approve any required changes. The Board has designated the corporate secretary and general counsel to assist in the interpretation and application of this policy, including matters which raise questions among management. This DoA is limited and subordinate to applicable laws and statutes, as well as the company's Certificate of Incorporation and By-Laws. This DoA applies to all company operations on a worldwide basis.

The purpose of the DoA is to ensure the efficient operation of the company while maintaining fiscal integrity and adherence to policy. Outlined herein are those situations in which the DoA is required. Procedures are referenced to provide additional detail for the execution of the policy. Accountability for the overall management of the property, assets, financial, and human resources of the company rests with the chief executive officer (CEO). Persons that have been assigned authority under the terms of the DoA must safeguard company resources by establishing and maintaining internal controls that deter and detect any potential misuse of resources.

Detailed Delegation

Detailed Delegation Statement

- **Delegation Process:** Authority cannot be delegated other than as specified in this document. Delegation requires approval of the delegator's immediate superior and must be documented with a delegation form. (Refer to Addendum 1) The delegation request form will include the name of the delegate, description of the scope of delegation, reason for delegation, effective dates of authority, and date of rescission of authority (delegations must not be open ended). The delegator must provide a copy of the form to the corporate secretary.

- **Defined Levels of Authority:** Operating unit management has the responsibility to provide instruction on the provisions of this DoA to all appropriate operating unit personnel. All personnel must understand the applicability of the provisions of this DoA in the performance of their respective responsibilities. Employees should confirm with the finance director of their operating unit what authority limits have been delegated to them. The chief of staff, general counsel, chief human resource officer, chief information officer, and the chief financial officer have the same financial delegation of authority as business unit leaders.

- **Responsibilities:** Each operating unit must maintain a written policy that deploys the DoA within that operating unit. Operating units have the authority to implement delegation procedures that are more stringent than the requirements of the policy if they believe it is in the best interests of the business. Each operating unit is required to review and update its DoA policy at least annually and to execute timely updates.

- **Approval Level Dollar Amounts:** All amounts of money indicated in this DoA to determine the approval level or the extent of authorization refer to the current U.S. dollar equivalent of the estimated valuation in local currency. The amounts indicated denote absolute limits and must not be exceeded, even in *de minimis* amounts.

- **Changes to the DoA Policy:** Only the Board can grant changes to the level of authority delegated to the CEO. All deviations or waivers with respect to the DoA must be in the form of a Board resolution. Other company policies should be administered so as not to conflict with the DoA.

- **Financial Commitment Delegation Structure:** For the purposes of the DoA, spending authority limits are specified in Section 1.2 and shown graphically below. The chief of staff, general counsel, chief human resource officer, chief information officer, and the chief financial officer have the same financial delegation of authority as business unit leaders. The diagram below depicts the "double-key" process required for the approval of financial commitments.

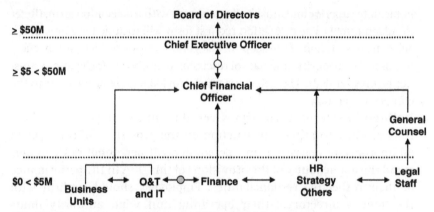

○ **Double Key:** reviewed proposals to the CFO and CEO for approval
◎ **Double Key:** reviewed proposals to Finance and BUL/O&T for approval

Restrictions/Exceptions/Powers Reserved

In addition to those items specified in the certificate of incorporation and by-laws, the Board reserves all authority not specifically delegated under the DoA, including the following:

Corporate Governance

- The establishment of policies governing the conduct of the company and its subsidiaries in relation to compliance with applicable laws and other such policies as the Board may deem to have significance
- Changes to the company's code of ethics
- The form and content of any proposed changes to the company's certificate of incorporation or by-laws, any proposed changes to this DoA, or any other change in the form of management governance and oversight of the company

Disclosure

- All public disclosures, including any filings on behalf of the company with the Securities and Exchange Commission (SEC) and other regulatory bodies
- Any other disclosures by the company to its shareholders and their representatives, the general public, and the business community

Financial Matters

- Declaration of dividends
- The issuance, repurchase, exchange, and redemption or conveyance of the right to any company equity securities
- Formation of debt facilities or issuance of long-term debt
- Mergers, consolidations, combinations, reorganizations, acquisitions or divestitures with a value of $50M or more, involving the company or any one of its subsidiaries
- Purchase or sale of a business, interest in a business or product line that is valued at $50M or more
- Purchase, sale, lease, or sale/leaseback of real estate or other property valued at $50M or more
- Recapitalizations, restructurings, spinoffs, splitoffs, Joint Ventures (JVs), strategic alliances and other transactions having a material effect on the capital structure of the company or its relationship to any subsidiary, group of subsidiaries or any third party
- Formation, sale, merger, or liquidation of a significant subsidiary
- Purchase or sale of equity securities or interests in another company of $50M or more
- Loans to other than affiliated companies of $5M or more
- Guarantees of indebtedness to other than affiliated companies of $5M or more
- Consolidated annual charitable contributions budget
- Business-as-usual commitments over $50M

Audit and Non-Audit Services

- Changes in accounting policy and principles
- Appointment of independent auditor
- Independent auditor's scope and fees
- Non-audit services provided by the external auditor
- Internal audit's scope

Compensation

- Maximum compensation level, salary changes, and salary ranges for all officers and employees of the company
- Retention programs for acquisitions, dispositions, facility closings, or other events

- Severance programs
- Duration of employment contracts
- Equity grants
- Selection and retention of compensation consultants

Officers

- Appointment, election, termination, and other actions related to company officers

Waivers

- Personal use of corporate assets
- Exemptions or exclusions from the company's Code of Ethics and Business Conduct

Other Matters

The Board also reserved the authority to review any other matter that it chooses. *Additionally, the Board must be informed of the following:*

- The settlement of suits and claims against the company to the extent that any required payments, agreements, consents, or commitments that may be deemed to significantly affect the corporate enterprise
- The establishment of company objectives and revisions to earnings, budgets, business plans, and capital expenditure plans
- Execution of contracts involving extraordinary obligations, risks or exposures, other than renewals with substantially unchanged terms and conditions
- Other matters judged by management to have significant and/or material impact to the company, its activities, employees, or customers

Delegation of Primary Authority

Officers and employees who delegate their authority remain responsible for monitoring and reviewing the actions of those to whom authority has been granted. Utmost care must be exercised in the selection of designees and the documentation, notification, and timely rescission of authority. Officers and employees are permitted to delegate their responsibilities and authorities to employees who report directly to them. It will be the responsibility of the individual who delegates to document in writing all delegations. Refer to the following table for permitted delegations of primary authority.

Primary Authority	Delegation to:
Board	Committees of the Board Officers of the Corporation Named individuals
Chief Executive Officer	Officers of the Corporation Business Unit Leaders Operations and Technology (O&T) Leader Named individuals
Chief of Staff	Named individuals
General Counsel	Individuals within the Law and Public Policy organization
Chief Ethics Officer	Individuals within the Ethics organization
Chief Strategy Officer	Individuals within the Strategy organization
Chief Human Resource Officer	Individuals within the Human Resources organization
Chief Information Officer	Individuals in the Information Technology Organization
Business Unit Leaders or Executive Leadership Team Members	Direct reports Named individuals
Direct Reports	Named individuals
Operations & Technology (O&T) Leaders	Direct reports to O&T Leader Named individuals
Direct Reports to O&T Leader	Named individuals
Facilities and Real Estate Leader	Individuals within the Facilities and Real Estate organization and operating unit Real Estate directors
Chief Financial Officer	Individuals within the finance organization Named individuals
Corporate Finance	Individuals within the corporate finance organization and operating unit finance directors
Chief Procurement Officer	Individuals within the procurement organization and operating unit procurement directors
Controller	Individuals within the controller's organization and operating unit finance directors
Treasurer	Individuals within the treasurer's organization
Chief Tax Officer	Individuals within the tax organization

Compliance and Controls

Compliance with this and all other company policies is mandatory. Any violation will be subject to disciplinary action, up to and including termination and prosecution. Where appropriate, the company will not limit itself to disciplinary actions but will pursue legal action against offending employees and other individuals involved.

The authorities here are always subject to the company's code of ethics. In all cases, good judgment should be used to identify risk and thus indicate where further consultation may be appropriate, consistent with the spirit and intent of the DoA.

All financial commitment approvals must include comprehensive and systematic assessments of the commitment's expected economic value, alignment with corporate strategy and plans, and associated risks that may affect the company's ability to achieve the intended results.

Definitions

Commitment by the company includes the execution of any written agreement or any other undertaking that obligates or binds the company in any respect (e.g. oral statements, electronic mail, or other representations), whether or not it involves the payment of money. Employees must never execute a document or otherwise commit the company unless they have clear authority to do so.

Company means the company and its worldwide operating subsidiaries.

Delegation of Authority is the formal written conveyance from one person to another of the authority to bind the company to a legally enforceable obligation. The authority to execute documents, make binding commitments, and authorize actions on behalf of the company is delegated to the appropriate corporate officer or those named in a specific delegation.

Delegation of Primary Authority applies to officers and employees who delegate their authority. These individuals remain responsible for monitoring and reviewing the actions of those to whom authority has been granted.

"Double-Key" process is management's approach to ensure that the right level and scope of approval has occurred for a transaction. Its definition is a principle: "For all materially important decisions, the manager responsible for the execution of the decision must obtain the concurrence of another manager at a comparable level of responsibility." Its usage derives from the two keys needed to unlock a safe deposit box in a bank vault.

The Board refers to the Board of Directors.

Example Delegation of Authority Matrix

Summary Delegation Of Authority Matrix	MCI Board	CEO	BUL O&T and IT	DR-BUL DR-O&T and IT	General Counsel	CFO	Controller	(8) Corporate Finance
SPENDING (7) Expenditures, Commitments, Leases, General Purchases, Disposals								
≥ 50MM	A (6)	P						
≥ 5MM		A (2)	P			A (2)	R(5)	R
≥ 1MM			A (3)	P			R(5)	A (3)
< 1MM				A (4)			R(5)	A(4)
ACQUISITIONS / MERGERS / DIVESTITURES / JOINT VENTURE/								
≥ 50MM	A (6)	P						
< 50MM		A (2)	P		A	A (2)	R	R
LEGAL SETTLEMENTS								
≥ 50MM	I	A (2)			A	A (2)	R	R
≥ 5MM		A (2)	P		A	A (2)	R	R
< 5MM			A (3)	P	A		R	A (3)
CONSULTING/CONTRACTOR AGREEMENTS								
≥ 1MM	A(1) (6)	A (2)	P		R	A (2)	R (1)	R
≥ 500K	A(1) (6)		A (3)	P	R		R (1)	A (3)
< 500K	A(1) (6)			A (4)	R		R (1)	A(4)

NOTE:
All approvals are subject to operating unit budget authorizations. R is Review, A is Approve, I is Inform, and P is Propose. DR is Direct Report. BUL is the Business Unit Leader. O&TL is the Operations and Technology Leader. (1) Non-Audit Accounting, Tax or Consulting Services offered by the external auditor. (2) The CEO and CFO will co-approve. (3) The BUL/O&TL and Corporate Finance will co-approve. (4) The DR-BUL/O&TL and Corporate Finance will co-approve. (5) Review for capital expenditures. (6) Approval on non-Business as Usual Transactions. (7) Augments require at least one-level higher approval than initial project (excluding CEO). (8) Procurement and Tax review considered as overall Corp Finance review and approval.

Operating unit means any subsidiary, joint venture, business group, function, or other business undertaking in which the company controls the activities of the business.

Subsidiaries are entities in which the company owns more than 50%, or owns 50% or less and exercises management control.

Subsidiary board refers to the boards of directors of individual subsidiaries of the company or its subsidiaries. To the extent that local legislation grants greater power to subsidiary boards than that afforded by this DoA, the narrower power provided for in this DoA will govern. It is recognized that in the case of separate legal entities, a review by a higher company body (e.g. an affiliate Board is subordinate to the Board) will sometimes be required.

EXAMPLE SEGREGATION OF DUTIES (SoD) POLICY

1.0 Introduction and Scope

This policy reflects the major business decisions that establish the objectives and provide direction for the company. Policies establish the basic process, fundamental philosophies, and major values upon which the organization must operate.

Policies differ from procedures in that procedures prescribe the means of accomplishing the policy. Procedures provide personnel with the guidelines and specific activities to ensure commonality, compliance, and control of policy related activities.

The overall approach is one of global consistency from budget preparation through consolidated reporting, with differentiated handling of processes for statutory or division specific requirements only.

The policy is divided into six sections:

1. **Introduction**
2. **Organizational Policy**
3. **Professional Standards**
4. **Risks and Internal Control Objectives Addressed by Policy**
5. **Functional Procedures**
6. **Addenda**

2.0 Organizational Policy

It is company's policy that an appropriate segregation of duties shall be maintained in accordance with the principles set forth in this document. The company shall identify, remediate, and maintain a separation of incompatible business functions. In permissible instances where business functions cannot be fully and appropriately segregated due to specific circumstances, management shall implement mitigating controls to compensate for such situations. As changes occur in the organizational, functional, and technological environments, assessments shall be performed to address the impact on the segregation of duties resulting from such changes.

The company's senior management shall review, revise, and enforce this policy as significant developments occur with respect to the segregation of duties.

2.1 Purpose of Segregation of Duties

Adequate segregation of duties reduces the likelihood that errors (intentional or unintentional) will remain undetected by providing for separate processing by different individuals at various stages of a transaction and for independent reviews of the work performed. The segregation of duties provides four primary benefits: (1) the risk of a deliberate fraud is mitigated as the collusion of two or more persons would be required in order to circumvent controls; (2) the risk of legitimate errors is mitigated as the likelihood of detection is increased; (3) the cost of corrective actions is mitigated as errors are generally detected relatively earlier in their lifecycle; and (4) the organization's reputation for integrity and quality is enhanced through a system of checks and balances.

Segregation of duties is a basic, key internal control and one of the most difficult to accomplish. In essence, there is greater assurance that internal control responsibilities will be fully deployed when there is increased dispersion of such responsibilities among multiple individuals and work groups.

2.2 Principles of Segregation of Duties

The key principle of segregation of duties is that an individual or small group of individuals should not be in a position to control all aspects of a transaction or business process. Basically, the general duties to be segregated are: planning/initiation, authorization, custody of assets, and recording or reporting of transactions. In addition, control tasks such as review, audit, and reconcile should not be performed by the same individual responsible for recording or reporting the transaction.

The principle of segregation of duties generally helps define the constructs which will govern the definition of processes, controls, and reporting structures of organizational units. Another element of segregation of duties is that within an organizational unit where an employee's compensation, commission, and performance evaluation are controlled or driven by the same Management Team, it is critical to ensure that employees are not pressured to override controls, processes, or segregation of duties constructs.

The principle of segregation of duties in an information system environment is also critical as it ensures the separation of different functions such as transaction entry, online approval of the transactions, master file initiation, master file maintenance, user access rights, and the review of transactions. In the context of application level controls, this means that one individual should not have access rights which permit them to enter, approve, and review transactions. Therefore, assigning different security profiles to various individuals would support the principle of segregation of duties.

The following general categories of duties or responsibilities are examined regarding segregation of duties:

- Formulating policy, plans, and goals
- Approving policy, plans, and goals
- Developing/analyzing business case justification
- Initiating a transaction
- Authorizing the transaction
- Recording the transaction
- Monitoring or having custody of physical assets
- Monitoring and/or reporting on performance results
- Reconciling accounts and transactions
- Authorizing master file transactions
- Processing master file transactions
- Providing information systems development, security administration, and other related support
- Following-up/resolving issues or discrepancies

In an ideal system, different employees would perform each of these major functions. Segregation of duties would imply that no one would have control of two or more of these responsibilities within a given sub-cycle or process. As a matter of degree of application, the more negotiable the asset is in the marketplace, typically the greater the need for proper segregation of duties—especially when dealing with cash, negotiable checks and inventories. It may be possible for one person to perform multiple responsibilities as long as they are across separate or segregated processes, activities, transactions, and other business matters. For example, a customer account representative may have responsibilities for obtaining credit information, updating customer profile information, verifying contract terms, and posting equipment changes.

2.3 Domains of Segregation of Duties

There are three strategic domains of segregation of duties that are addressed by this policy. These domains are organizational, functional, and technological. The organizational domain addresses segregation of duties issues that may develop due to the organizational structure of the company. The functional domain addresses segregation of duties issues that may develop due to the job functions for which individuals are assigned responsibility. Finally, technological domain addresses segregation of duties issues may develop due to the security configuration of various IT systems.

2.4 Use of Compensating Controls

In those instances where duties cannot be fully segregated, mitigating or compensating controls must be established. Mitigating or compensating controls are additional procedures designed to reduce the risk of errors or irregularities. For instance, if the record keeper also performs a reconciliation process, a detailed review of the reconciliation could be performed and documented by a supervisor to provide additional control over the assignment of incompatible functions. Segregation of duties is more difficult to achieve in a centralized, computerized environment. Compensating controls in this arena might include passwords, inquiry-only access, logs, dual authorization requirements, and documented reviews of input/output.

2.5 Relationship with Other Internal Control Measures

Segregation of duties is an integral part of the company's overall standards of internal control and is the foundation of the standards of internal control. It is a key control necessary to ensure that the other controls are effectively discharged by appropriate individuals and groups.

3.0 Professional Standards

This policy establishes standards and authoritative guidance for the company and all its subsidiaries.

4.0 Risks and Internal Control Objectives Addressed by Policy

Misstatement of financial accounts and management information due to: intentional or unintentional errors, omissions, and fraud

Loss of audit trail which validates detail analysis, approval, and implementation of transactions

Noncompliance with legal requirements

IT security weaknesses

4.1 Internal Control Objectives addressed by Policy

a) Section 1.5—General Control Requirements

Adequate segregation of duties and control responsibilities must be established and maintained in all functional areas of the company. In general, custodial, processing/operating, and accounting responsibilities should be separated to promote independent review and evaluation of company operations. Where adequate segregation cannot be achieved, other compensating controls must be established and documented.

5.0 Functional Procedures

5.1 Identification of Segregation of Duties Issues

a. Each functional business area shall be responsible for developing and implementing a schedule for assessing its area for potential or actual segregation of duties on a recurring basis.

b. Each functional business area shall formally evaluate its area for the existence of potential or actual segregation of duties issues on a periodic basis.

c. Organizational segregation of duties issues shall be considered during the periodic evaluations. The positioning of the business area in company, its relationships with other functional business areas, and the nature of its responsibilities shall be considered.

d. Functional segregation of duties issues shall be considered during the periodic evaluations. The assigned job functions of personnel in the business area shall be considered from a standpoint of incompatible duties.

e. Technological segregation of duties issues shall be considered during the periodic evaluations. The assigned system and application security of personnel shall be considered from a standpoint of access within systems to perform incompatible functions.

5.2 Remediation of Segregation of Duties Issues

a. Each functional business area shall document the segregation of duties issues identified during the formal periodic evaluations.

b. The nature of the issue, the domain (e.g. organizational, functional, or technological), and the involved parties/systems shall be included in the documentation of the segregation of duties issues.

c. Business area management shall review the documentation and determine remediation options for each issue.

d. Remediation options may include a combination of corrective or mitigating measures.

e. Business area management shall document the selected remediation method, along with the effective date of the remediation.

f. Company senior management and the internal audit department shall be provided copies of all documentation relating to segregation of duties analyses and remediation.

5.3 Maintenance of Segregation of Duties

a. In the course of regular decision-making, business area management shall contemplate the impact of segregation of duties issues.

b. Guidance provided in Section 6 shall serve as the foundation for evaluating business decisions in the context of segregation of duties.

6.0 Addenda

6.1 Overview of Segregation of Duties Matrices

a. The matrix in 6.2 provides general guidance regarding segregation of duties.

b. The matrices in 6.3 through 6.9 provide guidance for specific business processes. When appropriate, these matrices can be used in lieu of the general matrix in 6.2.

c. The matrices reflect the desired state of the segregation of duties, and they represent the basis upon which functional business areas should assess their current state.

d. Each row and column in a matrix represents a major business sub-process.

e. Where the intersection of a row and column is denoted by an "X," the corresponding business sub-processes represent incompatible functions that should be segregated.

f. The segregation of duties can exist and should be assessed at the organizational, functional, and/or systematic levels.

6.2 General Segregation of Duties Matrix

NATIVE SEGREGATION OF DUTIES MATRIX

PROCESS	SIC CODE	GROUP NAME	GROUP	01	02	03	04	05	06	07	08	09	10	11	12
GENERAL	1.5	FORMULATING PLANS AND GOALS	01							X				X	
GENERAL	1.5	DEVELOPING BUSINESS CASE JUSTIFICATIONS	02				X		X	X			X		X
GENERAL	1.5	INITIATING TRANSACTIONS	03		X		X					X	X		X
GENERAL	1.5	AUTHORIZING TRANSACTIONS	04		X	X			X			X	X	X	X
GENERAL	1.5	RECORDING TRANSACTIONS	05			X			X		X	X	X	X	X
GENERAL	1.5	CUSTODY OF PHYSICAL ASSETS	06		X			X				X	X	X	X
GENERAL	1.5	REPORTING ON PERFORMANCE RESULTS	07	X	X							X	X		X
GENERAL	1.5	RECONCILING ACCOUNTS AND TRANSACTIONS	08			X	X	X	X	X			X	X	X
GENERAL	1.5	AUTHORIZING MASTER FILE TRANSACTIONS	09		X	X	X	X	X	X	X			X	X
GENERAL	1.5	PROCESSING MASTER FILE TRANSACTIONS	10				X	X	X		X	X			X
GENERAL	1.5	PROVIDING IT SUPPORT	11	X	X	X	X	X	X	X	X	X			X
GENERAL	1.5	RESOLVING ISSUES OR DESCREPANCIES	12						X					X	

6.3 Revenue Segregation of Duties Matrix

		NATIVE SEGREGATION OF DUTIES MATRIX												
				CUSTOMER MASTER DATA	CREDIT MANAGEMENT	CUSTOMER INCENTIVES	CUSTOMER CONTRACTS	PRICING	ORDER ENTRY	A/R PAYMENTS	A/R ENTRY	BILLING	APPROVE BILLING	COLLECTIONS	POST A/R PAYMENTS
PROCESS	SIC CODE	GROUP NAME	GROUP	01	02	03	04	05	06	07	08	09	10	11	12
REVENUE		CUSTOMER MASTER DATA	01		X	X	X	X	X	X	X	X	X	X	X
	3.4.7	CREDIT MANAGEMENT	02	X		X	X	X	X	X	X	X	X		X
	3.11.6	CUSTOMER INCENTIVES	03	X	X		X								X
		CUSTOMER CONTRACTS	04	X	X	X		X		X	X	X	X	X	X
	3.10.3	PRICING	05	X	X		X			X	X		X	X	X
		ORDER ENTRY	06	X	X	X				X	X	X			X
	3.9.4	A/R PAYMENTS	07	X	X		X	X	X			X	X	X	X
	3.7.1	A/R ENTRY	08	X	X		X	X	X			X	X	X	X
	3.6.10	BILLING	09	X	X		X		X	X	X		X	X	X
		APPROVE BILLING	10	X	X		X	X		X	X.	X		X	X
		COLLECTIONS	11	X			X	X		X	X	X	X		X
	3.7.1	POST A/R PAYMENTS	12	X	X	X	X	X	X	X	X	X	X	X	

6.4 Bill Audit Segregation of Duties Matrix

		NATIVE SEGREGATION OF DUTIES MATRIX									
				NEGOTIATE CARRIER AGREEMENTS	APPROVE CARRIER AGREEMENTS	MAINTAIN CARRIER RELATIONSHIPS	RECEIVE / ENTER CARRIER BILLS	AUTHORIZE CARRIER BILLS FOR PAYMENT	COMPLETE BILL AUDIT	MANAGE CARRIER DISPUTES	UPDATE CIRCUIT INFORMATION AND CARRIER RATES
PROCESS	SIC CODE	GROUP NAME	GROUP	01	02	03	04	05	06	07	08
BILL AUDIT		NEGOTIATE CARRIER AGREEMENTS	01		X			X	X		X
		APPROVE CARRIER AGREEMENTS	02	X		X	X		X	X	X
		MAINTAIN CARRIER RELATIONSHIPS	03		X		X		X		
		RECEIVE / ENTER CARRIER BILLS	04		X	X		X	X	X	
		AUTHORIZE CARRIER BILLS FOR PAYMENT	05	X			X		X	X	X
	4.5.1	COMPLETE BILL AUDIT	06	X	X	X	X	X		X	X
		MANAGE CARRIER DISPUTES	07		X		X	X	X		
	4.5.7	UPDATE CIRCUIT INFORMATION AND CARRIER RATES	08	X	X			X	X		

6.5 Procurement Segregation of Duties Matrix

NATIVE SEGREGATION OF DUTIES MATRIX

PROCESS	SIC CODE	GROUP NAME	GROUP	01 Check Disbursement Management	02 Process and Print Payments	03 A/P Entry	04 A/P Payments	05 Purchase Requisitions	06 Release Purchase Requisitions	07 Purchase Orders	08 Release Purchase Orders	09 Vendor Master Data	10 Release Vendor Invoices	11 Vendor Pricing Agreement	12 Check Adjustments	13 Post A/P Payments
PROCUREMENT	6.6.1	CHECK DISBURSEMENT MANAGEMENT	01	—		×	×		×	×	×		×	×	×	×
	6.6.1	PROCESS AND PRINT PAYMENTS	02		—	×	×		×	×	×	×			×	×
	6.5.1	A/P ENTRY	03	×	×	—	×	×	×	×	×	×	×	×	×	×
	6.5.1	A/P PAYMENTS	04	×	×	×	—		×	×	×	×	×	×	×	×
	6.2.1	PURCHASE REQUISITIONS	05			×	×	—	×		×	×	×	×	×	
	6.2.1	RELEASE PURCHASE REQUISITIONS	06	×	×	×	×	×	—	×	×	×	×	×	×	×
	6.2.1	PURCHASE ORDERS	07		×	×	×		×	—	×	×	×	×	×	×
	6.2.1	RELEASE PURCHASE ORDERS	08	×	×	×	×	×		×	—	×	×	×	×	×
		VENDOR MASTER DATA	09	×	×	×	×	×	×	×	×	—	×	×	×	×
	6.6.1	RELEASE VENDOR INVOICES	10	×	×	×	×	×	×	×	×	×	—	×	×	×
		VENDOR PRICING AGREEMENT	11			×	×		×	×	×	×	×	—	×	×
	6.6.1	CHECK ADJUSTMENTS	12	×	×	×	×	×	×	×	×	×	×	×	—	×
	6.5.1	POST A/P PAYMENTS	13	×	×	×			×	×	×	×	×	×	×	—

6.6 Inventory Management Segregation of Duties Matrix

PROCESS	SIC CODE	GROUP NAME	GROUP	GOODS DELIVERIES 01	GOODS RECEIPTS 02	MATERIAL / SERVICE MASTER 03	GOODS MOVEMENTS 04	PHYSICAL INVENTORY COUNT 05	POST GOODS RECEIPTS 06	POSTING FOR INVENTORY MOVEMENTS 07	APPROVE INVENTORY DIFFERENCES 08	POST GOODS ISSUES 09
INVENTORY MANAGEMENT	6.4.2	GOODS DELIVERIES	01		X	X		X	X	X	X	X
	6.4.2	GOODS RECEIPTS	02	X		X				X	X	X
		MATERIAL / SERVICE MASTER	03	X	X		X	X	X		X	X
		GOODS MOVEMENTS	04			X			X		X	
	5.2.1	PHYSICAL INVENTORY COUNT	05	X		X			X	X	X	X
	5.2.1	POST GOODS RECEIPTS	06	X		X	X	X		X	X	X
		POSTING FOR INVENTORY MOVEMENTS	07	X	X			X	X		X	X
	5.2.1	APPROVE INVENTORY DIFFERENCES	08	X	X	X	X	X	X	X		X
	5.2.1	POST GOODS ISSUES	09	X	X	X		X	X	X	X	

Native Segregation of Duties Matrix

6.7 Asset Management Segregation of Duties Matrix

PROCESS	SIC CODE	GROUP NAME	GROUP	ASSET MASTER DATA 01	ASSET MAINTENANCE 02	PROJECT CREATE / CHANGE 03	RELEASE / BLOCK ASSET GROUP 04	PROJECT ACCOUNTING MANAGEMENT 05
ASSET MANAGEMENT		ASSET MASTER DATA	01		X	X		X
	5.1.12	ASSET MAINTENANCE	02	X			X	X
	5.1.12	PROJECT CREATE / CHANGE	03	X			X	X
	5.1.12	RELEASE / BLOCK ASSET GROUP	04		X	X		X
	5.1.12	PROJECT ACCOUNTING MANAGEMENT	05	X	X	X	X	

Native Segregation of Duties Matrix

6.8 General Ledger Accounting Segregation of Duties Matrix

NATIVE SEGREGATION OF DUTIES MATRIX								
				BANK / CHECK RECONCILIATIONS	FI MASTER DATA	COST / PROFIT CENTER ACCOUNTING	POST G/L ACCOUNTING	G/L JOURNAL ENTRY
PROCESS	SIC CODE	GROUP NAME	GROUP	01	02	03	04	05
G/L ACCOUNTING		BANK / CHECK RECONCILIATIONS	01		X	X	X	X
		FI MASTER DATA	02	X		X	X	X
		COST / PROFIT CENTER ACCOUNTING	03	X	X			
		POST G/L ACCOUNTING	04	X	X			X
		G/L JOURNAL ENTRY	05	X	X		X	

6.9 Human Resources/Payroll Segregation of Duties Matrix

NATIVE SEGREGATION OF DUTIES MATRIX											
				EDIT PAYROLL MASTER FILE	APPROVE SALARY / WAGE CHANGES	DETERMINE SALARY / WAGE RATES	RESOLVE EMPLOYEE PAYROLL INQUIRIES	DISBURSE PAYROLL	AUTHORIZE ELECTRONIC DISBURSEMENTS	PREPARE PAYROLL	INITIATE PAYROLL
PROCESS	SIC CODE	GROUP NAME	GROUP	01	02	03	04	05	06	07	08
HR / PAYROLL	7.1.2	EDIT PAYROLL MASTER FILE	01		X	X		X	X	X	X
	7.1.11	APPROVE SALARY / WAGE CHANGES	02	X		X				X	X
	7.1.11	DETERMINE SALARY / WAGE RATES	03	X	X		X	X	X	X	
		RESOLVE EMPLOYEE PAYROLL INQUIRIES	04			X				X	X
	7.2.7	DISBURSE PAYROLL	05	X		X			X	X	X
	7.2.7	AUTHORIZE ELECTRONIC DISBURSEMENTS	06	X		X		X		X	X
	7.1.11	PREPARE PAYROLL	07	X	X	X	X	X	X		X
	7.1.11	INITIATE PAYROLL	08	X	X		X	X	X	X	

EXAMPLE SYSTEM ACCESS (SA) POLICY

Introduction and Scope

The System Access (SA) policy applies to both domestic and international financial and operational systems and is an integral part of segregation of duties. The scope of the Systems Access policy is worldwide. The policy applies to the approval of new access requests and the establishment of an internal controls environment for general system access.

The SA policy ensures that transactions cannot be systematically generated to create segregation of duties control issues. There are two types of segregation of duties controls that must be in place: (1) Control of Security Object Privileges, and (2) Control of Multiple Security Profiles. The policy establishes a framework for incompatible functions as depicted in the chart below:

Record Keeping	Asset Custody
Creating and Maintaining Records	Access to and/or Control of Assets

Authorization	Reconciliation
Reviewing and Approving Transactions	Assurance that Transactions Are Proper

Responsibilities

System access will be defined based on individual employee roles and responsibilities within financial and operational processes. Business owners have the core responsibility for defining system access roles. Business owners will have responsibility for reviewing and approving all user access requests.

Risk Assessment: If system access controls are not implemented, control weaknesses can occur.

- Purchases can be authorized and goods can be received from the transaction at the user level.
- Inventory management and physical counts can be performed by the same user.
- Sales can be invoiced and cash applied by the same user.

- A sales order and the terms of sale can be approved by the same user.
- The same user can modify an evaluated receipts contract and receive against a purchase order.
- Products can be shipped and sales order tolerances modified.
- A vendor can be established in the accounts payable process and payments can be executed.
- An accounts payable user can create an erroneous accounts receivable transaction.
- A general ledger user can post and pay accounts payable invoices.

Process Flow and Control Mechanisms

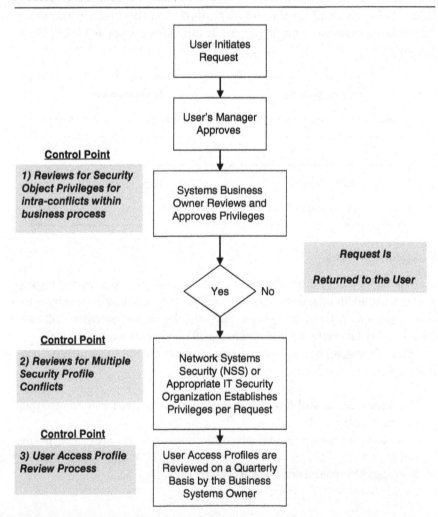

Control Mechanisms

1. Control of Security Object Privileges

If security object privileges are not properly defined, intra-conflicts can occur in which the user can have excessive or conflicting user access. A segregation-of-duties issue arises when profiles, roles, or classes are not well defined at the user level. The conflicting privileges introduce risk assigned to a user through a single security object.

2. Control of Multiple Security Profiles

If multiple security privileges are not properly defined, extra-conflicts can occurs in which the cumulative privileges of the user are excessive and conflicting. The conflicting privileges introduce risk when assigned to a user through multiple security objects.

3. Profile/Access Control Review Process

System access will be reviewed by the business system owner to ensure that conflicting privileges are not in place within the internal organization (intra-conflicts). The business systems owner will also review system access privileges to ensure that external organization cannot access processes that are the responsibility of the business owner's organization. Control gaps will be remediated as they are identified. If access is removed or modified, employees must reapply for access within 30 days of any change in department/cost center. This will ensure that system access adheres to all Audit requirements for direct line management and secondary approvals as well as policies regarding segregation of duties.

4. Validation and Control Review

Management will circulate application-level reports to the appropriate IT and business personnel for ongoing validation.

1. Validation of conflict definitions, which indicate the conditions that constitute a conflict in duties. Consider monitoring controls which may mitigate the risk of a conflict definition.
2. Validation of technical segregation of duties reports, which outline the existing conflicts. Internal Audit will perform testing as defined in their annual planning process.

EXAMPLE PRICING POLICY

Introduction and Scope

The pricing policy is an integral part of the segregation of duties requirements for the company's internal controls. Specially, the pricing process will report to the finance function to ensure segregation of duties from the contract administration and business analysis.

The pricing process includes standard and nonstandard pricing, management of the pricing model, analysis, and review. The finance and internal controls organizations are responsible for establishing the monitoring process as part of the controls environment.

The scope of this policy is worldwide and is applicable to enterprise markets, the company's International and Wholesale Markets, and U.S. Sales and Service.

Customer Contracts and Sales Offerings

The chief executive officer (CEO) shall determine the organizational responsibility for accepting customer contracts, establishing standard contract terms, and analyzing benefits and risks. Contracts may be entered into only by authorized company officers and employees or as authorized by the designated business unit leaders (BUL).

The CEO has the responsibility to determine the operating unit assignment for pricing policies and guidelines associated with sales offerings. The development and implementation of pricing policies and guidelines is the responsibility of the designated operating unit in consultation with law and public policy (LPP), marketing, and corporate finance. Corporate finance reviews the ability to bill and collect for each product offering. The controller reviews the accounting for new offerings and changes to existing offerings. LPP will review regulatory and contract law implications. The approval of pricing policy is the responsibility of the CFO. Included in these responsibilities are new product offerings, standard discounts, promotions, and special bids, as well as contract adjustments and amendments.

LPP prepares standard customer contracts for execution. Each operating unit shall execute its standard customer contracts and shall review and secure the approval of LPP for nonstandard customer contracts.

Control Mechanisms – Levels of Authority for Standard Customer Contracts and Sales Offerings

STANDARD CUSTOMER CONTRACTS AND SALES OFFERINGS	BUS. UNIT LEADER	SVP	VP	DIRECTOR	MANAGER/SR MGR	LAW & PUB. POLICY	CORPORATE FINANCE	REVENUE OPERATIONS	MARKETING	BUS. DEVELOPMENT	CONTROLLER	CUSTOMER SERVICE	SALES
—Create and maintain required cost models used to develop standard customer offerings		X				A	R						
—Determine accounting for new offerings and changes to existing offerings			X						A				
—Develop pricing guidelines and financial conditions associated with sales offerings based on approved cost models	X					A	A	R					
—Conduct on-going reviews of pricing policies, financial conditions and guidelines associated with sales offerings based on approved cost models and product positioning strategy		X			R	A	R						
—Develop new and revised customer offerings within approved policies and guidelines	X				R	A	A	R					R
—Obtain additional approvals required by Enterprise Markets Standard Pricing Approval Matrix		X			R	A							
—Verify that pricing and related terms are properly defined, offerings meets all regulatory requirements, and appropriate tariffs and price guides are filed			X		A	A							
—Create standard Non-Disclosure Agreements for use with customers as appropriate or required			X		A	A							
—Create standard customer contracts for execution			X		A	A	A	A					
—Acknowledge receipt of rates with all required approvals and certify that offerings meet applicable rate audit guidelines			X			A		A					
—Input approved rates into appropriate billing systems			X			A							
—Ensure that appropriate Field Sales Tools have been updated as appropriate and internal Field Sales Communication has occurred			X				A						
—Ensure that Customer Service is aware of and trained to support new and revised customer offerings			X				A	A		R			
—Ensure that appropriate management approvals are obtained for standard offers and pricing discounts, as required, prior to customer receiving offer/quote from MCI		X										A	
—Ensure proper acceptance and handling of standard customer contracts and offerings, including provisions for customer credit approvals and maintaining executed contracts as required				X	R	A	A	R			R		R

A = Approve
R = Review (minimum Director level review required unless otherwise provided)
Required approvals must be obtained before commitments are made.
Approval authorities listed are minimum levels. Department heads may add additional approval levels (beyond the minimum), if they choose.
In such cases, the department is responsible for ensuring that the additional approvals are obtained.

TESTING INTERNAL CONTROLS AND SELECTING SAMPLE SIZES

The purpose of this tool is to define a standard and consistent testing strategy and to establish a baseline of awareness related to the roles and responsibilities for testing internal controls throughout the payment process. This tool also provides a framework for the design of a test plan for individual business processes. Corporates should have a well-defined sample selection methodology documented and followed for each test of controls.

As general guidelines, internal control testing sample size should vary with the following aspects of the business controls:

- Frequency of control activity
- Inherent risk of business cycle
- Automated vs. manual control
- Complexity of the business cycle

Guiding Principles for Sample Size Selection

1. Management should be testing more than the minimum sample size requirements included in the methodology.

2. Sample sizes should be directionally and respectively consistent with the minimum requirements.

3. Sample sizes for testing of manual controls are based on frequency of the control and historical sizes remain the minimum.

4. Medium and higher risk areas should have larger sample sizes.

5. Minimum requirements for sample size are based on the frequency of each control. Management test samples must be representative and larger than these minimum size requirements.

6. Professional judgment should be used in determining the need to increase the sample size above the minimum. Several testing considerations for increasing the sample size include:

- Increased complexity of the internal control is a factor.
- According to Auditing Standard Number 5,[1] external auditors are permitted to place a certain amount of reliance on the testing performed by management, depending on:
  a. The nature of the test
  b. The degree to which the tests are routine/standard
  c. The competence and objectivity of the team performing the test

[1]Public Accounting Oversight Board (PCAOB), accessed December 18, 2018, https://pcaobus.org/Standards/Auditing/pages/auditing_standard_5.aspx.

When relying on management, auditors typically reduce the number of controls which they test, versus reducing the number of tests for each control.

- If management identified 10 controls that were performed multiple times a day the external auditors were relying on 80% of management's testing (low risk, high reliance), the auditors might test 2 controls with a minimum sample of 30.
- Control environment and walkthroughs must be performed 100% by the external auditor.

Sample Size Selection Table

Frequency of Control	Number of Items (Minimum Sample Size)
Annual	1
Quarterly	2
Monthly	3 to 6
Weekly	10, 15, 20
Daily	20, 30, 40
Multiple times a day	30, 45, 60

Indicators in Determining Auditor Reliance on Management Testing

Indicators for Reduced Auditor Sample Size and Relying on Management	Indicators for Full Independent Audit Testing
■ Low risk of material misstatement	■ Accounts with higher materiality, judgments, estimates, and/or risk of material misstatement
■ Low degree of judgement is required to evaluate the operating effectiveness of the control	■ Judgment required to evaluate operating effectiveness
■ Low potential for management override	■ Pervasive
	■ Higher potential for management override
	■ Fiscal-period-end testing is required

Testing Techniques

There are four different testing techniques that can be used to test internal controls. These testing techniques are summarized below:

1. **Inquiry of the process owner provides relevant information regarding the controls.** Obtain support for these discussions through corroborating inquiry with others, or by examining reports, manuals, or other documents used in or generated by the performance of the control. Inquiry alone does not provide sufficient evidence about whether a specific control is operating effectively and therefore must be used in combination with the others described below.
2. **Observation should be used if there is no, or limited, documentation of the operation of a control.** Observation is useful for physical controls (e.g. seeing that the warehouse door is locked, or that blank checks are safeguarded) and segregation of duties controls. (*Note*: While better than inquiry, the risk with observation is that the control may not be performed consistently.)
3. **Inspection** of evidence should be used to determine whether manual controls, like the follow-up of exception reports, are being performed. Evidence could include written explanations, checkmarks, initials, or other indications of follow-up documented on the exception report itself. The inspection of records, documents, reconciliations, and reports could serve as evidence that a control has been properly applied.
4. **Re-performance** of a control is used to further ensure (beyond inquiry, observation, and inspection of evidence) that a control is operating effectively.

Evaluating Internal Control Deficiencies

A deficiency is considered a significant deficiency or material weakness if, either individually or in the aggregate, after considering compensating controls, the likelihood and potential magnitude fall within the criteria in the table below.

Compensating controls must be at the same level of detail (i.e. budget-to-actual comparison is not a good compensating control), be considered in the process flow documentation, and be tested and operating effectively.

Classification of Deficiency	Likelihood of Misstatement		Potential Magnitude of Misstatement
Internal control deficiency	Remote (less than 5% to 10% chance)	**OR**	Inconsequential (less than 0.5% to 1.0% of pre-tax income)
Significant deficiency	More than remote (more than 5% to 10%)	**AND**	More than inconsequential (greater than 0.5% to 1.0% of pre-tax income)
Material weakness	More than remote (more than 5% to 10%)	**AND**	Material (greater than 4% to 5% of pre-tax income)

As part of the testing process, various exceptions may be identified that will be classified as a deficiency or weakness. Here is the process that controllers or owners of internal controls should use to properly address the deficiency.

1. Identify deficiency.
2. Understand and assess management's evaluation.
3. Identify compensating controls.
4. Assess likelihood of misstatement.
5. Assess potential magnitude of misstatement.
6. Determine classification of deficiencies.
7. Assess aggregation with other deficiencies.

Internal Controls Remediation

The length of time that remediated controls are expected to be in place to be considered operationally effective is as follows:

- If the control has been remediated > 90 days, then the normal sample size for the frequency of the control/level of risk should be tested.
- If the control has been remediated < 90 days, then the sample sizes below must be used:

Frequency of Control	Minimum time period of operation	Minimum number of items to be tested
Quarterly	2 quarters	1
Monthly	2 months	2
Weekly	4 weeks	2
Daily	30 days	10
Multiple times a day	30 days	30

Index

Page references followed by *t* indicate a table